BATTLESHIPS
AND
CARRIERS

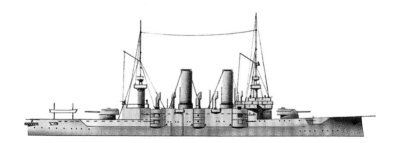

BATTLESHIPS
AND
CARRIERS

STEVE CRAWFORD

Grange
BOOKS

ISBN 1-84013-337-6

Editorial and design by Amber Books Ltd
Bradley's Close
74–77 White Lion Street
London N1 9PF
Design: Wilson Design Associates

Printed in Singapore

PICTURE CREDITS:
TRH Pictures

ARTWORK CREDITS
All artworks Istituto Geografico De Agostini S.p.A. except the following:
Aerospace Publishing: 16, 27, 39, 45, 58, 93, 186, 203, 204, 207, 229, 241, 254,
258, 269, 279, 281
Bob Garwood: 50, 126

CONTENTS

Introduction

In any country's navy, the battleship and aircraft carrier are not just its biggest and most powerful vessels, they are also a symbol of that nation's maritime strength, its ambition, and its wealth. The ships described and illustrated in this book cover a huge variety of types and sizes of vessel, from coastal defence ships of the nineteenth century such as the *Arminius* of Prussia, to the vast nuclear-powered aircraft carriers like USS *Enterprise* of today's US Navy.

All the ships illustrated in this book were all built to fight. That is their ultimate purpose, and the technical innovations which have attempted to give one ship a fighting edge over another has always been the driving force behind their design and construction. What began in the 1850s with steam engines in the hulls of wooden three-deckers, such as the French *Bretagne*, created within 40 years the big-gun battleship, epitomised by Japan's armoured giant *Yamato* of World War II; the main gun turrets of which would weigh more than the whole of *Bretagne* under full sail. Ships such as the *Yamato* are the archetypal 'big' warship, but smaller vessels of previous centuries are also classified as capital ships. The reader should be aware that the definition of a battleship is a large, heavily armed armoured vessel armed with large-calibre guns. Thus the *Ark Royal* of 400 years ago

Above: The nuclear-powered aircraft carrier USS George Washington. *Aircraft carriers are the capital ships of the modern age, able to project air power into remote areas.*

Above: The American battleship USS Iowa *unleashes a salvo from her nine 16in guns.*

was one of Queen Elizabeth I's battleships, just as the *Stonewall* was for the Confederacy 200 years later.

The logical progression of this development is quite clear in the history of many of the ships featured in this book. The *Agincourt* of 1862, for example, had her guns in broadside exactly the same as the *Ark Royal* of 300 years before. She had a steam engine, but still relied on her sails at sea. Her armour was made up of iron plates backed onto a greater thickness of wood, making her literally an 'ironclad'. Like many of her time, however, she was already being fitted with rifled, breech-loading guns, which were more accurate and had a longer range than the old smoothbore muzzle-loading weapons. Her guns would also be firing explosive shells. Perfected by the French in the 1840s, they had proved their destructiveness in 1853, during the Battle of Sinope between the Russians and Turks.

So guns were becoming more effective and munitions more destructive, and the answer to that threat lay in more defensive armour. The French *Gloire* of 1859 boasted a wide wrought iron belt running from below the waterline to her upper deck, backed by up to 650mm (25.6 in) of wooden hull. But wood was becoming obsolete. *Warrior*, launched the following year for the Royal Navy was the first ship to have an iron hull. She carried four 70-pounder and ten 110-pounder guns, which outclassed *Gloire* and made *Warrior* the most powerful warship in the world. But not for long.

A Royal Navy officer called Cowper Coles wrote to the Admiralty in 1861 claiming he could disable and capture *Warrior* in an hour using a ship of his own design which cost half as much as *Warrior* to build, and which employed half the men. His secret was the gun turret. The Lords of the Admiralty accepted Cowper Coles' challenge. The *Prince Albert* was launched in 1864 and proved the potential of the gun turret, which could after all bring guns to bear on a target far faster than any ship with guns ranged along the hull. However, she could never match *Warrior* as a sea-going vessel, being too lightly rigged with sail, and her steam engine was not powerful enough for the weight of the armoured hull and the armoured turrets, each of which weighed 112 tonnes (111 tons) and had to be worked by hand.

Refusing to be discouraged, Cowper Coles went on to try and prove the viability of a sea-going turreted warship when he built *Captain* in 1869. She was fully rigged and, to prevent the masts getting in the way, the turrets were placed very low to the water. Unfortunately all this made her unseaworthy, and she capsized in a storm during her trials, taking most of the crew and Cowper Coles with her.

THE TRIUMPH OF TURRETED WARSHIPS

By the early 1870s armoured warships with turrets had proved themselves in combat. In 1862, during the American Civil War, *Monitor* of the US Navy had beaten the CSS *Virginia* in the first gun duel between completely armoured steam-driven vessels. But the combat was in shallow coastal waters and *Monitor* was later to suffer the same fate as *Captain* – she tried to take to the open sea and foundered in heavy weather. It seemed as if such designs would always be restricted to coastal defence and shallow waters.

The drawbacks to armour and steam, however, did not curb the ambitions of either designers, ship builders or navies. It was clear that the advantages of a fighting ship with steam power, armour plate and big guns were too great to be ignored for the sake of the practical problems involved in getting the right balance of all three. A ship needed enough armour to defend itself against the guns of an enemy vessel, a hull big enough to house the engines necessary to propel that weight at sufficient speed, and guns big enough to match, if not outrange, any others. It was a technical conundrum which the greatest technical minds of the age tried to solve, and which resulted in the 1870s and 1880s in a huge variety of ship designs.

The position of guns in these vessels posed a special problem, particularly until the mid-1870s, when guns and turrets had to be positioned around the full rig of sails and masts most capital ships still carried. The guns needed to be sufficiently protected, but had to be high enough off the waterline to avoid being flooded and taking the ship down. Some vessels, such as the Turkish *Lufi Djelil*, had hinged bulwarks that could be lowered to allow their turrets clear fields of fire, while others such as *Caimen* of France had guns placed in raised armoured redoubts called barbettes. Another solution, seen in France's massive battleship *Dévastation*, was to have the main armament amidships inside a central battery.

THE RAM BOW

One feature, however, which characterised most ocean-going capital ships of the period was the ram bow. Designers were greatly influenced by the ramming and sinking of the Italian battleship *Re d'Italia* at the Battle of Lissa in 1866. Despite the fact that the biggest naval guns now had a range of over 2742m (3000 yds), many saw the fate of the *Re d'Italia* as proof that ramming was a viable naval tactic and a practical use for an iron hull. For the next 30 years warships would feature the chisel-like ram bow, and some, such as the Confederate commerce raider *Stonewall*, would be built specifically as rams.

This period of experimental warship design, however, could not go on indefinitely. A fleet could not be sent to sea if every vessel in it was of a different type, with different sailing characteristics and carrying a different calibre gun. In 1889, the British Admiralty called a halt and ordered the building of an entirely new fleet of 70 ships, including eight standard first-class battleships. The resulting capital class vessel of this fleet was the *Royal Sovereign* of 1892. Her hull and guns were of steel, she was protected by armour plate up to 450mm (17.7in) thick and carried guns of 343mm (13.5in) calibre. Even though she displaced nearly 16,000 tonnes (15,744 tons), she could still make 16 knots.

The era of the big-gun battleship had arrived. But the economic cost was enormous. Naval expenditure in Britain rose by 290 per cent during the 1890s, and by the end of the decade the cost of each new Royal Navy battleship was approaching £1.5 million. Not that such considerations caused any slow-down in warship construction. The world had embarked on its first great arms race, and every industrialised country – and many, such as Brazil, who weren't – saw the possession of a navy, and particularly battleships, as a mark of their power and self-esteem. The competitive spirit

Above: The British battleship HMS Warspite. *She was one of the Royal Navy's most important ships, fighting in many key engagements in both world wars.*

in this race was particularly strong in the new world powers such as Imperial Germany and the United States, who both spent twice as much as the British on their navies in an effort to catch up.

But the British had begun this arms race, to all intents and purposes, and were not going to risk losing their naval supremacy. Quality was what was going to keep the Royal Navy ahead, even though official policy (known as the Two Power Standard) stated that they maintain a navy bigger than any other two of the largest navies in the world combined. In 1906 they launched HMS *Dreadnought*, a ship which combined every single technical advance to date, from new steam turbine engines to electrically controlled gun turrets. *Dreadnought* made obsolete every other battleship in the world, including those in her own navy, and gave her name to an entirely new class of warship.

As with many of the record-breaking vessels of the past, however, *Dreadnought*'s time as the world's number one did not last very long. By 1908 the Royal Navy was building so-called 'Super-Dreadnoughts', ships such as *Iron Duke*, which were over 8128 tonnes (8000 tons) heavier.

The future of the capital ship seemed to lay in bigger and bigger battleships carrying guns of ever-increasing size. But in the years just prior to World War I questions were being asked as to the battleship's future. While the sheer technical achievement in building them was celebrated, many – including senior Royal Navy officers – were wondering exactly how useful in battle these huge floating gun batteries would be.

Countries such as Germany were ceding the battleship contest and were beginning to develop other warship types like the battle cruiser, vessels designed for fast commerce raiding rather than naval battles, which would find ultimate expression in the great German raiders of World War II, such as *Scharnhorst* and *Bismarck*. More ominously, Germany was also investing in a fleet of torpedo-carrying submarines.

THE FIRST AIRCRAFT CARRIERS

It was to be the aircraft, though, which would ultimately make the battleship redundant. Recognised as a potential weapon in naval warfare as far back as 1894, it was the Americans who began work trying to fly an aircraft off a warship, when in January 1911 Lieutenant Theodore G. Ellyson landed a biplane on the converted deck of the cruiser *Pennsylvania*.

Aircraft were used for reconnaissance and target-spotting during World War I, but their offensive capabilities were not fully explored until the 1920s. Pioneers such as Brigadier-General 'Billy' Mitchell in the United States proved that ships could be destroyed by bombardment from the air. In trials in 1921 his aircraft even sunk the ex-German dreadnought *Ostfriedland*, though it took two days of attacks and 19 bomb hits to complete the job. The United States Navy, though, was convinced, and in 1922 its first aircraft carrier, *Langley*, was launched. Four years later plans for specially designed carrier-based aircraft were on the drawing board.

There was a new offensive weapon in the naval arsenal, but throughout the 1920s and 1930s traditionalists held firm that any future naval warfare would be decided by battleships, despite the fact that they were restricted by international disarmament treaties in 1921 and 1930 which effectively stopped battleship construction for 10 years and restricted gross tonnage when building began again.

At the beginning of World War II, battleships such as *Haruna* of Japan and the Royal Navy's HMS *Nelson* still represented the most powerful war machines made by man. But by 1942 the type had been completely eclipsed by the practicalities of a new kind of warfare, and faith in the power of the battleship had vanished forever. Air raids by torpedo planes on Taranto and Pearl Harbor, the sinking of *Repulse* and *Prince of Wales* off Malaya, the attacks on British battleships *Barham*, *Warspite*, *Queen Elizabeth* and *Valiant* in the Mediterranean, all proved that a battleship could not exist without control of the air space above it. And while there were a few successes for the old style gunnery warfare, the sinking of *Haruna* by USS *Washington* off Guadalcanal, for example, it was clear that the best practical use for a

Above: The Russian Kiev class carrier's angled deck is optimised for short take-off and landings.

battleship was in shore bombardment or as a gun platform for scores of anti-aircraft guns. The age of the aircraft carrier as a capital ship, had arrived.

The US Navy's carrier battle group represents the apogee of the aircraft carrier as the most powerful naval vessel currently in service. A carrier battle group consists of one or two carriers, each capable of deploying an air wing (which on average contains nine squadrons of aircraft, ranging from F/A-18 and F-14 fighters to SH-60 helicopters). This represents a massive capability for force projection. And yet the carriers require substantial naval assets to protect them from both air and submarine attack: guided-missile cruisers, guided-missile destroyers, anti-submarine warfare destroyers, anti-submarine warfare frigates and even one or two nuclear submarines – proof that the capital ship, no matter how powerful, is always vulnerable.

Admiral Graf Spee

Limited by the 1919 Treaty of Versailles to a maximum displacement of 10,200 tonnes (10,039 tons), Germany produced the cleverly designed 'pocket' battleship. Great savings were achieved by using electric welding and light alloys in the hull. *Admiral Graf Spee*, with her two sister ships, *Deutschland* and *Admiral Scheer*, were intended primarily as commerce-raiders. The ship was scuttled off Montevideo, Uruguay, after engaging three British cruisers, *Exeter*, *Ajax* and *Achilles*, in the Battle of the River Plate in December 1939. This ship was officially classified as being an 'armoured ship' by the Germans, though it was popularly referred to as being a 'pocket' battleship, a title which stuck. In actual fact neither term is strictly correct, for she was in reality an armoured cruiser of an exceptionally powerful type.

Country of origin:	Germany
Crew:	926
Weight:	10,160 tonnes (10,000 tons)
Dimensions:	186m x 20.6m x 7.2m (610ft 3in x 67ft 7in x 23ft 7in)
Range:	37,040km (20,000nm) at 15 knots
Armour:	76mm (3in) belt, 140 – 76mm (5.5 – 3in) on turrets, 38mm (1.5in) on deck
Armament:	Six 279mm (11in), eight 150mm (6in) guns
Powerplant:	Eight sets of MAN diesels, two shafts
Performance:	26 knots

Affondatore

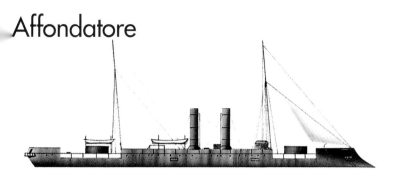

An iron-hulled schooner rigged vessel, *Affondatore* had a pronounced wrought iron ram. She had two turrets, each designed by the British Navy's Captain Cowper Coles. She acted as the flagship of Admiral Persano's fleet at the Battle of Lissa in July 1866, and remained in service with the Italian Navy for a further 41 years. The battle was the culmination of Italo-Austrian rivalry in the Adriatic, and was the only fleet action of the ironclad era. The tactics of the Austrian commander, Admiral Tegetthof, relied on the ram as his artillery was especially weak (his Krupp guns had not been delivered as Austria and Prussia were at that time at war). When his flagship, the *Ferdinand Max*, rammed the *Re d'Italia* the ram instantly became the preferred weapon of many naval commanders. This thinking was entirely misplaced, as the Italian ship had been dead in the water, her rudder shot away.

Country of origin:	Italy
Crew:	460
Weight:	4070 tonnes (4006 tons)
Dimensions:	93.9m x 12m x 6.3m (308ft x 39ft 4in x 20ft 8in)
Range:	2779km (1500nm) at 10 knots
Armour:	127mm (5in) belt and turrets
Armament:	Two 254mm (10in) muzzle-loading rifled (MLR) guns
Powerplant:	Single screw, horizontal compound engines
Performance:	12 knots

Agamemnon

Agamemnon was one of the Lord Nelson class and the last of Britain's pre-dreadnoughts. Laid down in 1904, her construction coincided with that of HMS *Dreadnought*. As a result *Agamemnon*'s completion was delayed until 1908, by which time *Dreadnought* had made history and the Lord Nelson class was launched into virtual obsolescence. Characterised by their large secondary armament, which differed of course from the all big-gun dreadnoughts, the class was known at the time for having a rather French look to its design, with a high superstructure and low unequal-sized funnels. *Agamemnon* served in the eastern Mediterranean during World War I, and saw action in the Dardenelles. During these operations she was hit over 60 times, and on 15 May 1916 her gunners shot down Zeppelin L85 at Salonika.

Country of origin:	Great Britain
Crew:	810
Weight:	16,347 tonnes (16,090 tons)
Dimensions:	124m x 135m x 24m (410ft x 44ft 6in x 79ft 6in)
Range:	17,000km (9180nm) at 10 knots
Armour:	304mm – 203mm (12in – 8in) belt, 178mm – 304mm (7.1 – 12in) on citadel and turrets
Armament:	Four 304mm (12in), ten 234mm (9.2in), 24 12-pounder guns, five torpedo tubes
Powerplant:	Twin shaft four cylinder engine
Performance:	18 knots

Agincourt

Agincourt was constructed with all her guns placed in one long armoured battery, while her two sister ships, *Northumberland* and *Minotaur*, had the distinction of being the longest single-screw warships ever built. *Agincourt* was also one of the last British ships to be fitted with muzzle-loading guns. These guns were to be replaced in the 1860s with breech-loading weapons. *Agincourt* and her two sister vessels, each had five masts and two funnels. *Minotaur* served as flagship during her active career; *Northumberland* was armed with the new 8in guns and had her side armour reduced. *Agincourt* was first laid down as HMS *Captain*. After being paid off she was used as a training ship. She was to end her days (from 1908 onwards) as a coal hulk at Sheerness. *Agincourt* was not broken up until 1960.

Country of origin:	Great Britain
Crew:	800
Weight:	10,812 tonnes (10,642 tons) full load
Dimensions:	124m x 18.2m x 85m (406ft 10in x 59ft 9in x 278ft 10in)
Range:	5067km (2825nm) at 10 knots
Armour:	127mm (5in) belt and battery with 254mm (10in) wood backing
Armament:	Four 229mm (9in) guns and 24 178mm (7in) muzzle-loading rifled guns
Powerplant:	Single shaft two cylinder engine
Performance:	14.8 knots

Agincourt

Originally ordered in Britain by the Brazilian Government and named *Rio de Janiero* when she launched in 1913, the Brazilians found they could not afford her. She was sold on to Turkey as *Sultan Osman I*, but never delivered. Completed in August 1914, she was appropriated by the Royal Navy for war service and renamed *Agincourt*. In design she had many unusual features, not least her length and big main armament of 14 304mm (12in) guns on seven twin turrets. However, this huge amount of weight weakened her hull which was in any case woefully underprotected. She was nevertheless known in her time as a good sea boat. Her tripod main mast was reduced to a pole in 1917 and later removed. After World War I, *Agincourt* was unsuccessfully offered for sale back to Brazil, and sold for scrap in the 1920s.

Country of origin:	Great Britain
Crew:	1270
Weight:	27,940 tonnes (27,500 tons)
Dimensions:	204.7m x 27.1m x 8.2m (671ft 6in x 89ft x 27ft)
Range:	8100km (4500nm) at 12 knots
Armour:	229mm – 102mm (9in – 4in) belt, 152mm (6in) on bulkheads
Armament:	14 304mm (12in), 20 152mm (6in), 10 76mm (3in) guns
Powerplant:	Four shaft geared turbines
Performance:	22 knots

Akagi

A kagi was designed as a 41,820 tonne (41,161 ton) battlecruiser but, while still on the stocks, the Washington Naval Treaty of 1922 (whereby Japan was forced to restrict her naval programme) caused the design to be altered. Built to dispatch up to 60 aircraft, she was modified to carry heavier aircraft and more light guns. As converted, she had three flight decks forward, no island and two funnels on the starboard side, one pointing up, the other out and down. During reconstruction (1935–38) the two lower flight decks forward were removed and the top flight deck extended forward to the bow. An island was added on the port side. *Akagi* led the Japanese carrier assault on Pearl Harbor on 7 December 1941, but was destroyed seven months later by bombs dropped by US Navy divebombers at the decisive Battle of Midway.

Country of origin:	Japan
Crew:	2000
Weight:	29,580 tonnes (29,114 tons)
Dimensions:	249m x 30.5m x 8.1m (816ft 11in x 100ft x 26ft 7in)
Range:	14,800km (8000nm) at 14 knots
Armour:	152mm (6in) belt
Armament:	10 203mm (8in), 12 119mm (4.7in) guns, 91 aircraft
Powerplant:	Four shaft turbines
Performance:	32.5 knots

Almirante Cochrane

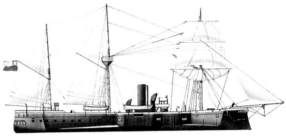

*A*lmirante Cochrane and her sister ship, *Blanco Encalada*, both combined good protection with a powerful armament on a small displacement. *Almirante Cochrane*'s guns were in an armoured box. Both of these battleships took part in the war with Peru when Chile seized large parts of the Peruvian coastline. *Blanco Encalada* was the first battleship to have the dubious honour of being sunk by a modern torpedo. Launched in 1874, *Almirante Cochrane* was named in honour of Thomas, Lord Cochrane (1775–1860), Earl of Dundonald, the British naval officer who commanded the Chilean Navy in the war of independence. *Almirante Cochrane* fought on the Congressional side during the civil war of 1891; she was subsequently used as a torpedo and gunnery school ship, and was broken up in 1934.

Country of origin:	Chile
Crew:	300
Weight:	3631 tonnes (3574 tons)
Dimensions:	64m x 13.9m x 6.7m (210ft x 45ft 7in x 22ft)
Range:	2223km (1200nm) at 10 knots
Armour:	229mm (9in) belt, 203mm – 152mm (8in to 6in) on central battery
Armament:	Six 209mm (8.2in) guns
Powerplant:	Twin shaft horizontal compound engine
Performance:	12.75 knots

America

The *Kitty Hawk* class were the first aircraft carriers not to carry conventional guns. Intended to be larger and improved versions of the earlier Forrestal class, *Kitty Hawk* (CV 63) and *Constellation* (CV 64) were the first two built. The third, *America* (CV 66), was launched in 1964, and incorporated further improvements based on operational experience. Her dimensions are slightly different to those of her sisters, with a narrower smokestack. She was the first carrier to be equipped with an integrated Combat Information Centre (CIC) and is also fitted with a bow-mounted sonar. A fourth ship, *John F. Kennedy* (CV 67), was built after the US Congress refused to sanction a nuclear-powered vessel in 1964. Policy has since changed, and all large US carriers since then have used nuclear propulsion, leaving *America* and her sisters as the largest conventionally driven vessels in service.

Country of origin:	USA
Crew:	3306, 1379 with air group
Weight:	81,090 tonnes (79,813 tons) fully loaded
Dimensions:	324m x 77m x 10.7m (1063ft x 252ft 7in x 35ft)
Range:	21,600km (12,000nm) at 12 knots
Armour:	Belt 51mm (2in)
Armament:	Three Mark 29 launchers for NATO Sea Sparrow SAMs, three 20mm (0.79in) Phalanx CIWS (Close-in Weapons System), 90 aircraft
Powerplant:	Four shaft geared turbines
Performance:	33 knots

Ammiraglio di Saint Bon

Launched in 1897, *Ammiraglio di Saint Bon* was a compact, heavily protected vessel. A flagship of the Italian Navy, *Ammiraglio di Saint Bon* was a fine example of the emphasis that Italian naval planners of the time were putting on armour. For example, her 152mm (6in) guns were housed in an armoured central battery. Improvements in metallurgical technology in the late 1800s meant that the ship's speed would not be impaired by her solid build. *Ammiraglio di Saint Bon* took part in the Italo-Turkish War; in 1912 she supported Italian forces occupying Tripoli, and in the same year she operated in the Aegean Sea in support of Italian forces occupying the island of Rhodes during the Balkan War. During World War I she was based on Venice for operations in the Adriatic. She was decommissioned in June 1920.

Country of origin:	Italy
Crew:	450
Weight:	10,156 tonnes (9996 tons)
Dimensions:	105m x 21m x 7.6m (344ft 6in x 69ft x 25ft)
Range:	3200km (2000 miles) at 10 knots
Armour:	254mm (10in) steel plate
Armament:	Four 254mm (10in), eight 152mm (6in) guns
Powerplant:	Two vertical triple expansion engines developing 14,000hp; 12 cylindrical boilers
Performance:	18 knots

Andrea Doria

Laid down in 1912, and launched four years later in 1916, *Andrea Doria*, and her sister ship *Caio Duilio*, both underwent a very rigorous reconstruction programme from 1937 to 1940. *Andrea Doria*'s top speed was increased from 21.5 to 27 knots and in addition she was given improved armour on her turrets and engine rooms. During World War I she operated in the southern Adriatic, and subsequently in 1919 she operated in the Black Sea, supporting the Allied Intervention Force operating in South Russia on the loyalist side during the civil war. During World War II *Andrea Doria* took part in convoy battles and in some notable actions, including the First Battle of Sirte. She was placed on the Reserve in 1942, and in the following year she surrendered to the British at Malta. Both ships remained in service until 1958.

Country of origin:	Italy
Crew:	1198
Weight:	26,115 tonnes (25,704 tons)
Dimensions:	176m x 28m x 8.8m (577ft 5in x 91ft 10in x 28ft 10in)
Range:	8784km (4800nm) at 10 knots (before reconstruction)
Armour:	229mm (9in) belt, 229mm (9in) turrets, 127mm (5in) on guns
Armament:	13 304mm (12in), 16 152mm (6in) guns
Powerplant:	Twin shaft geared turbines
Performance:	26 knots

Appalachian

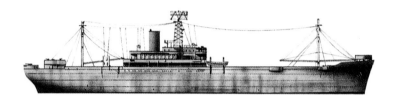

Appalachian was one of an important group of ships that acted both as the headquarters ship and as air control for the amphibious assaults on Japanese-held islands during World War II. In January 1945 she was headquarters ship for Amphibious Group 3, which operated in support of the large-scale US landings at Lingayen Gulf in the Philippines. The landings were heavily contested by Japanese Kamikaze suicide pilots, who managed to sink a US carrier and damage several more, but *Appalachian* escaped unharmed. *Appalachian*, which was designated *AGC.1*, was the first of seventeen US amphibious force flagships, which served in all theatres of war. She later served briefly as Pacific Fleet flagship in 1947, before being removed from the active list that same year. She was broken up in 1960.

Country of origin:	USA
Crew:	507 and 368 HQ personnel
Weight:	14,133 tonnes (13,910 tons)
Dimensions:	132.6m x 19.2m x 7.3m (435ft x 63ft x 24ft)
Range:	5560km (3000nm) at 16 knots
Armour:	Varied, depending on protection of key points
Armament:	Two 127mm (5in), eight 40mm (1.6in) guns
Powerplant:	Single shaft turbine
Performance:	17 knots

Aquila

A *quila* began her life as the 33,764-tonne (33,232 ton) cruise ship *Roma*.
She was requisitioned by the Italian Navy in 1941 for conversion into the
first Italian aircraft carrier. Several improvements were undertaken during
World War II. For example, more powerful engines were installed as well as an
enormous second underwater keel, into which cement was poured to increase
stability. In September 1943, when almost completed at Genoa, *Aquila* was seized
by the Germans following Italy's surrender, and on 19 April 1945 she was severely
damaged by Italian human torpedoes to prevent her being used by the Germans as
a blockship. She was intended to carry an air group of 51 aircraft, and her turbines
were taken from the uncompleted cruisers *Silla* and *Emilio*. *Aquila* never saw
service and was broken up in 1951.

Country of origin:	Italy
Crew:	1165 and 24 air personnel
Weight:	28,810 tonnes (28,356 tons)
Dimensions:	231.5m x 29.4m x 7.3m (759ft 6in x 96ft 5in x 24ft)
Range:	5400km (4150nm) at 18 knots
Armour:	Not fitted
Armament:	Eight 135mm (5.3in) guns, 36 aircraft
Powerplant:	Four shaft geared turbines
Performance:	32 knots

Arapiles

A rapiles was originally planned as a wooden screw frigate, but she was altered
while still on the stocks to become a broadside ironclad with a midship
armour belt that added over 200 tonnes (203 tons) to the displacement. In 1873
Arapiles grounded off Venezuela and was sent to New York for repairs. This
removal coincided with the crisis that had arisen between Spain and the USA
over the seizure of the American steamer *Virginius* by a Spanish cruiser off Cuba.
During this crisis, a sunken lighter effectively prevented any attempt to effect her
escape from dry dock. In the end, the poor state of *Arapiles*' wooden hull meant
that it was uneconomic to carry out repairs. The name of the vessel was taken from
the site of the Battle of Salamanca (1812), in which the Duke of Wellington defeated
the French.

Country of origin:	Spain
Crew:	350
Weight:	5791 tonnes (5700 tons)
Dimensions:	85.4m x 16.5m (280ft x 54ft)
Range:	Not known
Armour:	121mm (4.8in) iron belt
Armament:	Two 254mm (10in), five 203mm (8in) guns
Powerplant:	100nhp steam engine
Performance:	12 knots

Arizona

*A**rizona***, like her sister ship *Pennsylvania*, was an improved and enlarged version of the Nevada class, her main armament being housed in four triple turrets. Launched in 1915, and completed the following year, *Arizona* did not see any action during World War I. In 1941 she sailed to the Pacific to join the US fleet based at Pearl Harbor. On the morning of 7 December the Japanese launched an air attack without warning. One of the first ships hit was *Arizona*. A bomb is believed to have struck one of her forward turrets which detonated the magazine beneath. The ship blew up taking over a thousand of her crew with her. *Arizona* was one of four US battleships sunk at Pearl Harbor; a fifth was beached and three more damaged. Today her remains still lie in the shallow waters of the harbour where she is preserved as a war grave.

Country of origin:	USA
Crew:	1117
Weight:	32,045 tonnes (32,567 tons)
Dimensions:	185.4m x 29.6m x 8.8m (608ft x 97ft 1in x 28ft 10in)
Range:	14,400km (8000nm) at 10 knots
Armour:	343mm – 203mm (13.5in – 8in) belt, 450mm – 229mm (18in – 9in) on turrets
Armament:	12 356mm (14in), 22 127mm (5in) guns
Powerplant:	Four shaft geared turbines
Performance:	21 knots

Ark Royal

Built for Sir Walter Raleigh in 1587 (he intended to use her in his project for the colonisation of North America), and originally named *Anne Royal*, this ship was purchased by Queen Elizabeth I for £5,000 and renamed *Ark Royal*. She was the flagship of Lord Howard of Effingham at the battle against the Spanish Armada of 1588 and was one of the largest vessels in the English fleet. *Ark Royal* had two gun decks, a double forecastle, a quarter deck and a poop deck right aft. She had an elegant outline and none of the cluttered superstructure then common on such large vessels. Her armament ranged from 19kg to 2.7kg (41.8lb to 5.9lb) guns. Britain was the first nation to adopt the galleon, in the reign of Henry VIII, while Spain was the last great maritime nation to adopt it. *Ark Royal* was accidentally burnt while in dock.

Country of origin:	Great Britain
Crew:	340 sailors, 268 gunners, 100 soldiers
Weight:	813 tonnes (800 tons)
Dimensions:	88.7m x 13.1m x 7.3m (291ft x 43ft x 24ft)
Range:	–
Armour:	–
Armament:	55 guns
Powerplant:	–
Performance:	–

Ark Royal

*A*rk Royal was the first large purpose-built aircraft carrier to be constructed for the Royal Navy, with a long flight deck some 18m (60ft) above the deep water load line. The aircraft carrier's full complement was 60 aircraft, although she never actually carried this many as such a load would have reduced her fighting capability. During her war operations, she took part in the Norwegian campaign of 1940 and was subsequently transferred to the Mediterranean Theatre, where she joined 'Force H' at Gibraltar. In May 1941 one of her Swordfish aircraft torpedoed the German battleship *Bismarck*, destroying the warship's steering gear – an act that led to *Bismarck* being sunk some hours later by the British Fleet. In November 1941 *Ark Royal* was torpedoed by the German submarine *U81* and capsized after 14 hours.

Country of origin:	Great Britain
Crew:	1580
Weight:	28,164 tonnes (27,720 tons)
Dimensions:	243.8m x 28.9m x 8.5m (800ft x 94ft 9in x 27ft 9in)
Range:	14,119km (7620nm) at 20 knots
Armour:	114mm (4.5in) belt, 76mm (3in) bulkheads
Armament:	16 114mm (4.5in) guns, 60 aircraft
Powerplant:	Triple shaft geared turbines
Performance:	31 knots

Armide

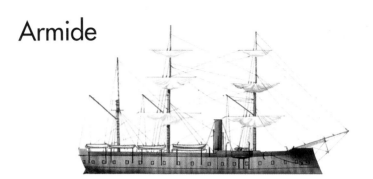

*A*rmide and her six sisters were designed as central battery ships for service on far flung foreign stations. The larger battleships then in service were too costly to build and maintain away from Europe, so *Armide* was ideally suited to arenas where she was unlikely to meet an opponent stronger than herself. In 1870 *Armide* operated in the North Sea and the Baltic, implementing the naval blockade of Prussia during the Franco–Prussian war (a blockade which, incidentally, persuaded the Germans that they needed a powerful, modern fleet) and in 1873 she undertook a blockade of Cartagena, Spain, during a period of civil unrest there. She was broken up in 1887. *Armide* had a wooden hull and was barque-rigged, with a sail area of 1,450 square metres (14,500 sq ft). Alma class were 'handy' ships, with a turning circle of 330m (360yds).

Country of origin:	France
Crew:	316
Weight:	3569 tonnes (3513 tons)
Dimensions:	70m x 14 x 7m (229ft 8in x 46ft x 23ft)
Range:	2233km (1460nm) at 10 knots
Armour:	152mm (6in) belt, 120mm (4.7in) on battery
Armament:	Six 193mm (7.6in) guns
Powerplant:	Single shaft horizontal compound
Performance:	11.9 knots

Arminius

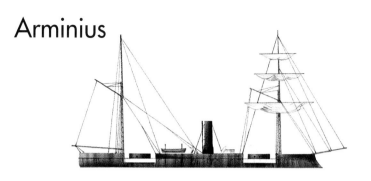

In the 1860s Prussia was anxious to defend herself against the Danes. Unable to build suitable warships herself, Prussia purchased *Arminius*, a ship that was being built in England. She was launched in 1864 and hastily completed, but arrived too late in the Baltic to take part in the war with Denmark. One of a type designed by Captain Cowper Coles of the Royal Navy – the man instrumental in developing the gun turret – *Arminius* became the first battleship to join what was to become the German Navy. She became a coastal defence vessel, helping to protect the River Elbe in the Franco-Prussian war of 1870. In October 1870 she was damaged in a collision with the despatch vessel *Falcke* off Wilhelmshaven. After repair she was an engineering training ship, then an icebreaker. She was broken up in 1902 at Hamburg.

Country of origin:	Germany
Crew:	132
Weight:	1917 tonnes (1887 tons)
Dimensions:	63.2m x 10.9m x 4.6m (207ft 5in x 35ft 9in x 15ft)
Range:	1853km (1000nm) at 8 knots
Armour:	114mm (4.5in) belt with wooden backing
Armament:	Four 208mm (8.2in) guns
Powerplant:	Single screw, single horizontal two-cylinder engine
Performance:	11.2 knots

Arpad

A rpad was developed as a small battleship type which was intended for service in the Adriatic. Although the vessel was fairly well protected, her main armament was weak. Nevertheless, her secondary battery was certainly as powerful as that of any battleship in service at the time. *Arpad* was one of the first warships to rely heavily on electricity in order to work the main guns, hoists and ventilators. *Arpad* was one of the Hapsburg class of pre-Dreadnought battleships. She took her name from the 10th-century chief of the Magyars, who was also the national hero of Hungary. Launched in 1899 and completed in 1903, *Arpad* then underwent a substantial refit in 1911–12. At the end of World War I she was put to use as a training ship; she was interned at Pola in 1918 and broken up in Italy in 1920.

Country of origin:	Austria
Crew:	638
Weight:	8965 tonnes (8823 tons)
Dimensions:	114.8m x 19.9m x 7.5m (376ft 6in x 65ft 2in x 24ft 6in)
Range:	6670km (3600nm) at 10 knots
Armour:	220mm (8.6in) thick belt, 280mm (11in) turrets and centre casement
Armament:	Three 240mm (9.5in), 12 152mm (6in) guns
Powerplant:	Twin screw triple expansion engines
Performance:	19.6 knots

Asahi

In 1896 Japan began a naval expansion programme. Because her own shipyards were not yet ready to accommodate such a programme, *Asahi* and her three sister ships were ordered from British yards. All four vessels were designed by G.C. Macrow along the lines of the Royal Navy's Canopus class. *Asahi* saw extensive operational service in the 1904–05 war with Russia serving as Admiral Togo's flagship. She took part in the blockade of Port Arthur, where she was moderately damaged by a mine, and on 27 May 1905 she sustained nine shell hits in the decisive Battle of Tsushima. She was later preserved as a memorial. In 1923 *Asahi* was converted to a submarine depot ship. Finally, on 25 May 1942 she was torpedoed and sunk by the US submarine *Salmon* in the South China Sea.

Country of origin:	Japan
Crew:	836
Weight:	15,443 tonnes (15,2000 tons)
Dimensions:	133.5m x 23m x 8.4m (438ft x 75ft 6in x 27ft 6in)
Range:	16,677km (9000nm) at 10 knots
Armour:	229mm – 102mm (9in – 4in) belt, 356mm – 203mm (14in – 8in) around guns
Armament:	Four 304mm (12in), 14 152mm (6in) guns
Powerplant:	Twin screw, vertical triple expansion engines
Performance:	18 knots

Assar-i-Tewfik

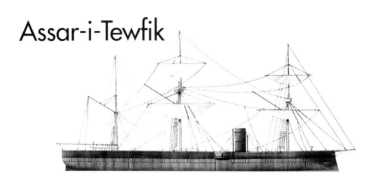

Formerly known as the Egyptian ironclad *Ibrahmieh*, which had been launched in 1868, the ship was renamed *Assar-i-Tewfik*. She had six of her heavy guns concentrated in an armoured battery, which also protected the funnel base. As a further improvement, two more guns were mounted directly above the battery. This new arrangement helped reduce the average size of battleships, and resulted in greater manoeuvrability. In December 1916 *Assar-i-Tewfik* went into action off the Dardanelles in the Balkan war against Bulgaria, receiving some damage. Then, on 11 February 1912, she ran aground near Podima in the Bosphorus while supporting troops in action and had to be abandoned. Defined as a coastal battery ship, *Assar-i-Tewfik* was similar to the French Trident class of vessel.

Country of origin:	Turkey
Crew:	320
Weight:	4762 tonnes (4687 tons)
Dimensions:	83m x 16m x 6.5m (272ft 4in x 52ft 6in x 21ft 4in)
Range:	2965km (1600nm) at 10 knots
Armour:	Belt 76 – 140mm (2.98 – 5.5in), battery 127mm (4.99in)
Armament:	Eight 228mm (9in) muzzle-loading guns
Powerplant:	Single shaft compound engines
Performance:	13 knots

Attu

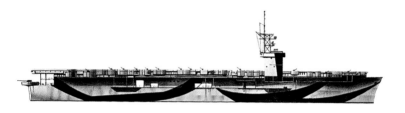

In 1942, shipbuilder Henry J. Kaiser was employed in the mass production of cargo vessels to replace those that had been lost in action. It was decided at that time to complete 50 of the unfinished hulls as escort carriers. The resultant vessel was named *Attu* (*CVE 102*). Her 49 sister ships of the Casablanca class, were all completed within a single year. The Casablanca class carried an air group of nine bombers, nine torpedo bombers and nine fighters. They were the first vessels of their kind to be built as escort carriers from the keel up. All of the Casablanca class went on to serve in the Pacific, with the exception of *Guadalcanal* and *Kasaan Bay*, both of which saw service in the Atlantic. In 1947, *Attu* was converted for mercantile use and renamed *Gay*. She was subsequently scrapped at Baltimore in 1949.

Country of origin:	USA
Crew:	860
Weight:	11,076 tonnes (10,902 tons)
Dimensions:	156.1m x 32.9m x 6.3m (512ft 3in x 108ft x 20ft 9in)
Range:	18,360km (10,200nm) at 10 knots
Armour:	Flight deck unarmoured
Armament:	One 127mm (5in), 38 40mm (1.5in) guns, 27 aircraft
Powerplant:	Twin screw reciprocating engines
Performance:	15 knots

Audacious

*A*udacious saw extensive service in the almost continuous warfare that Britain was engaged in at the turn of the 18th century. Her type was considered to be the best balance between offensive power and sailing ability, and formed the backbone of the battleline. Vessels like *Audacious* were virtually floating gun platforms, their primary task being to undertake offensive operations against an enemy fleet. Launched in 1785, *Audacious* took part in many actions, including the Battle of the Nile in August 1798, when she fought and overcame the French ship *Conquérant*. However, British vessels of the period were built to a standard pattern and were considered too small for the number of guns carried. French vessels had a better underwater hull form and could usually outsail their British counterparts. She was broken up in 1815.

Country of origin:	Great Britain
Crew:	550
Weight:	1422 tonnes (1400 tons)
Dimensions:	54.8m x 14.9m (180ft x 49ft)
Range:	–
Armour:	–
Armament:	36 32-pounders on the lower deck, 34 24-pounders on the main gun deck, 10 18-pounders on the upper deck
Powerplant:	–
Performance:	–

Audacious

Built in answer to the growing strength and ambition of the German Navy, *Audacious*, one of the King George V class, was part of the 1911 British battleship expansion programme. She carried the foremast before the funnels, giving better vision to fire control when underway, a standard arrangement on all subsequent dreadnoughts. While on patrol in October 1914, *Audacious* struck a mine off Ireland and all attempts to tow her to safety failed. She was the first major British warship lost in World War I. Of the other two vessels in her class, *King George V* served as a gunnery training ship after World War I, and was broken up in 1926, and *Centurion* went on to see service in World War II as a floating AA battery in the Mediterranean. She was sunk off Normandy in June 1944 to form part of an artificial harbour.

Country of origin:	Great Britain
Crew:	782
Weight:	26,111 tonnes (25,700 tons)
Dimensions:	182.1m x 27.1m x 8.7m (597ft 6in x 89ft x 28ft 6in)
Range:	12,114km (6730nm) at 10 knots
Armour:	305 – 203mm (12.8 – 7.9in) main belt with 280mm (11in) on turrets
Armament:	10 342mm (13.5in), 16 102mm (4in) guns
Powerplant:	Four shaft geared turbines
Performance:	21 knots

Australia

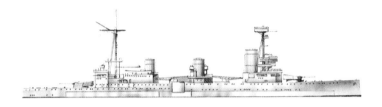

*A*ustralia was a new type of cruiser. Improvements in speed had been achieved by reducing armour protection, and by reducing the main guns by two. In addition, the middle group of turrets, placed in échelon, had a greater field of fire. *Australia* was built on the Clyde in 1913, and after completion she sailed to the Pacific to become the flagship of the Royal Australian Navy. She returned to Britain mid-way through World War I, but was unable to take part in the Battle of Jutland as the result of a collision with the battlecruiser *New Zealand* in fog. In December 1916 *Australia* was damaged in another collision, this time with the battlecruiser *Repulse*. *Australia* was decommissioned in December 1921, and was subsequently used as a target ship, until she was sunk off Sydney in April 1924.

Country of origin:	Australia
Crew:	800
Weight:	21,640 tonnes (21,300 tons)
Dimensions:	180m x 24.3m x 9m (590ft x 80ft x 30ft)
Range:	11,394km (6330nm) at 10 knots
Armour:	152mm (6in) belt
Armament:	Eight 304mm (12in) guns
Powerplant:	Four screw geared turbines
Performance:	26.9 knots

Baden

Baden and her sister *Bayern* were completed in 1916. In contrast to earlier classes in the Imperial German Navy, such as the König, their main armament was increased from 304mm (12in) to 380mm (15in). This was to match the guns rumoured to be carried on the new British Queen Elizabeth class. Unusually for a battleship of the period *Baden* was coal-fired, since wartime fuel oil supplies in Germany were too unpredictable. Commissioned too late to have much impact on World War I, *Baden* was Fleet Flagship from October 1916, replacing *Friedrich der Grosse*, and surrendered in 1918. She was not scheduled to be surrendered, but was substituted for the incomplete *Mackensen*. She was unsuccessfully scuttled at Scapa Flow in 1919, and after being salvaged by the Royal Navy was used as a gunnery target, then sunk.

Country of origin:	Germany
Crew:	1271
Weight:	32,197 tonnes (31,690 tons) deep load
Dimensions:	179.8m x 30m x 8.43m (589ft 10in x 98ft 5in x 27ft 8in)
Range:	9000km (5000nm) at 10 knots
Armour:	356mm – 120mm (14in – 4.7in) belt, 304mm – 140mm (12in – 5.5in) bulkheads, 356mm – 102mm (14in – 4in) turrets
Armament:	Eight 380mm (15in), 16 150mm (5.9in) guns
Powerplant:	Three shaft turbines
Performance:	22 knots

Barham

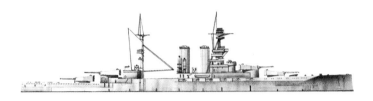

Barham and her three sisters were designed to compete with new battleships (with 355mm [14in] guns) being designed by Germany, Japan and the USA. The class was equipped with newly designed 380mm (15in) guns, which proved more accurate than the previous 343mm (13.5in) guns, and also carried a much bigger bursting charge. *Barham* was badly damaged at Jutland in 1916. All ships in the class underwent modernisation in the early 1930s. *Barham* was sunk with heavy loss of life off Sollum in the Mediterranean by *U331* on 25 November 1941. The other ships in Barham's class were *Malaya, Queen Elizabeth, Valiant* and *Warspite*. After extensive war service, they were broken up in 1947–48. *Valiant* and *Queen Elizabeth* were badly damaged in a daring attack by Italian frogmen in Alexandria harbour in 1941.

Country of origin:	Great Britain
Crew:	951
Weight:	32,004 tonnes (31,500 tons)
Dimensions:	196m x 27.6m x 8.8m (643ft x 90ft 6in x 29ft)
Range:	26,100km (14,500nm) at 10 knots
Armour:	330mm – 152mm (13in – 6in) belt, 330mm (15in) turrets
Armament:	Eight 381mm (15in), 14 152mm (6in) guns
Powerplant:	Four shaft turbines
Performance:	24 knots

Barrozo

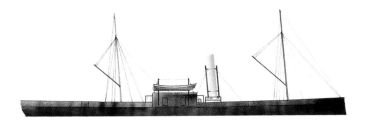

As a country with a long coastline, Brazil always maintained a substantial navy, almost from the moment the country gained its independence from Portugal in 1822. During the conflict with Paraguay it acquired a fleet of small armoured monitors which, like *Barrozo*, waged a river campaign in the interior of the South American continent. *Barrozo* was an armoured central battery ship with a wooden hull, which served extensively in the 1865-70 war with Paraguay. Towards the end of the war in July 1870, the Paraguayans tried to capture *Barrozo* and *Rio Grande* by drifting down river in canoes and then boarding the ships. *Rio Grande* was boarded first, and most of her crew were killed. Meanwhile, *Barrozo* had steamed alongside and was able to kill all the boarders on *Rio Grande*'s deck with grape shot. *Barrozo* was discarded in 1885.

Country of origin:	Brazil
Crew:	70
Weight:	1375 tonnes (1354 tons)
Dimensions:	57m x 11.2m x 2.4m (186ft x 37ft x 8ft)
Range:	1853km (1000nm) at 8 knots
Armour:	95mm – 62mm (3.8in – 2.5in) iron belt
Armament:	Two 178mm (7in), three 120mm (4.7in) guns
Powerplant:	Single screw single expansion engine
Performance:	9 knots

Basileus Georgios

***B**asileus Georgios* was a small central battery ship with a full length armour belt. The armour made up 340 tonnes (335 tons) of the displacement, giving the diminutive battleship greater offensive and defensive capabilities on a small displacement than any other battleship of her time. The battery was placed forward of centre and ahead of the funnel, with end ports in the corners to enable firing ahead or astern. *Basileus Georgios*, named after George I, King of Greece (1845–1913) was one of two small ironclads which had been acquired in the mid-19th century. These remained the principal vessels in service with the Greek Navy until the advent of the three small battleships of the Hydra class (*Hydra*, *Psara* and *Spetsai*) in 1887. No further measures were taken to enhance Greek sea power until 1900.

Country of origin:	Greece
Crew:	152
Weight:	1802 tonnes (1774 tons)
Dimensions:	61m x 10m x 4.8m (200ft x 33ft x 16ft)
Range:	2409km (1300nm) at 12 knots
Armour:	178mm – 152mm (7in – 6in) iron belt, 152mm (6in) round battery
Armament:	Two 229mm (9in) guns
Powerplant:	Twin screw compound engines
Performance:	12.2 knots

Béarn

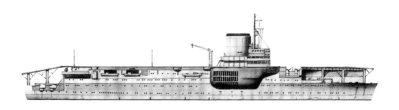

The aircraft carrier *Béarn* was converted from the incompleted hull of a Normandie class battleship, and her original turbine propulsion was replaced by the combined system which was designed for that vessel. In October 1939 she formed a key element of a hunting group (Force L) based on Brest, which, together with other British and French naval forces, was engaged in the search for the German pocket battleship *Admiral Graf Spee*. Apart from that, *Béarn* was not used as a frontline carrier in World War II because of her low speed, but she gave valuable service as an aircraft ferry. After the fall of France in 1940, *Béarn* was captured and held at Martinique to prevent her return to France. After the war she served off Indo-China (Vietnam) during France's conflict there. She was scrapped in 1949.

Country of origin:	France
Crew:	875
Weight:	28,854 tonnes (28,400 tons)
Dimensions:	182.5m x 27m x 9m (599ft x 88ft 11in x 30ft 6in)
Range:	14,824km (6000nm) at 10 knots
Armour:	94mm (3.75in) belt, 25mm (1in) flight deck
Armament:	Eight 152mm (6in) guns, 40 aircraft
Powerplant:	Four screw geared turbines, triple expansion engines
Performance:	21.5 knots

Belleisle

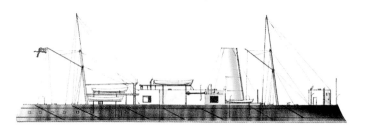

B*elleisle* and her sister ship *Orion* were originally laid down for the Turkish Navy. British neutrality during the Russo-Turkish war of 1878 meant that these ships could not be delivered, so they were bought by the Royal Navy. Their 305mm (12in) guns were mounted in a large central battery, where they could fire ahead and astern as well as in broadside. Poor sea-keeping capabilities meant that the vessels were used in coastal defence. The armour belt ran the full length of the hull, and supported a 2.4m (8ft) solid-forged ram, already an anachronism in 1876. In 1886 she was fitted with extra light guns and a torpedo net. The last British central battery ship, *Belleisle* briefly had a square rig when she was completed, and had her short funnel raised in 1879. From 1900, she was used as a target hulk. She was broken up in 1904.

Country of origin:	Great Britain
Crew:	250
Weight:	1802 tonnes (1774 tons)
Dimensions:	61m x 10m x 4.8m (200ft x 33ft x 16ft)
Range:	3726km (2000nm) at 10 knots
Armour:	304mm – 152mm (12in – 6in) belt, 262mm – 203mm (10.5in – 8in) battery, 229mm – 127mm (9in – 5in) bulkheads
Armament:	Two 228mm (9in) guns
Powerplant:	Twin screw compound engines
Performance:	13 knots

Bellerophon

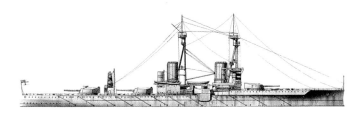

Launched in 1907, *Bellerophon* and her sisters *Temeraire* and *Superb* closely followed the dimensions of HMS *Dreadnought*, though their torpedo defences were increased with improvements to bulkhead armour and secondary armament. When completed in 1909 the Bellerophon class also had masts in front of funnels. This avoided the smoke problems to the command top encountered on *Dreadnought*, which had a single mast behind its forward funnel. *Bellerophon* had an unlucky early career, being damaged in a collision with the battlecruiser *Inflexible* in 1911 and subsequently with the merchant vessel *St Clair* in 1914. She served with the Home Fleet and fought at Jutland in 1916. After World War I she was converted to a gunnery training ship and scrapped under the terms of the Washington Treaty of the 1920s.

Country of origin:	Great Britain
Crew:	735
Weight:	22,245 tonnes (22,102 tons)
Dimensions:	160.3m x 25.2m x 8.3m (526ft 6in x 82ft 6in x 278ft 3in)
Range:	10,296km (5720nm) at 12 knots
Armour:	254mm – 380mm (10in – 15in) belt, 203mm (8in) bulkheads
Armament:	10 305mm (12in), 16 102mm (4in) guns, three torpedo tubes
Powerplant:	Four shaft, geared steam turbines
Performance:	21 knots

Ben-my-Chree

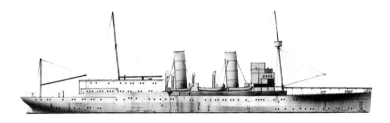

*B*en-my-Chree, a former passenger vessel on the Isle of Man route, was converted into a seaplane carrier in 1915. She was fitted with a large hangar aft, plus a flying-off ramp on the fore deck. She was equipped with the new Sopwith Schneider seaplane fighters. This aircraft had a 100hp rotary engine, an upward-firing Lewis gun and the ability to climb to 3048m (10,000ft) in a little over 30 minutes. With such improvements as these, the Sopwith Schneider presented the first serious threat to the Zeppelin airships which were attacking targets in Great Britain. Later, armed with two torpedo-carrying Short seaplanes, *Ben-my-Chree* served in the Dardanelles campaign, her aircraft sinking two Turkish vessels. While anchored in Kastelorgio harbour in 1917, *Ben-my-Chree* was attacked by Turkish shore batteries and sunk.

Country of origin:	Great Britain
Crew:	250
Weight:	3942 tonnes (3880 tons)
Dimensions:	114m x 14m x 5.3m (375ft x 46ft x 17ft 6in)
Range:	2223km (1200nm) at 10 knots
Armour:	None
Armament:	Four, Short 184 seaplanes
Powerplant:	Twin screw turbines
Performance:	24.5 knots

Benbow

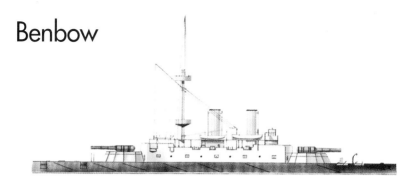

B*enbow* was one of the Rodney class of battleship built in answer to the French Formidable class then under construction. Original armament was to have been four 343mm (13.5in) and eight 152mm (6in) guns, but the Woolwich Arsenal was unable to deliver these and so two 112-tonne (111-ton) guns were mounted instead, in large open barbettes, one fore and one aft. The weight saved was used to install an extra pair of 152mm (6in) guns. There were many problems with the main armament, and the entire battleship class was delayed, *Benbow* herself taking six years to complete. *Benbow* was named after Admiral John Benbow (1653–1702) who was killed in action in the West Indies. The warship spent most of her active service life in the Mediterranean before being paid off in 1904. She was scrapped in 1909.

Country of origin:	Great Britain
Crew:	523
Weight:	10,770 tonnes (10,600 tons)
Dimensions:	99m x 21m x 8.2m (325ft x 68ft x 27ft 10in)
Range:	9265km (5000nm) at 8 knots
Armour:	450mm – 203mm (18in – 8in) belt, 400mm – 178mm (16in – 7in) bulkheads, 356mm – 304mm (14in – 12in) barbettes
Armament:	Two 412mm (16.25in), 10 152mm (6in) guns
Powerplant:	Twin screw inverted compound engines
Performance:	17.5 knots

Benedetto Brin

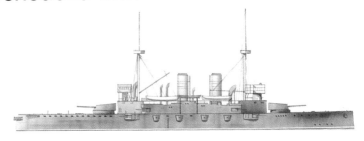

B*enedetto Brin* was designed by one of the world's leading naval architects at the time and on completion was named after him. The warship's design was a compromise, with her protection being reduced in favour of both speed and firepower. *Benedetto Brin* and her sister *Regina Margherita* were unique ships and had good sea-keeping capabilities. Launched in 1901 and completed in 1905, the warship *Benedetto Brin* was involved in naval operations off Tripoli in 1911 and subsequently in the Aegean Sea in the following year. On 27 September 1915, *Benedetto Brin* was destroyed by a magazine explosion in Brindisi harbour, either as a result of Austrian sabotage or of an accident involving unstable cordite. About half her crew – 421 men – perished in the incident.

Country of origin:	Italy
Crew:	812 – 900
Weight:	13,426 tonnes (13,215 tons)
Dimensions:	138.6m x 23.8m x 8.8m (449ft 6in x 78ft 3in x 29ft)
Range:	18,000km (10,000nm) at 12 knots
Armour:	152mm (6in) side, 76mm (3in) deck, 203mm (8in) turrets
Armament:	Four 304mm (12in), four 203mm (8in), 12 152mm (6in) guns
Powerplant:	Twin screw, triple expansion engines
Performance:	20.3 knots

Benton

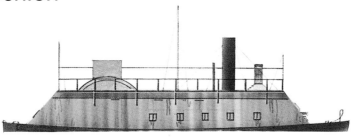

***B**enton* was originally the catamaran-hulled salvage vessel *Submarine No. 7*. She was converted by planking over the space between the hulls, adding a new bow and building a two-tier casement housing the main armament over most of her hull. Her armour was removed in 1865 and she was sold at auction for a fraction of her original cost. *Benton* was typical of the 'panic' warship conversions that emerged at the start of the American Civil War. These vessels all followed a similar pattern, with casement upperworks mounting two to four guns. Most were inadequately armoured. Those which were incomplete at the end of the war were sold abroad. After that time, interest in the navy faded, the thinking being that America would need only to defend her coastline, for which only monitors would be necessary.

Country of origin:	USA
Crew:	50
Weight:	643 tonnes (633 tons)
Dimensions:	61.5m x 22m (202ft x 72ft 9in)
Range:	1482km (800nm) at 6 knots
Armour:	50mm (2in) casement
Armament:	Two 279mm (11in) guns
Powerplant:	Inclined engines driving a single stern wheel
Performance:	–

Bismarck

The 1919 Treaty of Versailles imposed tight restrictions on German naval developments. In spite of this, the Germans managed to carry out secret design studies, and when the Anglo-German Naval Treaty of 1935 came into force, were able to respond quickly. They began the construction of two battleships, *Bismark* and *Tirpitz*. As they had been unable to properly test new hull forms, they used the World War I *Baden* design. While they were equipped with powerful modern engines and were fine, well-armed warships, the dated armour configuration meant that the steering gear and much of the communications and control systems were poorly protected. In May 1941, Bismarck was sent on a raiding mission into the Atlantic, but the Royal Navy caught up with her. In the ensuing battles she sunk *Hood*, before suffering so much damage that her crew scuttled her.

Country of origin:	Germany
Crew:	2039
Weight:	50,955 tonnes (50,153 tons)
Dimensions:	250m x 36m x 9m (823ft 6in x 118ft x 29ft 6in)
Range:	15,000km (8100nm) at 18 knots
Armour:	312mm – 262mm (12.5in – 10.5in) belt, 362mm – 178mm (14.5in – 7in) main turrets
Armament:	Eight 380mm (15in), 12 152mm (6in) guns, six aircraft
Powerplant:	Three shaft geared turbines
Performance:	29 knots

Bouvet

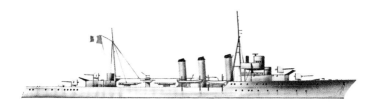

Named after Admiral Pierre François Henri Bouvet (1775–1860), commander of the French naval forces during the Napoleonic Wars, *Bouvet* was the last of the basic Charles Martel design and was thought to be the best of the group. She lacked the massive superstructure of the preceding group, and had a built-up stern which improved seaworthiness. In January 1903, she was damaged in a collision with the battleship *Gaulois* in the Mediterranean. After a substantial refit in 1913 she escorted Mediterranean convoys after the outbreak of World War I. In March 1915, *Bouvet* took part in an attack in the Dardanelles, during which she was seriously damaged by Turkish guns before running onto a mine. She rapidly filled with water, and her bulkheads collapsed. She sank in two minutes with the loss of 660 lives.

Country of origin:	France
Crew:	710
Weight:	12,200 tonnes (12,007 tons)
Dimensions:	118m x 21m x 8.3m (386ft 6in x 70ft 2in x 27ft 6in)
Range:	7412km (4000nm) at 10 knots
Armour:	400mm – 203mm (16in – 8in) belt, 380mm (15in) turrets
Armament:	Two 305mm (12in), two 275mm (10.8in) guns
Powerplant:	Triple screw, vertical expansion engines
Performance:	18 knots

Bretagne

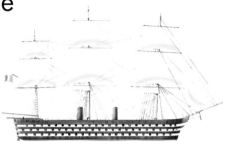

French naval weakness had become brutally apparent in 1840, when she was forced to back down over the Syrian confrontation. French battleships at that time were steam-powered with sail assistance, and tended to suffer from poor sailing qualities. British ships of the same period were designed with sail as their main motive force, and steam as an auxiliary source of power. During the 1850s, attempts were made to build up a strong French Navy, but these were countered by the British. *Bretagne* was one of the new style of French steam battleships of the period. She had three decks housing 130 of the new pattern of long gun, and a full rig of canvas with boiler rooms placed either side of the huge main mast. Built at Brest, *Bretagne* was the second largest wooden three-decker ever built. In 1866 she was removed from the French Navy list.

Country of origin:	France
Crew:	500
Weight:	6878 tonnes (6770 tons)
Dimensions:	12m x 18m (265ft 8in x 59ft 4in)
Range:	1853km (1000nm) under steam
Armour:	None
Armament:	130 32-pounders plus various other weapons
Powerplant:	Single screw compound engine
Performance:	12 knots

Bretagne

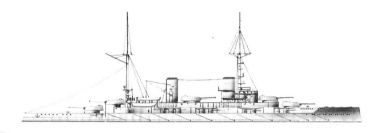

Because France found herself falling behind in the dreadnought naval race, *Bretagne* and her sisters *Provence* and *Lorraine* were based on the design of the preceding Courbet class to cut down construction time. *Bretagne* served in the Mediterranean from 1916–18, then underwent a series of extensive modernisations in 1921–23, 1927–30 and 1932–35. With the surrender of France in 1940, *Bretagne* and other French naval warships were called upon to join a British alliance, but the French admiral Gensoul refused. British warships, their gunfire directed by Swordfish spotter aircraft from the carrier *Ark Royal*, opened fire on the French vessels in their anchorage at Oran in Algeria. Heavy shells tore into the magazine of *Bretagne*, which blew up and capsized with the loss of 1012 lives.

Country of origin:	France
Crew:	1133
Weight:	29,420 tonnes (28,956 tons)
Dimensions:	166m x 27m x 10m (544ft 8in x 88ft 3in x 32ft 2in)
Range:	8460km (4700nm) at 10 knots
Armour:	279mm (11in) belt, 254mm – 380mm (10in – 15in) turrets
Armament:	10 340mm (13.4in) guns
Powerplant:	Quadruple screw geared turbines
Performance:	20 knots

Caiman

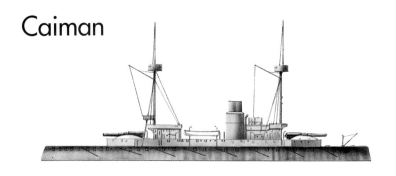

At the end of the 1870s, France abandoned the broadside ironclad battleships in her use, and instead adopted the barbette system of mounting the heavy guns high above the waterline away from any damage that could be caused by rough seas. *Caiman* was laid down in 1878. She was one of four large coastal defence vessels which were noted for their heavy armour and ordnance, with two heavy guns placed in barbettes. The other vessels in this class were *Indomptable*, *Requin* and *Terrible*. All of the vessels except *Terrible* were rebuilt between 1895 and 1901 to include both new boilers and new armament. *Requin*, rebuilt with two funnels on the centreline and military masts, survived to serve in World War I. *Caiman* ended her days as a discarded hulk at Rochefort in 1910; she was broken up in 1927.

Country of origin:	France
Crew:	373
Weight:	7650 tonnes (7259 tons)
Dimensions:	82.6m x 18m x 8m (271ft x 59ft x 26ft 2in)
Range:	3243km (1750nm) at 10 knots
Armour:	203mm – 500mm (8in – 19in) shallow armour belt at waterline
Armament:	Two 420mm (16.5in) guns
Powerplant:	Twin screw, vertical compound engines
Performance:	15 knots

Cairo

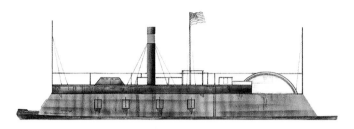

The Union ship *Cairo* was a converted low-draught paddle steamer. Typical of the type of craft which fought along the rivers during the American Civil War, *Cairo* and hundreds like her were instrumental in denying the rebels use of the continent's waterways, which effectively split up the Confederacy. These craft served with the Western Flotilla and took part in a number of notable actions; on 6 February 1862, for example, they bombarded the rebel-held Fort Henry, commanding the Tennessee River, into submission. *Cairo* had a low wooden hull surmounted by a large armoured casement with sloping sides. Muzzle-loading guns were stationed broadside and forward. Additional armour was constructed round the engines and rear paddle. *Cairo* was sunk by a Confederate mine in the Mississippi on 2 December 1862.

Country of origin:	USA
Crew:	50
Weight:	902 tonnes (887 tons)
Dimensions:	53m x 16m x 2m (173ft 9in x 4ft 9in x 6ft 6in)
Range:	Not known
Armour:	3in (75mm) casement
Armament:	Three 203mm (8in), three 178mm (7in) guns
Powerplant:	Single stern wheel driven by two non-condensing reciprocating engines
Performance:	8 knots

Canada

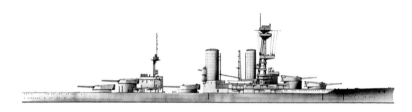

In 1911 Chile had two new battleships under construction, but all work on these vessels ceased in 1914 and *Almirante Latorre*, the most advanced of the two, was subsequently bought by the Royal Navy and renamed *Canada*. Her sister ship, the *Almirante Cochrane*, was also taken over by the British and renamed *Eagle*. *Canada* was a lengthened 'Iron Duke' type battleship. She had two large unequal funnels and a high tripod foremast and pole mainmast. Completed in 1915, *Canada* spent her entire war service with the Grand Fleet at Scapa Flow. She was one of the most effective battleships in the fleet; she saw action at the Battle of Jutland in 1916, and took part in the blockade of Germany. *Canada* was returned to Chile in 1920 and continued to see service as one of that country's capital ships.

Country of origin:	Chile
Crew:	1176
Weight:	32,634 tonnes (32,120 tons)
Dimensions:	202m x 28m x 9m (660ft 9in x 92ft x 29ft)
Range:	8153km (4400nm) at 10 knots
Armour:	229mm – 112mm (9in – 4.5in) belt, 254mm (10in) barbettes, 152mm (6in) turrets
Armament:	10 355mm (14in) guns
Powerplant:	Quadruple screw geared turbines
Performance:	22.8 knots

Canberra

Originally commissioned in 1941 as a Baltimore class cruiser, *Canberra* saw much war service in the central Pacific from 1944, in the battle for Truk and in heavy raids on Japanese-held islands as part of the US Task Group 58. In October 1944, she was badly damaged by a torpedo off Okinawa. She was rebuilt and recommissioned in 1955 as one of two Boston class missile cruisers. *Canberra* and her sister *Boston* were the first US Navy vessels specifically designed as anti-aircraft missile ships and were rushed into service during the Cold War. Armed with Terrier missiles in place of their aft turrets, their forward turrets were also to be replaced with missiles, though this never occurred. Instead, other ships were converted to increase the US Navy's anti-aircraft missile capability. *Canberra* was stricken in 1973.

Country of origin:	USA
Crew:	1,544
Weight:	18,234 tonnes (17,947 tons)
Dimensions:	205.4m x 21.25m x 7.6m (673ft 5in x 69ft 8in x 24ft 11in)
Range:	13,140km (7300nm) at 12 knots
Armour:	51mm (2in) belt
Armament:	Two Terrier surface-to-air missiles (72 missiles per launcher), six 203mm (8in), 10 127mm (5in) guns
Powerplant:	Four shaft geared turbines
Performance:	33 knots

Canopus

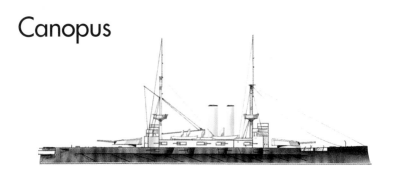

Canopus class battleships were intended for service on the Pacific station where the growing power of Japan and Russia was causing concern. The Canopus class were the first British battleships to have water tube boilers, which provided higher power and greater economy. They were also some of the last pre-dreadnoughts. At full speed *Canopus* used 10 tonnes (9 tons) of coal per hour. Launched in 1897, she was stationed at the Falkland Islands during World War I, and was briefly in action against von Spee's cruiser squadron in December 1914, though she did not engage. She later took part in the Dardanelles operation in 1915, before returning to home waters. The only damage *Canopus* sustained during her career was in August 1904, when she was in collision with the battleship *Barfleur* in Mounts Bay. She was sold in 1920.

Country of origin:	Great Britain
Crew:	750
Weight:	14,520 tonnes (14,300 tons)
Dimensions:	118m x 23m x 8m (390ft x 74ft x 26ft)
Range:	14,824km (8000nm) at 10 knots
Armour:	152mm (6in) belt, 305mm (12in) on barbettes
Armament:	Four 304mm (12in), 12 152mm (6in) guns
Powerplant:	Twin screw, triple expansion engines
Performance:	18.5 knots

Capitan Prat

During 1887 the Chilean government decided to modernise its navy by purchasing the latest type of warships from Europe. A 6096-tonne (6000-ton) battleship was part of the programme. The French firm of Forges et Chantiers de la Méditerranée won the contract, and *Capitan Prat* was laid down in 1888. Her 239mm (9.4in) guns were mounted singly in turrets, one at each end of the vessel and one on each side of the hull. A secondary battery of eight 120mm (4.7in) guns was mounted in twin turrets on the upper deck. Armour alone took up one third of her displacement. Until World War I, *Capitan Prat* was Chile's most powerful warship. After reconstruction in 1909–10 she served as a submarine depot ship. The vessel, named after a naval officer killed in action when his ship was sunk by a Peruvian ironclad, was stricken in 1935.

Country of origin:	Chile
Crew:	480
Weight:	7011 tonnes (6910 tons)
Dimensions:	100m x 18.5m x 7m (328ft x 60ft 8in x 22ft 10in)
Range:	8616km (4650nm) at 10 knots
Armour:	295mm – 195mm (11.8in – 7.8in) belt, 270mm – 203mm (10.8in – 8in) barbettes, 77.5mm (3.1in) citadel
Armament:	Four 239mm (9.4in) guns
Powerplant:	Twin screw, horizontal triple expansion engines
Performance:	18.3 knots

Captain

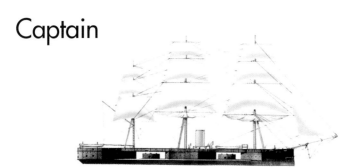

Captain was designed by Cowper Coles, who was a vigorous supporter of the idea that a few guns mounted in heavily armoured turrets, and with a wide field of fire, were better than a large number of guns spread along the side of a vessel and protected by thin armour. Also, he thought it possible to give the turret ship, usually employed on coastal defence duties, a full set of canvas, making it a true ocean-going battleship. *Captain* performed well during trials. However, in September 1870 she sank during a storm in the Bay of Biscay with the loss of 473 men, including Coles who was aboard to observe how his ship performed at sea. The ship had floated too deeply because of overweight material used in her construction, giving a freeboard of only 1.95m (6ft 5in) instead of the designed 2.5m (8ft 6in), which was already low.

Country of origin:	Great Britain
Crew:	473
Weight:	7892 tonnes (7767 tons)
Dimensions:	98m x 16m x 7.8m (320ft x 53ft 3in x 25ft 6in)
Range:	3706km (2000nm) at 10 knots
Armour:	Belt 102 – 178mm (4 – 7in)
Armament:	Four 304mm (12in) guns
Powerplant:	Twin screw, horizontal truck engines
Performance:	14 knots

Carl XIV Johan

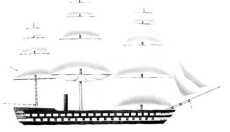

The Swedes were impressed with the performance of British steam battleships during the 1854–55 Baltic campaign against Russian forces. Fearing that Russia would improve her fleet, Sweden sought assistance from Britain in late 1855. The existing sailing battleship *Carl XIV Johan* had already been undergoing conversion, but her final transformation was not a success, partly because Scandinavian battleships were built with small displacements and shallow draughts designed for the Baltic, and in consequence the hull form did not lend itself to a conversion along the lines of British battleships. *Carl XIV Johan* was broken up in 1867. Although a neutral power since 1860, Sweden afterwards maintained a strong defensive navy. Although united with Norway under the Swedish crown until 1905, the Swedish and Norwegian fleets were separate entities.

Country of origin:	Sweden
Crew:	350
Weight:	26,424 tonnes (26,008 tons)
Dimensions:	54m x 14m (176ft 11in x 48ft 2in)
Range:	3706km (2000nm) at 2 knots
Armour:	50mm (2in) belt
Armament:	68 guns
Powerplant:	Single screw reciprocating engine
Performance:	6.5 knots

Castelfidardo

Castelfidardo was originally completed with a schooner rig. This was later altered to a barque rig, and finally towards the end of her career to two military masts. The vessel took part in the attack upon the Austrian fortress on the island of Lissa in July 1866 and was part of Rear Admiral Vacca's squadron. During the subsequent action against the Austrian fleet she was set on fire aft but managed to survive the blaze. In 1869 she was damaged by a boiler explosion when at Brindisi; following repairs she took part in the liberation of Rome in the following year, and after a refit she operated off Tnnis and in the Red Sea in support of Italian colonial interests. *Castelfidardo* was reconstructed in 1889–90 becoming a coastal defence vessel and then a torpedo school ship before being broken up in 1910.

Country of origin:	Italy
Crew:	485
Weight:	4560 tonnes (4527 tons)
Dimensions:	82m x 15m x 6m (268ft 4in x 49ft 9in x 20ft 10in)
Range:	3057km (1650nm) at 10 knots
Armour:	109mm (4.3in) belt
Armament:	Four 203mm (8in), 22 164mm (6.5in) guns
Powerplant:	Single screw reciprocating engine
Performance:	12.1 knots

Centurion

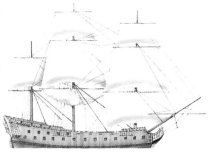

In 1739 war broke out between England and Spain. *Centurion*, a wooden fourth-rate battleship, became the flagship of George Anson who had orders to engage the Spanish in the South Atlantic and Pacific. The squadron set out in September 1740 but the voyage was a disaster, with over 1,300 men losing their lives, though only four died through enemy action. This was mainly due to the fact that most of the military personnel on the voyage were elderly pensioned-off veterans, pressed into service against their will, who easily succumbed to disease and malnutrition. During the long voyage *Centurion* fought many actions against the Spanish, and captured *Nostra Signora de Cabadonga*. *Centurion* was badly damaged while rounding Cape Horn, but in June 1744 arrived back in Britain. She later underwent a major refit during which her armament was reduced to 50 guns.

Country of origin:	Great Britain
Crew:	400
Weight:	1021 tonnes (1005 tons)
Dimensions:	44m x 12m x 5m (144ft 1in x 40ft 1in x 16ft 5in)
Range:	Unlimited, depending on provisions and weather
Armour:	None
Armament:	60 guns, including 24-pounders, 9-pounders and 6-pounders
Powerplant:	–
Performance:	3 knots

Centurion

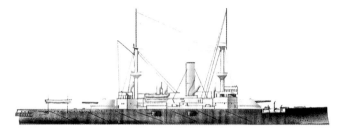

Centurion and her sister vessel *Barfleur* were second-class battleships that formed part of the large expansion programme for the Royal Navy begun in 1889. They were intended to counteract the powerful armoured cruisers of the Russian Navy in the Pacific. The relatively light draught of the vessels enabled them to navigate China's rivers with ease. From 1894 to 1901, *Centurion* saw action on the China Station, helping to protect British and Allied interests in the various Boxer uprisings. After reconstruction work in 1901–03, in which she was rearmed and had her foremast removed, *Centurion* returned to China, where in 1904 she was badly damaged in a collision with the battleship *Glory*. In 1910 *Centurion* was sold for scrap and subsequently broken up at Morecambe, Cumbria.

Country of origin:	Great Britain
Crew:	620
Weight:	10,668 tonnes (10,500 tons)
Dimensions:	110m x 21m x 7.7m (360ft x 70ft x 25ft 6in)
Range:	11,118km (6000nm) at 10 knots
Armour:	304mm – 229mm (12in – 9in) belt, 229mm – 127mm (9in – 5in) barbettes, 203mm (8in) bulkheads
Armament:	Four 254mm (10in) guns
Powerplant:	Twin screw, triple expansion engines
Performance:	18.5 knots

Charlemagne

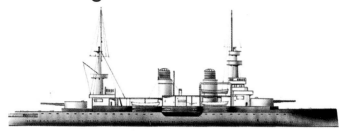

With *Charlemagne* and her two sister ships, France followed the design trend of other great powers at the time and adopted twin mountings for the main armament. Completed in 1899, her design tried to achieve too much on a small displacement, but even so she was a good economical steamer. She burnt less than 10 tonnes (9 tons) of coal per hour at full speed. In March 1903, she was in collision with one of her sister vessels, the *Gaulois* (the other was the *Saint Louis*) but she escaped damage. In World War I *Charlemagne*'s role was to escort Mediterranean convoys. The steamer also took part in operations at Salonika and in the Dardanelles, where she was damaged by shore batteries. Returning to service after repair and refit, *Charlemagne* was stricken in 1918 and broken up in 1920.

Country of origin:	France
Crew:	694
Weight:	11,277 tonnes (11,100 tons)
Dimensions:	114m x 20m x 8m (374ft x 66ft 5in x 27ft 6in)
Range:	7783km (4200nm) at 10 knots
Armour:	203 – 368mm (8in – 14.5in) belt, 380mm (15in) on turrets
Armament:	Four 304mm (12in) guns
Powerplant:	Triple screw, triple expansion engines
Performance:	18 knots

Charles Martel

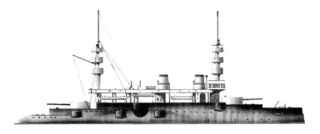

L aid down in 1891, *Charles Martel* was part of the French naval programme
intended to replace all their wooden-hulled ironclads by 1900. In the usual
French practice she had her main armament laid out in lozenge or diamond fashion.
The two 304mm (12in) guns were mounted fore and aft in armoured turrets, while the
two 274mm (10.8in) weapons were in smaller turrets, on sponsons which protruded
from each side of the hull. Her secondary armament was eight 140mm (5.5in) guns
in electrically driven turrets on the main and upper deck. She had a distinctive
appearance, with a high forecastle, and a covered flying bridge linking both masts.
Her interior was also broken up into dozens of separate watertight compartments,
which helped reduce the chance of catastrophic damage from a penetrating hit. She
saw service throughout World War I and was stricken and scrapped in 1922.

Country of origin:	France
Crew:	644
Weight:	11,880 tonnes (11,693 tons)
Dimensions:	115m x 22m x 8m (378ft 11in x 71ft 2in x 27ft 6in)
Range:	6022km (3520nm) at 10 knots
Armour:	254 – 457mm (10 – 18 in) belt
Armament:	Two 304mm (12in), two 274mm (10.8in) guns
Powerplant:	Twin screw, triple expansion engines
Performance:	18 knots

Chen Yuen

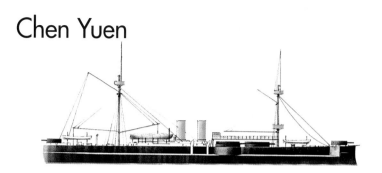

By the end of the 1870s the Chinese had decided to modernise their navy along the lines of powers in the West. As a consequence, a major programme was begun in the 1880s, and *Chen Yuen* and her sister *Ting Yuen* became China's only battleships. Both were steel-hulled, and featured a strongly armoured central citadel which covered the engines, boilers and magazines. Both were German-built by the Vulcan shipyards at Stettin, and sailed to China under the German mercantile flag. In September 1894, *Chen Yuen* was severely damaged in the Battle of the Yalu during the Sino-Japanese War and later went aground at Wei Hai Wei, where she was damaged again by Japanese batteries and foundered. In 1895, she was captured by the Japanese, refloated and commissioned in the Imperial Japanese Navy. She was scrapped in 1914.

Country of origin:	China
Crew:	350
Weight:	7792 tonnes (7670 tons)
Dimensions:	94m x 18m x 6m (307ft 9in x 59ft x 20ft)
Range:	8338km (4500nm) at 10 knots
Armour:	356mm (14in) belt, 356mm – 305mm (14in – 12in) barbettes
Armament:	Four 304mm (12in), two 152mm (6in) guns
Powerplant:	Twin screw, horizontal compound engines
Performance:	15.7 knots

Clémenceau

*C*lémenceau was one of three French battleships laid down between 1935 and 1939. The others were *Richelieu* and *Jean Bart*; a fourth – *Gascoigne* – was ordered but later cancelled. When France fell in 1940, the Germans found *Clémenceau*'s incomplete hull in dock at Brest. When the Allies invaded France, the Germans considered using it to block the harbour entrance, but she was sunk during a bombing raid in August 1944. The illustration shows her as she would have looked if completed according to the 1940 plans. Her two sister ships both saw service; *Richelieu* was taken over by the Allies and served in the Indian Ocean in 1944–45, and *Jean Bart*, having been damaged by gunfire during the Allied landings in North Africa in 1942, was completed after the war and took part in the Anglo-French Suez operations in 1956.

Country of origin:	France
Crew:	1550
Weight:	48,260 tonnes (47,500 tons)
Dimensions:	247.9m x 33m x 9.6m (813ft 2in x 108ft 3in x 31ft 7in)
Range:	(est): 15,750km (8500nm) at 14 knots
Armour:	337mm – 243mm (13.5in – 9.75in) belt
Armament:	Eight 381mm (15in) guns
Powerplant:	Quadruple screw, geared turbines
Performance:	(est): 25 knots

Clémenceau

*C*lémenceau (*R98*) and her sister *Foch* (*R99*) were originally intended as part of a class of six fleet carriers, but only two were built. *Clémenceau* was ordered from Brest dockyard in May 1954, while *Foch* began construction at St Nazaire and was completed at Brest. They were the first French purpose-built carriers, and *Clémenceau* underwent constant modification during design and construction. She has served the French Navy well, operating in the Pacific, off the coast of Lebanon, and taking part in the 1991 Gulf War. During her career she has been extensively modernised, with new defensive weapons and command systems added. Her air wing normally comprised 16 Super Étendards, 3 Étendard IVP, 10 F-8 Crusaders, 7 Alizé, plus helicopters. In recent years she has operated more helicopters than fixed-wing aircraft. She is due to be replaced by the nuclear-powered *Charles de Gaulle*.

Country of origin:	France
Crew:	1338, or 984 (as a helicopter carrier)
Weight:	33,304 tonnes (32,780 tons)
Dimensions:	257m x 46m x 9m (843ft 2in x 150ft x 28ft 3in)
Range:	13,500km (7500nm) at 12 knots
Armour:	Flight deck, superstructure and bridges 50mm (2in)
Armament:	Eight 100mm (3.9in) guns, 40 aircraft
Powerplant:	Twin screw geared turbines
Performance:	32 knots

Colbert

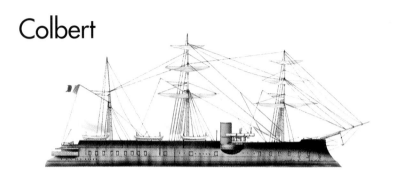

Colbert and her sister ship *Trident* were the last wooden-hulled French capital ships to be built. Launched in September 1875, she was in many ways obsolete even before she put to sea – the age of wooden-hulled warships was fast coming to an end. In an attempt to save coal, and also to safeguard against machinery breakdown, *Colbert* was fully rigged with 2044 square metres (22,000 sq ft) of sail. Her armour belt extended 1.8m (6ft) above and below the waterlines. *Colbert* was named after Jean Baptiste Colbert, Marquis de Seigneley, (1619–1683) the statesman who initiated construction of a large French navy to challenge the maritime power of England and Holland. The warship saw only one period of action, when she was used to bombard dissident forces at Sfax in Tunisia in 1881. She was removed from the list in 1900.

Country of origin:	France
Crew:	774
Weight:	8890 tonnes (8750 tons)
Dimensions:	97m x 17m x 9m (317ft 7in x 57ft 3in x 29ft)
Range:	6114km (3300nm) at 10 knots
Armour:	217mm – 178mm (8.7in – 7in) iron belt, 157mm (6.3in) battery
Armament:	Eight 270mm (10.8in), two 238mm (9.4in), eight 140mm (5.5in) guns
Powerplant:	Single screw, horizontal return engines
Performance:	14 knots

Collingwood

Collingwood was the prototype of the new British Admiral battleship class laid down in the summer of 1880. Later units varied, especially in the fitting of heavier guns, but she was to set the overall design for British battleships for the next 20 years. A transverse water chamber was fitted at each end of the vessel to steady her when rolling. The main deck ran from end to end of the hull, upon which were carried the four heavy guns mounted in pairs in two barbettes on the centreline. Because of her low freeboard, *Collingwood* was very wet in a seaway. In 1886 she was damaged when a faulty 12in gun burst on trials. In 1887 she joined the Mediterranean Fleet and served with it for 10 years before returning home for a refit as a coastguard ship. She was placed on the reserve in 1903 and scrapped in 1909.

Country of origin:	Great Britain
Crew:	498
Weight:	9652 tonnes (9500 tons)
Dimensions:	99m x 21m x 8m (324ft 10in x 68ft x 26ft 3in)
Range:	12,917km (7000nm) at 10 knots
Armour:	203mm – 457mm (8in – 18in) waterline belt
Armament:	Four 304mm (12in), six 152mm (6in) guns
Powerplant:	Twin screw, inverted compound engines
Performance:	17 knots

Colossus

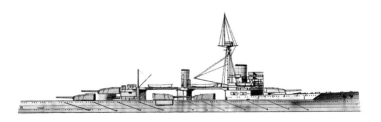

Colossus and her sister ship *Hercules* formed part of the rapid British naval expansion programme of 1909. *Colossus* had an improvement over previous dreadnoughts in that she was built with stronger armour protection. To save weight the aftermast was omitted, but the foremast, with its vital fire control centre, was placed behind the first funnel, although this meant that she suffered severely from smoke interference. *Colossus* was one of the last British battleships to mount 305mm (12in) guns; the next major group would carry the new 343mm (13.5in) weapons. During the Battle of Jutland in 1916, where she was flagship of the Battle Fleet's 5th Division, she was hit by two shells. She subsequently served as a cadet training ship before being sold for scrap and broken up at Alloa, Scotland, in 1922.

Country of origin:	Great Britain
Crew:	755
Weight:	23,419 tonnes (23,050 tons)
Dimensions:	166m x 26m x 9m (546ft x 85ft x 28ft 9in)
Range:	12,024km (6680nm) at 12 knots
Armour:	279mm – 178mm (11in – 7in) belt, 279mm – 102mm (11in – 4in) barbettes
Armament:	10 305mm (12in) guns
Powerplant:	Four shaft turbines
Performance:	21 knots

Commandant Teste

Commandant Teste served in the Mediterranean until World War II. She was scuttled at Toulon when France surrendered, and was not raised again until the end of the war. The scuttling was somewhat premature; although a large part of the French fleet was disarmed under the terms of the armistice, it was agreed that no vessels were to be handed over to the Germans. At that time there were two battleships, two large destroyers, eight smaller destroyers, seven submarines and 200 small craft in British harbours, with the rest of the French fleet at Oran. After refitting, she served as a store ship. In the late 1940s there were plans to convert her to a flush-decked aircraft carrier, but the plans were never effected. She was scrapped in 1950, after serving for nearly 30 years in one role or another, albeit with a short stay under the waves!

Country of origin:	France
Crew:	400
Weight:	11,684 tonnes (11,500 tons)
Dimensions:	167m x 27m x 7m (548ft x 88ft 7in x 22ft 9in)
Range:	7412km (4000nm) at 15 knots
Armour:	Unknown
Armament:	13mm (3.9in) guns
Powerplant:	Twin screw turbines
Performance:	21.4 knots

Connecticut

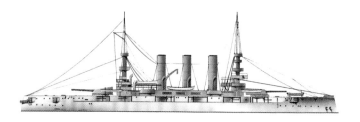

Part of a six-strong class, *Connecticut* was an enlarged version of the previous Virginia class and repeated the use of three different calibres for the main armament, except that the 152mm (6in) weapons were updated to 178mm (7in). Both the 304mm (12in) and 203mm (8in) gun turrets were electrically powered. The main armour belt ran from 1.2m (4ft) above to 1.5m (5ft) below the waterline. *Connecticut* compared very favourably with British and Japanese capital ships of the same period. She was flagship of the US Atlantic Fleet in 1906–07, and saw service with the Atlantic fleet during World War I. She was fitted with AA guns in 1916, and at the end of World War I she made four voyages as a troop transport. She saw service with the Pacific Fleet in 1921–22, and was decommissioned in 1923.

Country of origin:	USA
Crew:	881
Weight:	17,948 tonnes (17,666 tons)
Dimensions:	140m x 23m x 7m (456ft 4in x 76ft 10in x 24ft 6in)
Range:	9265km (5000nm) at 10 knots
Armour:	279mm – 152mm (11in – 6in) belt, 254mm – 152mm (10in – 6in) barbettes, 304mm – 203mm (12in – 8in) turrets
Armament:	Four 305mm (12in), eight 203mm (8in) and 12 178mm (7in) guns
Powerplant:	Twin screw, vertical triple expansion engines
Performance:	18 knots

Conqueror

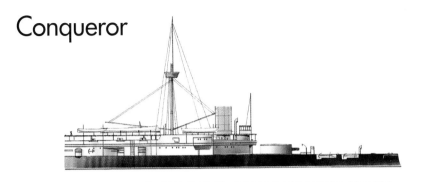

Conqueror was an unusual design in that the vessel combined the gun with the ram (note that there is nothing missing from the illustration above). *Conqueror* and her sister ship *Hero* were larger versions of the unusual rams of the 1870s and featured their main armament forward. *Conqueror* was the last coastal defence vessel to be built for the Royal Navy. She proved too small for ocean-going operations, but at the same time too large for coastal defence. Her in-service career was consequently inauspicious, and she spent most of it on harbour service as tender to a gunnery school. In July 1900 she went aground, and two years later she was paid off and laid up to await disposal. She was broken up in 1907, while her sister *Hero* was sunk as a gunnery target the following year.

Country of origin:	Great Britain
Crew:	330
Weight:	6299 tonnes (6200 tons)
Dimensions:	88m x 18m x 7m (288ft x 58ft x 23ft 6in)
Range:	9635km (5200nm) at 10 knots
Armour:	304mm – 203mm (12in – 8in) waterline belt, 280mm (11in) turret
Armament:	Two 304mm (12in) guns
Powerplant:	Twin screw, inverted compound engines
Performance:	14 knots

Conqueror

An increase in displacement over the previous class enabled *Conqueror* and her three sisters to mount the new 343mm (13.5 in) guns, making these vessels the first of the so-called 'super dreadnoughts'. *Conqueror* also carried the 533mm (21in) torpedo instead of the 450mm (18in) version. While she featured a more sleek design than the early dreadnoughts, there was one major weakness in *Conqueror*'s layout. The vitally important fire control mast was positioned between the funnels, resulting in severe smoke interference at high speeds. In December 1914 she was damaged in collision with the battleship *Monarch*; after repair she rejoined the Grand Fleet and fought in the Battle of Jutland in 1916. She was sold and broken up in 1922. Her sister ships were *Monarch*, *Orion* and *Thunderer*.

Country of origin:	Great Britain
Crew:	752
Weight:	26,284 tonnes (25,870 tons)
Dimensions:	177m x 27m x 9m (581ft x 88ft 7in x 28ft)
Range:	12,470km (6730nm) at 10 knots
Armour:	304mm – 203mm (12in – 8in) waterline belt, 280mm (11.2in) on turrets
Armament:	10 343mm (13.5in) guns
Powerplant:	Quadruple shaft turbines
Performance:	21 knots

Conte di Cavour

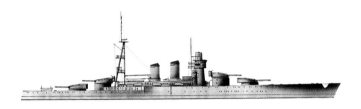

*C*onte di Cavour was designed in 1908 as an improved version of *Dante Alighieri*. Completed in 1914, *Conte di Cavour* saw war service in the southern Adriatic, and in 1919 she engaged in a cruise to the USA. In 1923 she operated in support of Italian troops occupying the island of Corfu. She was extensively rebuilt between 1933 and 1937 and emerged as a virtually new ship. She had new machinery and her hull was lengthened. Sunk at Taranto by torpedoes launched from British aircraft flying from *Illustrious*, *Conte di Cavour* was later refloated and towed to Trieste. She was rebuilt but, following the Italian surrender, she was seized by the Germans in September 1943, and eventually sunk during an air raid in 1945. Her wreckage was broken up at the end of World War II.

Country of origin:	Italy
Crew:	1200
Weight:	29,496 tonnes (29,032 tons)
Dimensions:	186m x 28m x 9m (611ft 6in x 91ft 10in x 30ft)
Range:	8640km (4800nm) at 10 knots
Armour:	254mm (10in) side and turrets
Armament:	10 320mm (12.6in), 12 120mm (4.7in) guns
Powerplant:	Twin screw turbines
Performance:	28.2 knots

Conte Verde

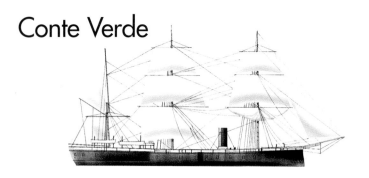

*C*onte Verde was an unusual wooden-hulled broadside battleship in that only parts of the bow and stern were armoured with iron plates, the rest of the hull being protected by thick wooden timbers. She was one of a group of three vessels originally laid down as frigates, but converted into ironclad battleships while still on the stocks. *Conte Verde*'s armament was altered to six 254mm (10in) guns and one 203mm (8in) gun on or near her completion in 1871. She was discarded in 1880 and scrapped in 1898. *Conte Verde* (Green Count) was named after *Amedeo VI*, Count of Savoy (1334–1383), who favoured green costumes. Her sister ships were *Messina* and *Principe de Carignano*. *Messina* took part in the Liberation of Rome in September 1870, while *Principe de Carignano* fought in the Battle of Lissa, 1866.

Country of origin:	Italy
Crew:	572
Weight:	3928 tonnes (3866 tons)
Dimensions:	74m x 15m x 6.5m (241ft 10in x 50ft x 21ft 4in)
Range:	2160km (1200nm) at 8 knots
Armour:	118mm (4.75in) side plates
Armament:	18 160-pounders, four 72-pounders
Powerplant:	Single screw, single expansion engine
Performance:	10 knots

Courageous

Courageous and her sister *Glorious* were completed in 1917 as fast cruisers for service in the Baltic. They were heavily armed with four 380mm (15in) guns, but had very little armour. By the 1920s, Britain was anxious to increase her carrier strength, so both vessels, and their near sister *Furious*, were converted to aircraft carriers. The conversion of *Courageous* was completed in March 1928. Her superstructure and armament were replaced by an aircraft hangar running almost the length of the ship. The forward 18m (59ft) of the hangar was an open deck, which could be used to fly off slow-flying aircraft such as the Swordfish. Above this was an open flight deck, with two large elevators set into it. All three ships served through the 1930s, and formed the backbone of the British carrier force at the start of World War II. In the opening days of the war *Courageous* was torpedoed and sunk by *U20*.

Country of origin:	Great Britain
Crew:	828
Weight:	26,517 tonnes (26,100 tons)
Dimensions:	240m x 27m x 8m (786ft 5in x 90ft 6in x 27ft 3in)
Range:	5929km (3200nm) at 19 knots
Armour:	75mm – 50mm (3in – 2in) belt
Armament:	16 120mm (4.7in) guns, six flights of aircraft
Powerplant:	Quadruple screw turbines
Performance:	31.5 knots

Courbet

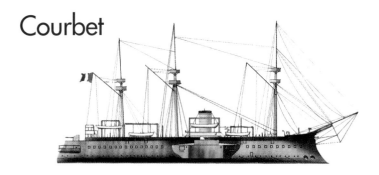

The largest central battery ships ever built, *Courbet* and her sister *Dévastation* were laid down by the French immediately after the Franco-Prussian War of 1870, in order to strengthen the navy (though why they did so remains a mystery as it was on land that they had been decisively beaten by the Prussians in a war that had revealed France's glaring military deficiencies). They were powerful fighting units and were handy sea-going vessels. Two funnels set side-by-side rose up through the main battery. By the 1890s *Courbet*'s rig had been modified, with each mast carrying two fighting tops. She suffered two serious accidents during her career, the first in 1895 when she went aground in the Iles d'Hyeres during manoeuvres, and the second in 1898 when she was holed by an anchor at Cadiz. She was removed from the navy list in 1910.

Country of origin:	France
Crew:	689
Weight:	9855 tonnes (9700 tons)
Dimensions:	95m x 20m x 7.6m (312ft x 67ft x 25ft)
Range:	3706km (2000nm) at 10 knots
Armour:	380mm – 178mm (15in – 7in) iron belt, 238mm (9.4in) battery
Armament:	Four 340mm (13.4in), four 266mm (10.5in) guns
Powerplant:	Twin screw, vertical compound engines
Performance:	15 knots

Couronne

Couronne was the first iron-hulled capital ship to be laid down. Upon completion in 1862 she proved a better seaboat than her wooden-hulled contemporaries, and she was still afloat 70 years after her launch. Originally her guns were in broadside battery behind her armour, but she underwent several armament changes during her career. In 1885 she became a gunnery training ship, having had all her armour removed. *Couronne* was hulked in 1910, and was not broken up until 1934. Originally launched in March 1861, her long career compares sharply to those wooden-hulled warships of the mid-nineteenth century, and was proof, if proof were needed, that the iron-hulled warship was the future as far as warfare at sea was concerned. That said, the placing of her guns along the sides was a throwback to a bygone age.

Country of origin:	France
Crew:	570
Weight:	6173 tonnes (6076 tons)
Dimensions:	80m x 17m x 8m (262ft 5in x 54ft 9in x 27ft)
Range:	4465km (2410nm) at 10 knots
Armour:	102mm – 80mm (4in – 3.2in) iron belt
Armament:	30 163mm (6.4in) guns
Powerplant:	Single screw, horizontal return engines
Performance:	13 knots

Custoza

Custoza was the second Austrian iron-hulled capital ship and was designed to make effective use of the ram. She was one of the largest central battery ships ever built and had a long career. In 1877 her full rig was reduced, and in the early 1880s additional smaller weapons were added, plus three 350mm (13.8in) torpedo tubes. *Custoza* was converted into a barracks ship in 1914. In 1920 she was handed over to Italy as a war reparation and scrapped soon after. Launched in August 1872, it is curious how the ram was seen as a dominant factor in naval warfare at this time. One would have thought that the development of more accurate and deadly cannons would have led to naval theorists believing that the future lay with gun duels at long ranges rather than closing with the enemy, but this was not the case.

Country of origin:	Austria
Crew:	548
Weight:	7730 tonnes (7609 tons)
Dimensions:	95m x 17.6m x 8m (311ft 8in x 58ft x 26ft)
Range:	3000km (1620nm) at 10 knots
Armour:	203mm (8in) belt, 178mm (7in) casemates
Armament:	Eight 260mm (10.2in), six 89mm (3.5in) guns
Powerplant:	Single screw, horizontal compound engines
Performance:	13.7 knots

Cyclops

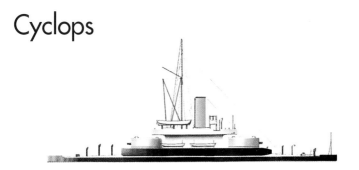

Cyclops and her three sisters, *Gorgon, Hecate* and *Hydra,* were well-armoured, low freeboard ships with an upper hull structure amidships that protected the base of the two turrets. The overhanging bridge carried the ship's boats which were handled by a single boom attached to the mast. Although designed specifically for harbour defence, these vessels were also used for general coastline protection. Between 1887 and 1889 all four vessels underwent extensive refits. Although launched in 1871, *Cyclops* was not completed until 1877, after which time she spent most of her career in reserve until she was sold in 1903. Her sister vessels all proved to be unsatisfactory as ironclads. They all served in the Royal Navy's Particular Service Squadron, and all were sold for scrap in the same year, 1903.

Country of origin:	Great Britain
Crew:	150
Weight:	3535 tonnes (3480 tons)
Dimensions:	68.5m x 14m x 5m (225ft x 45ft x 16ft 4in)
Range:	6000km (3000nm) at 10 knots
Armour:	152mm – 203mm (6in – 8in) on sides of hull, 203mm – 228mm (8in – 9in) upperhull, 228mm – 254mm (9in – 10in) turrets
Armament:	Four 254mm (10in) guns
Powerplant:	Twin screw, horizontal direct acting engines
Performance:	11 knots

Danmark

L aunched in 1864, the ironclad *Danmark* was originally named *Santa Maria*.
She was ordered from Thompson of Glasgow by Lieutenant North of the
Confederate Navy. Unfortunately Confederate funds were low at the time, and
delays in paying the installments postponed her completion. She was finally sold to
Denmark, which was at war with Prussia, and was re-named *Danmark*. Launched
in 1864, she was reconstructed prior to completion and commissioned on 1 June
1869. After undergoing a refit in 1876–77 she was used as an accommodation ship,
being a poor sea boat and little used in her true role. She was broken up in 1907.
Ironically, Denmark possessed one of the finest ironclads in the world at this time;
she was *Rolf Krake*, the only ironclad in service at the time of the war with Austria
in 1864.

Country of origin:	Denmark
Crew:	530
Weight:	4823 tonnes (4747 tons)
Dimensions:	82m x 15m x 6m (270ft x 50ft x 19ft 2in)
Range:	3335km (1800nm) at 6 knots
Armour:	112mm (4.5in) iron plate
Armament:	12 152mm (6in), 12 203mm (8in) guns
Powerplant:	Single screw compound engines
Performance:	8.5 knots

Dante Alighieri

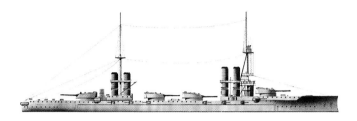

Designed by Engineering Admiral Masdea, the *Dante Alighieri* was the first battleship to mount triple turrets on the centreline; she was also the first Italian dreadnought to be built. Laid down in 1909 she was completed in 1912. She was reconstructed in 1923 and given a tripod mast. In World War I she was the flagship of the Italian Fleet in the southern Adriatic, although she saw no action. When Italy entered the war in 1915 the fleet included six dreadnoughts, with four more under construction. The main operational base was originally Trieste, but the main body of the fleet later moved to Taranto to escape Austrian air attacks. Although the Italian battle fleet did little during the war, its ships carried out a successful blockade of the eastern Adriatic coastline. *Dante Alighieri* was scrapped in 1928.

Country of origin:	Italy
Crew:	981
Weight:	22,149 tonnes (21,800 tons)
Dimensions:	168m x 26.5m x 10m (551ft 2in x 87ft 3in x 31ft 10in)
Range:	9265km (5000nm) at 10 knots
Armour:	152mm – 249mm (6in – 9.8in) on belt
Armament:	12 304mm (12in), 20 120mm (4.7in) guns
Powerplant:	Quadruple screw turbines
Performance:	22 knots

Danton

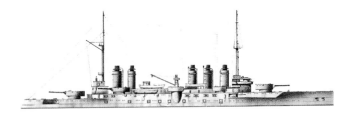

***D**anton* and her five sisters were the last battleships to be built for the French Navy before the British all-big-gun battleship *Dreadnought* appeared on the scene and revolutionised naval development. Although *Danton*'s class contained powerful vessels, it was too late to provide a serious challenge to the dreadnoughts then entering service. Named after Georges Jacques Danton, a leader of the French Revolution, the battleship was laid down at Brest in 1908 and launched in July 1909. She was completed in 1911 and saw initial war service in escorting Mediterranean convoys. In 1915 she was on station in the Adriatic and in 1916 in the Aegean. On 19 March 1917, en route from Toulon to Corfu, she was hit by two torpedoes from the German submarine *U64* and sank southwest of Sardinia with the loss of 296 lives.

Country of origin:	France
Crew:	753, later 923
Weight:	19,761 tonnes (19,450 tons)
Dimensions:	146.5m x 25.8m x 9m (481ft x 84ft 8in x 28ft 8in)
Range:	6066km (3370nm) at 10 knots
Armour:	270mm (10.8in) belt, 300mm (11.75in) main turrets
Armament:	Four 304mm (12in) guns
Powerplant:	Quadruple screw turbines
Performance:	19.3 knots

Dauphin
Royale

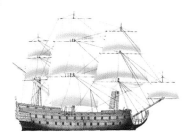

When Cardinal Richelieu came to power in 1624, he set about improving the sorry state of France's once powerful navy. He ordered five ships from Holland and from these beginnings grew the large fleet, which included *Dauphin Royale*, that fought the Anglo-Dutch fleet off Beachy Head in June 1690. *Dauphin Royale* was a large vessel with two main gundecks and one upper deck. The French fleet at Beachy Head totalled 70 ships of the line, with 4,600 guns and 28,000 crew. At this time part of the English fleet was in the Mediterranean and part was escorting William of Orange to Ireland, so the Anglo-Dutch force numbered only 55 ships against the French force's 80, the latter having 4600 guns and 28,000 crew. Although the French were held at bay, their commander, Admiral Tourville, failed to press his advantage and threw away the chance of a resounding victory.

Country of origin:	France
Crew:	350
Weight:	1077 tonnes (1060 tons) approx
Dimensions:	Not known
Range:	Not known
Armour:	None
Armament:	104 guns
Powerplant:	None
Performance:	8 knots approx

Dédalo

***D**édalo* was formerly the US Navy ship *Cabot*, which had been laid down in 1942 as a cruiser, but completed the following year as a carrier of the Independence class. After service in World War II, *Cabot* was decommissioned in 1947. In 1967 she was lent to Spain, who purchased her in 1972, renaming her *Dédalo*. Her normal air wing comprised four air groups, one with eight Matador (Harrier) V/STOL aircraft, one with four Sea King ASW helicopters, one with four Agusta-Bell 212 ASW/electronic warfare helicopters, and one with four specialised helicopters (for example, Bell AH-1G attack helicopters to support an amphibious landing.) A maximum of seven four-aircraft groups could be handled aboard the carrier. She remained in service until the carrier *Principe de Asturias* entered service in 1987.

Country of origin:	Spain
Crew:	1112
Weight:	16,678 tonnes (16,416 tons)
Dimensions:	190m x 22m x 8m (622ft 4in x 73ft x 26ft)
Range:	13,500km (7500nm) at 12 knots
Armour:	127mm (5in) belt
Armament:	26 40mm (1.6in) guns, seven VSTOL aircraft, 20 helicopters
Powerplant:	Quadruple screw turbines
Performance:	30 knots

Demologos

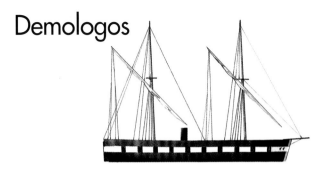

***D**emologos* was the first steam-powered warship in the world. She was designed
for coast-defence service during the war then in progress against Britain.
Originally named *Fulton the First*, the twin-hulled ship was laid down in June
1814. A single paddle wheel was positioned in the gap between the two hulls,
where it was well protected against enemy fire. The ship was completed with two
masts carrying lateen sails, plus a set of jibs. The war with Britain ended before
she saw action, and *Demologos* was laid up in New York as a store ship. On 4 June
1829 she was destroyed by an internal explosion. The next steam driven warship
for the US Navy was to be *Fulton II* in 1837. It would have been interesting to see
how *Demologos* would have fared in action against British warships, for in this
short conflict American frigates recorded some brilliant sucesses.

Country of origin:	USA
Crew:	150
Weight:	2514 tonnes (2475 tons)
Dimensions:	47.5m x 17m x 3m (156ft x 56ft x 10ft)
Range:	2965km (1600nm) at 6 knots
Armour:	None
Armament:	20 32-pounder guns
Powerplant:	Paddle wheel, inclined steam cylinder, compound engines
Performance:	7 knots

Denver

Denver is one of the Austin class of 11 ships which are enlarged versions of the previous Raleigh group. They have increased troop and vehicle capacity, being able to carry over 900 troops and 2540 tonnes (2500 tons) of cargo. *Denver* also has a comprehensive docking facility forming the stern of the vessel, capable of holding 20 landing craft. Access to the dock is via massive lock gates in the stern. Unlike the Raleigh group, the Austin class features a helicopter hangar big enough for six helicopters in transit or two in operation. Under normal operational conditions, one Raleigh and five Austin class ships serve with the Atlantic fleets, while six Austin class and and one Raleigh serve with the Pacific fleets. All the Austin class vessels underwent refits in the 1980s to extend their service life by 15 years.

Country of origin:	USA
Crew:	447 and up to 930 troops
Weight:	9477 tonnes (9328 tons)
Dimensions:	174m x 30.5m x 7m (570ft 3in x 100ft x 23ft)
Range:	14,824km (8000nm) at 15 knots
Armour:	100 – 175mm (4 – 7in) belt
Armament:	Eight 76mm (3in) guns
Powerplant:	Twin screw turbines
Performance:	20 knots

Derfflinger

On 16 December 1914, *Derfflinger* was part of a force of German warships that bombarded Scarborough and Whitby, on the northeast coast of England; shortly afterwards, in January 1915, she was seriously damaged in the Battle of Dogger Bank. In the following year, 1916, *Derfflinger* took part in the Battle of Jutland and blew up the British battlecruiser *Queen Mary* with 11 salvos. During that same battle, however, she was hit by ten 380mm (15in) and ten 304mm (12in) shells. Despite fires on board, severe flooding and damage to her after-turrets she survived the battle. *Derfflinger* and her two sister ships, *Hindenburg* and *Lutzow*, all of which had been launched in 1913, were arguably the best capital ships of their day. *Derfflinger* was scuttled at Scapa Flow in 1919 and raised for scrap in 1934.

Country of origin:	Germany
Crew:	1112
Weight:	30,706 tonnes (30,223 tons)
Dimensions:	210m x 29m x 8m (689ft x 95ft 2in x 27ft 3in)
Range:	10,080km (5600nm) at 12 knots
Armour:	300mm (11.8 in) waterline belt
Armament:	Eight 304mm (12in) guns
Powerplant:	Quadruple screw turbines
Performance:	28 knots

Deutschland

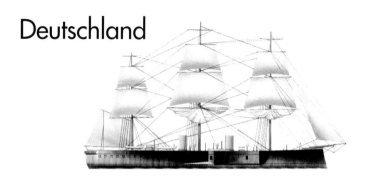

Before the foundation of the German Empire in 1871, Prussia retained only a small navy for coastal defence. It was the blockade by the French Navy during the Franco-Prussian war that finally convinced the German government of the pressing need for a larger navy. As a consequence, throughout the 1870s nine capital ships were begun, mainly in German yards. *Deutschland*, one of the Kaiser class, was an exception, and was the last German capital ship to be built abroad, being launched in Britain in 1874. She was a powerful central battery ship, with her main armament concentrated in an armoured box amidships. In 1882 her armament was altered, and in 1895 she was rebuilt as a heavy cruiser with military masts replacing her original sailing rig. *Deutschland* was taken out of service in 1906 and broken up in 1909.

Country of origin:	Germany
Crew:	656
Weight:	8939 tonnes (8799 tons)
Dimensions:	90m x 19m x 8m (293ft x 62ft 4in x 26ft)
Range:	4576km (2470nm) at 10 knots
Armour:	254mm – 127mm (10in – 5in) belt, 203mm – 229mm (8in – 7in) casement
Armament:	Eight 254mm (10in) guns
Powerplant:	Single screw, horizontal single expansion engine
Performance:	13 knots

Deutschland

Deutschland was part of Germany's last pre-dreadnought class laid down between 1903 and 1905. They differed slightly from the previous class in that they had more 89mm (3.5in) guns plus improved protection, but other weaknesses remained – as was shown at the Battle of Jutland in 1916 when one vessel in the class, *Pommern,* suffered a magazine explosion after only one hit from a torpedo. Small tube boilers were used for the Deutschland class, and these became standard for all vessels employed in the German Navy. Two ships of the class, *Schlesien* and *Schleswig-Holstein,* survived to serve in World War II and were lost in action. *Schleswig-Holstein* was sunk in an air attack in December 1944, and *Schlesien* ran on a mine in the Baltic in April 1945. *Deutschland* was scrapped in 1922.

Country of origin:	Germany
Crew:	743
Weight:	14,216 tonnes (13,993 tons)
Dimensions:	127.6m x 22m x 8m (418ft 8in x 73ft x 27ft)
Range:	8894km (4800nm) at 12 knots
Armour:	248mm (9.75in) belt, 280mm (11in) on main turrets
Armament:	14 170mm (6.7in), four 279mm (11in) guns
Powerplant:	Twin screw, triple expansion engines
Performance:	18.5 knots

Deutschland

***D**eutschland* was the first West German naval ship to exceed the post-war limit of 3048 tonnes (3000 tons), and entered service in May 1963. She was a light cruiser that could also operate as a minelayer, and she carried a varied armament for training purposes, including 100mm (3.9in) and 40mm (1.6in) guns, depth-charge launchers and torpedo tubes. Two types of machinery were also installed to maximise training opportunities for the 267 cadets. *Deutschland*'s total complement was 550. She would have been an important minelaying asset in a cold war. The naval mine was used by the Prussians to bar Kiel harbour against the Danes during the Schleswig-Holstein crisis of 1848–51, and mines were laid by the Russians during the Crimean War to prevent British and French naval units from shelling the Baltic naval base Kronshtadt.

Country of origin:	Germany
Crew:	172 plus cadets
Weight:	5588 tonnes (5500 tons)
Dimensions:	65m x 8.9m x 5.3m (213ft 3in x 29ft 2in x 17ft 5in)
Range:	6840km (3800nm) at 10 knots
Armour:	50 – 125mm (2 – 5in)
Armament:	Four 100mm (3.9in) guns
Powerplant:	Triple screw diesel motors, turbines
Performance:	22 knots

Devastation

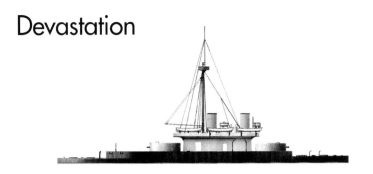

The 1869 design for the breastwork turret ship *Devastation* was a major step in the evolution of the battleship, producing a good balance of speed, protection and armament. As originally designed, the breastwork did not extend to the full width of the ship, and a passage was left on each side of the main deck. This area was later covered with a superstructure that extended to the sides of the ship. A recess in the aft superstructure allowed the guns to fire with maximum depression. Launched in 1871, *Devastation* was refitted in 1879, and between 1891 and 1892 she was given triple expansion engines. The refit included the installation of torpedoes, searchlights and machine guns. After 1892 she was used as a guardship at Gibraltar, where she was damaged by a gun explosion in 1900. *Devastation* was sold in 1908.

Country of origin:	Great Britain
Crew:	358
Weight:	9448 tonnes (9300 tons)
Dimensions:	87m x 20m x 8m (285ft x 65ft 3in x 26ft 8in)
Range:	4632km (2500nm) at 10 knots
Armour:	305mm – 212mm (12in – 8.5in) belt with 450mm – 400mm (18in – 16in) wood backing, 304mm – 254mm (12in – 10in) on turrets, 75mm – 50mm (3in – 2in) on deck
Armament:	Four 305mm (12in) guns
Powerplant:	Twin screw trunk engines
Performance:	13.8 knots

Dévastation

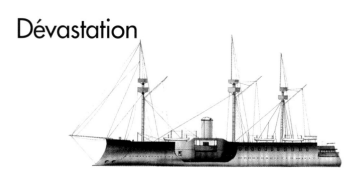

The massive central battery ship *Dévastation* was among the first vessels completed after France's war with Prussia in 1870. Designed by de Bussy, she and her sister vessel, *Courbet*, were improved Redoutable types with heavier guns and were believed to be superior to contemporary English vessels, which was probably correct, though France as a naval power lagged far behind Britain . This naval inferiority would not be made up with a handful of central battery ships. Her hull was of steel and iron with a double bottom. Lightly rigged and with two funnels abreast, she carried four guns in her central battery, two in barbettes and the remainder on deck. The main battery was never satisfactory and was continually updated. New machinery was installed 1901. *Dévastation* was scrapped in 1922.

Country of origin:	France
Crew:	689
Weight:	10,617 tonnes (10,450 tons)
Dimensions:	95m x 21m x 8m (311ft 6in x 69ft 9in x 27ft)
Range:	5188km (2800nm) at 10 knots
Armour:	380mm – 178mm (15in – 7in) iron belt
Armament:	Four 274mm (10.8in), four 340mm (13.4in) guns
Powerplant:	Twin screw, vertical compound engines
Performance:	15.5 knots

Dictator

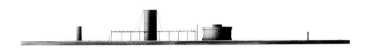

The huge monitor *Dictator* was a true ocean-going vessel, unlike the earlier smaller monitors then in service with the Union Navy. Launched in 1863, she was designed to have a speed of 16 knots, combined with a large radius of action due to her 1016-tonne (1000-ton) coal capacity. But in practice, she could only carry half that amount at half the designed speed. Mechanically weak, machinery failure prevented her taking part in perhaps her only action of the Civil War. After the war, interest in the navy faded and monitors were thought to be the only vessels necessary for the purely coastal defence role envisaged. No money was appropriated for new vessels and any funding was allocated to new ships based on foreign designs, with the result that monitors became obsolete as support grew for new ships. *Dictator* was sold in 1883.

Country of origin:	USA
Crew:	75
Weight:	4509 tonnes (4438 tons)
Dimensions:	95m x 15m x 6m (312ft x 50ft x 20ft 6in)
Range:	Unknown
Armour:	152mm – 25mm (6in – 1in) iron sides, 380mm (15in) turret, 50mm (2in) deck
Armament:	Two 380mm (15in) guns
Powerplant:	Single screw, vibrating lever engines
Performance:	9 knots (approx)

Dixmude

***D**ixmude* was one of three escort carriers which were built in the USA for lease to Britain. The carrier's original name was *Rio Parana*. Launched in 1940, the flight deck was increased to 134 metres (440ft) on arrival in Britain, and in 1942 her US weapons were replaced with British 102mm (4in) Mk V guns. Renamed *Biter*, she mostly served on convoy escort duties. Escort carriers such as the *Biter* did much to turn the Battle of the Atlantic in the Allies' favour. She was returned to the USA in 1945 and handed over to France, where she became the *Dixmude* and served as an aircraft transport. She saw action in Indo-China during 1946–48. In the early 1950s she was disarmed, and in 1960 she was hulked as an accommodation ship. *Dixmude* was returned to the USA in 1966 and subsequently scrapped.

Country of origin:	France
Crew:	555
Weight:	11,989 tonnes (11,800 tons)
Dimensions:	150m x 23m x 7.6m (490ft 10in x 78ft x 25ft 2in)
Range:	7412km (4000nm) at 15 knots
Armour:	50 – 100mm (2 – 4in)
Armament:	Three 102mm (4in) guns, 15 aircraft
Powerplant:	Single screw diesel engines
Performance:	16.5 knots

Dreadnought

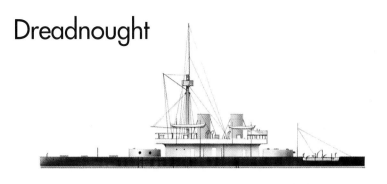

This vessel was originally designed by Edward J. Reed as a unit of the Devastation class to be called *Fury*. Work was suspended while she was on the stocks, pending a report on stability, protection and armament that was being prepared by the Committee of Designs. As *Dreadnought*, the ship was eventually completed in 1879 as a larger version of *Devastation*, and she incorporated many modifications on the earlier design. The 317mm (12.5in) guns were of a new specification, and were carried by *Dreadnought* throughout her entire career. The complete armour belt was the thickest continuous protection carried by a British warship. Commissioned in 1884, she served with the Mediterranean Fleet for 10 years before returning for a refit. She was used as a torpedo boat depot ship at Devonport, then broken up in 1908.

Country of origin:	Great Britain
Crew:	369
Weight:	11,060 tonnes (10,886 tons)
Dimensions:	104.5m x 19.4m x 8m (343ft x 63ft 10in x 26ft 3in)
Range:	9635km (5200nm) at 10 knots
Armour:	356mm – 203mm (14in – 8in) belt, 356mm – 279mm (14in – 11in) on citadel
Armament:	Four 317mm (12.5in) guns
Powerplant:	Twin screw, vertical compound engines
Performance:	14.5 knots

Dreadnought

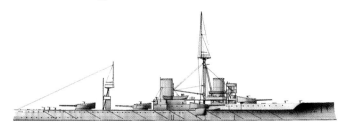

With the launching of *Dreadnought* in 1906, a new and more advanced era of warship construction began. *Dreadnought* was the first 'all-big-gun' battleship, so much so that she made all existing battleships obsolete. *Dreadnought* saw active service in World War I, being surpassed only by even larger ships of her type, to which she gave her generic name. Despite her warlike reputation, during World War I she only sank one enemy vessel, a German submarine which she rammed. The Royal Navy's Dreadnought fleet at the outbreak of World War I was thinly stretched, and after two months of hostilities ships had to be sent to their home ports on the south coast for refit. This meant that two or three of the Grand Fleet's most important vessels were absent from active duty at any one time. She was scrapped in 1923.

Country of origin:	Great Britain
Crew:	695 – 773
Weight:	22,194 tonnes (21,845 tons)
Dimensions:	160.4m x 25m x 8m (526ft 3in x 82ft x 26ft 3in)
Range:	11,916km (6620nm) at 10 knots
Armour:	203mm – 279mm (8in – 11in) belt, 280mm (11in) on turrets
Armament:	10 304mm (12in) guns
Powerplant:	Quadruple screw turbines
Performance:	21.6 knots

Duguesclin

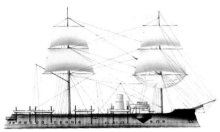

*D*uguesclin, a battleship of the Vauban class, had a wooden hull sheathed in copper, together with armour manufactured from standard wrought iron. Completed in 1886, she originally carried a heavy brig rig, but was later given two masts with military tops. Her crew numbered 440. *Duguesclin* had one sister, named *Vauban*. *Duguesclin* was a typical French battleship design of its day, characterised by a heavy squat appearance. During this period French naval thinking placed the emphasis on torpedo boats for defence and on cruisers for attacking enemy trade. Nevertheless, the construction of smaller second-class battleships, such as *Duguesclin*, continued, although naval policy was prone to change overnight as one minister succeeded another. *Duguesclin* was stricken in 1904.

Country of origin:	France
Crew:	440
Weight:	6210 tonnes (6112 tons)
Dimensions:	81m x 17.4m x 7.6m (265ft 9in x 57ft 3in x 25ft)
Range:	3335km (1800nm) at 10 knots
Armour:	152 – 254mm (6 – 10in) on waterline belt, 203mm (8in) on barbettes
Armament:	Six 140mm (5.5in), one 193mm (7.6in), four 240mm (9.4in) guns
Powerplant:	Twin screw, vertical compound engines
Performance:	14.5 knots

Duilio

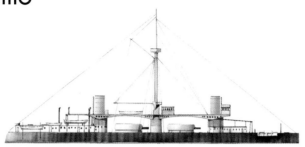

Duilio and her sister *Enrico Dandolo* were turret ships designed by Benedetto Brin, and upon completion were the most powerful warships in the world. They were the first warships to be rigged with just a military mast and to be armed with giant guns. Although laid down in 1873, *Duilio* was not completed until 1880. She was modernised in 1890, and again in 1900. After providing good service, *Duilio* was stripped of her armament in 1909 and became a floating oil tank. *Duilio*'s designer, Benedetto Brin, was a brilliant engineer whose designs did much to keep Italy at the forefront of maritime power. Vessels such as *Duilio* and *Dandalo*, with their massive guns, inspired competitive designs in other countries. Several of Brin's creations were exported to other countries, such as Spain, Argentina and Japan.

Country of origin:	Italy
Crew:	420, later 515
Weight:	12,264 tonnes (12,071 tons)
Dimensions:	109m x 19.7m x 8.3m (358ft 2in x 64ft 8in x 27ft 3in)
Range:	6768km (3760nm) at 10 knots
Armour:	537mm (21.5in) on the sides, 425mm (17in) on turrets and citadel
Armament:	Four 450mm (17.7in) guns
Powerplant:	Twin screw, vertical compound engines
Performance:	15 knots

Duilio

Completed in 1916 as members of the Doria class, *Duilio* and her sister *Andrea Doria* underwent several changes in their careers, for example, receiving seaplanes in 1925. Extensive modernisation between 1937 and 1940 upgraded both their armour and guns and turned both vessels into virtually new ships. *Duilio* was damaged in the British air attack on Taranto naval base, in November 1940. She was towed to Genoa for repair and narrowly escaped further damage when the port was bombarded by British warships in February 1941. Returned to active service later that year, she was employed on convoy interception and escort duty before being placed on the Reserve in 1942. After her surrender to the Allies at Malta in September 1943 she was used as a training ship. She was broken up at La Spezia in 1957.

Country of origin:	Italy
Crew:	1198
Weight:	29,861 tonnes (29,391 tons)
Dimensions:	187m x 28m x 8.5m (613ft 2in x 91ft 10in x 28ft 2in)
Range:	8640km (4800nm) at 12 knots
Armour:	254mm (10in) on sides, 279mm (11in) on turrets
Armament:	10 320mm (12.6in) guns
Powerplant:	Twin screw turbines
Performance:	27 knots

Duke of Wellington

The *Duke of Wellington* was laid down at Pembroke Dock in May 1849. In early 1852, with the growing threat of war with France, a hurried conversion programme was put in hand, and she was converted into a steam vessel with engines that developed 900hp. However, it would be nearly another 30 years before sails completely disappeared from warships in favour of engine power alone. She was hulked for harbour service in Portsmouth in 1863, and broken up in 1909. The last fleet action wholly under sail took place at Navarino on 20 October 1827, when a force of British, French and Russian ships under the command of Sir Edward Codrington destroyed a Turkish-Egyptian fleet and played a major part in securing Greek autonomy. The first practical steamboat was built by William Symington in 1802.

Country of origin:	Great Britain
Crew:	970
Weight:	5922 tonnes (5829 tons)
Dimensions:	73m x 18m x 7.5m (240ft x 60ft x 25ft)
Range:	4632km (2500nm) at 8 knots
Armour:	None
Armament:	10 203mm (8in) guns, plus 121 smaller weapons
Powerplant:	Single screw compound engines
Performance:	10 knots

Dunderberg

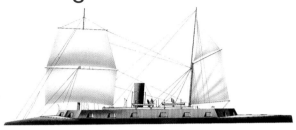

***D**underberg* was a brigantine-rigged casemate ironclad with a double bottom, collision bulkhead and a massive solid oak ram. Although laid down in late 1862, she was not completed in time for service in the American Civil War due to a shortage of materials and skilled labour. Upon completion she was one of the largest and most powerful vessels built for the US Navy. Her builder bought her back from the US Navy and sold her on to France, where she was renamed *Rochambeau*. The vessel arrived in France with no armament, which was installed; her bow was rebuilt, the ram being dispensed with, and her engines improved. She served with the French Navy on North Sea patrol and took part in the blockade of Prussia in 1870, but apart from that she saw little service. *Rochambeau* was stricken in 1872.

Country of origin:	USA
Crew:	590
Weight:	7173 tonnes (7060 tons)
Dimensions:	115m x 22m x 6.4m (377ft 4in x 72ft 10in x 21ft)
Range:	4447km (2400nm) at 8 knots
Armour:	89mm – 62.5mm (3.5in – 2.5in) iron belt, 112mm (4.5in) casemate
Armament:	Eight 279mm (11in), two 380mm (15in) guns
Powerplant:	Single screw, back-acting engines
Performance:	12 knots

Dunkerque

Based on the British Nelson class battleships, *Dunkerque* was the first French warship to be laid down after the Washington Treaty of 1922. She was the culmination of a series of design studies that resulted in an answer to the German Deutschland class of the early 1930s. A hangar and a catapult were provided for the four scout planes which she was to carry. In October 1939, as flagship of the Brest-based Force L, she joined the Royal Navy in the hunt for the German pocket battleship *Admiral Graf Spee*. She was employed on convoy escort duty until the surrender of France, and in July 1940 she was severely damaged by British warships at Mers-el-Kebir and by a torpedo attack three days later, with the loss of 210 lives. She was scuttled in Toulon harbour in 1942, and raised and sold for scrap in 1953.

Country of origin:	France
Crew:	1431
Weight:	36,068 tonnes (35,500 tons)
Dimensions:	214.5m x 31m x 8.6m (703ft 9in x 102ft 3in x 28ft 6in)
Range:	13,897km (7500nm) at 15 knots
Armour:	243mm – 143mm (9.75in – 5.75in) main belt, 331mm – 152mm (13.25in – 6in) on turrets
Armament:	16 127mm (5in), eight 330mm (13in) guns
Powerplant:	Quadruple screw turbines
Performance:	29.5 knots

Eagle

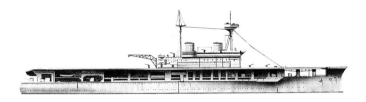

*E*agle was originally laid down in 1913 as the Chilean Navy's super-dreadnought *Almirante Cochrane*. With the outbreak of World War I work stopped and it only began again in 1917 after her purchase by the Royal Navy. Construction of the ship then continued, and the vessel was turned into an aircraft carrier. Eventually, she entered service in 1924. When Italy entered the war on the Axis side in June 1940, *Eagle* was the only aircraft carrier at the disposal of the British in the Mediterranean, and she performed sterling service in ferrying fighter aircraft to the besieged island of Malta. She had previously operated in the Indian Ocean and the South Atlantic, based in Ceylon, her main task being to search for German commerce raiders. In August 1942, *Eagle* was sunk in the Mediterranean by *U73* while attempting to deliver aircraft to Malta.

Country of origin:	Great Britain
Crew:	950
Weight:	27,664 tonnes (27,229 tons)
Dimensions:	203.4m x 32m x 8m (667ft 6in x 105ft x 26ft 3in)
Range:	5559km (3000nm) at 15 knots
Armour:	112mm – 25mm (4.5in – 1in) belt, 100mm (4in) bulkhead, 37.5mm – 25mm (1.5in – 1in) decks
Armament:	Five 102mm (4in), nine 152mm (6in) guns, 21 aircraft
Powerplant:	Quadruple screw turbines
Performance:	22.5 knots

Eagle

With the completion of the naval construction programmes of 1936 and 1937 and with the construction of the Illustrious class carriers of 1938 in progress, designs were prepared in 1942 for their successors. These designs allowed for two complete hangars to be built together with the ability to handle the heavier aircraft that were expected to be introduced. *Eagle* entered service in October 1951, was decommissioned in January 1972, and was sent for breaking-up in 1978. She was the sister ship of HMS *Ark Royal*. During her service career she took part in many peacekeeping actions, but she is perhaps best remembered for her offensive role in the Anglo-French Suez operations, when her aircraft carried out numerous strikes on targets in the Suez Canal Zone in support of Anglo-French ground forces.

Country of origin:	Great Britain
Crew:	2740
Weight:	47,200 tonnes (46,452 tons)
Dimensions:	245m x 34m x 11m (803ft 9in x 112ft 9in x 36ft)
Range:	7412km (4000nm) at 20 knots
Armour:	112mm (4.5in) belt, 112mm – 37.5mm (4.5in – 1.5in) bulkheads
Armament:	16 112mm (4.5in) guns
Powerplant:	Quadruple screw turbines
Performance:	32 knots

Ekaterina II

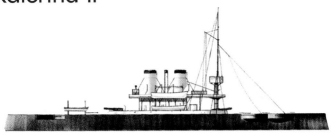

Russia's geography meant that its navy was divided into separate fleets in the Baltic, Black Sea and in the Far East, each with a different operational role. Until the 1870s the main arm of the Russian Navy comprised cruisers for commerce raiding, but as Russia sought to expand its power, so its naval strength was increased with the deployment of new warships. *Ekaterina II* was built for the Black Sea Fleet, and was one of the first major warships to have triple expansion engines. She and her sisters were among the most powerful battleships of their day, with their six guns mounted on a pear-shaped redoubt amidships. *Ekaterina II* was reclassified as a second-class battleship in 1906, and a year later became a target ship. She was sunk during target practice off Tendra harbour in 1907.

Country of origin:	Russian
Crew:	674
Weight:	11,224 tonnes (11,048 tons)
Dimensions:	100.9m x 21m x 8.5m (331ft x 68ft 11in x 27ft 11in)
Range:	2500km (1350nm) at 12 knots
Armour:	400mm – 203mm (16in – 8in) belt, 305mm (12in) redoubt
Armament:	Six 304mm (12in) guns
Powerplant:	Twin screw, vertical triple expansion engines
Performance:	16 knots

Emanuele Filiberto

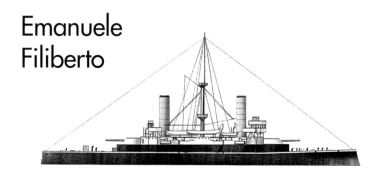

*E*manuele Filiberto was laid down in 1893, launched in 1897, and completed in 1902. However, her firepower was too light for a battleship of the line. Her speed and sea-keeping qualities were also inadequate, due to the low 4.4m (14ft 6in) freeboard forward and 3m (10ft) clearance aft. She had a high superstructure amidships, holding the twin funnels, a single military mast and her boats. Her four 254mm (10in) main guns were mounted in two armoured turrets, placed above barbettes to give clearance in heavy seas. Her secondary armament of eight 152mm (6in) guns were mounted in broadside on the main superstructure. In 1911, in the war with Turkey, she operated off Tripoli in support of Italian forces, and in 1912 formed part of the task force that occupied Rhodes. She served throughout World War I in the Adriatic. Despite her weaknesses she was not discarded until 1920.

Country of origin:	Italy
Crew:	565
Weight:	10,058 tonnes (9897 tons)
Dimensions:	111.8m x 21m x 7.2m (366ft 10in x 69ft 3in x 23ft 10in)
Range:	9900km (5500nm) at 12 knots
Armour:	248mm – 122mm (9.8in – 4in) belt
Armament:	Eight 152mm (6in), four 254mm (10in) guns
Powerplant:	Twin screw, triple expansion engines
Performance:	18 knots

Engadine

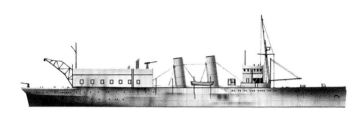

At the outbreak of World War I, the British Admiralty took over a number of fast cross-channel steamers for conversion into seaplane carriers. *Engadine* and her sister *Riviera* were two such ships and both were quickly converted to carry three aircraft. By December 1914 they were in action against the German airship sheds at Cuxhaven. *Engadine* was modified in 1915. She then served with the Grand Fleet, carrying out North Sea sweeps and anti-submarine patrols, and pursuing the German airships then beginning to increase their attacks upon the British mainland. During the Battle of Jutland in 1916, a Short 184 seaplane from *Engadine* made the first-ever air reconnaissance of a fleet in action, transmitting the position of the German warships by means of wireless telegraphy. *Engadine* later served in the Mediterranean. She was returned to her owners in 1919.

Country of origin:	Great Britain
Crew:	250
Weight:	1702 tonnes (1676 tons)
Dimensions:	96.3m x 12.5m (316 ft x 41ft)
Range:	2779km (1500nm) at 18 knots
Armour:	50mm (2in) belt
Armament:	Two 102mm (4in), one 6-pounder gun, six seaplanes
Powerplant:	Triple screw turbines
Performance:	21 knots

Engadine

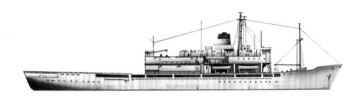

Engadine was laid down in August 1965 and was designed for the training of helicopter crews in deep-water operations. Although she does not carry her own aircraft, these can be embarked as necessary and housed in the large hangar aft of the funnel. At any one time, *Engadine* can carry four Wessex and two WASP helicopters, or two of the larger Sea Kings. Complement is 81, plus an additional 113 training crew. *Engadine* can also operate pilotless target aircraft. She is a unique vessel, giving a thorough training to the helicopter crews that form a major part of the anti-submarine defence of surface ships. *Engadine* forms part of the Royal Fleet Auxiliary (RFA), which consists of support vessels such as logistics ships, oilers and tankers. She is fitted with Denny Brown stabilisers to provide greater ship control during helicopter operations.

Country of origin:	Great Britain
Crew:	75 plus 113 training crews
Weight:	9144 tonnes (9000 tons)
Dimensions:	129.3m x 17.8m x 6.7m (424ft 3in x 58ft 5in x 22ft)
Range:	9265km (5000nm) at 14 knots
Armour:	None
Armament:	None
Powerplant:	Single screw diesel engines
Performance:	16 knots

Enrico Dandolo

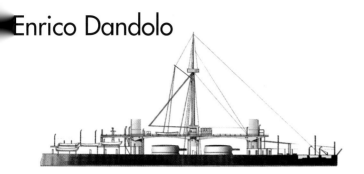

After the Battle of Lissa in 1866, Italian Navy budgets were severely cut, but during the second administration of Augusto Riboty the situation improved, and funds were made available for the construction of thoroughly modern vessels. Riboty was succeeded by Saint Bon, who allowed Benedetto Brin full rein to develop heavily armed, well-protected, fast capital ships. *Enrico Dandolo* and her sister *Duilio* were the first of such vessels, and were the first battleships with giant guns and no provision for sailing. *Enrico Dandolo* served as a a guard ship at Tobruk, Libya, in 1913, and then as a floating battery at Brindisi and Venice during World War I, and was discarded in 1920. The vessel was named after Enrico Dandolo (1108–1205), the doge of Venice, who captured Constantinople in the Fourth Crusade.

Country of origin:	Italy
Crew:	550
Weight:	12,461 tonnes (12,265 tons)
Dimensions:	109.2m x 19.7m x 8.8m (358ft 3in x 64ft 8in x 28ft 10in)
Range:	1830km (1000nm) at 10 knots
Armour:	550mm (21.7in) thick belt amidships, 400mm (16in) on turrets and central citadel
Armament:	Four 450mm (18in) guns
Powerplant:	Twin screw, vertical triple expansion engines
Performance:	15.6 knots

Enterprise

Early *Enterprise* designs had a flush deck, but this was thought to pose a smoke threat to landing aircraft, and an island structure to carry funnel uptakes and provide control centres was devised. The aircraft hangars were light structures independent from the hull, that could be closed off with rolling shutters. *Enterprise* was refitted in 1942 after action at the Battle of Midway, during which her dive bombers helped sink three Japanese carriers. Apart from Midway, her World War II battle honours included Guadalcanal, the Eastern Solomons, the Gilbert Islands, Kwajalein, Eniwetok, the Truk raid, Hollandia, Saipan, the Battle of the Philippine Sea, Palau, Leyte, Luzon, Taiwan, the China coast, Iwo Jima and Okinawa. She received five bomb hits and survived two attacks by Kamikazes off Okinawa. She was sold in 1958, despite efforts to preserve her as a memorial.

Country of origin:	USA
Crew:	2175
Weight:	25,908 tonnes (25,500 tons)
Dimensions:	246.7m x 26.2m x 7.9m (809ft 6in x 86ft x 26ft)
Range:	21,600km (12,000nm) at 12 knots
Armour:	102mm - 62.5mm (4in – 2.5in) belt, 37.5mm (1.5in) armoured deck
	102mm (4in) bulkheads
Armament:	Eight 127mm (5in) guns
Powerplant:	Quadruple screw turbines
Performance:	37.5 knots

Enterprise

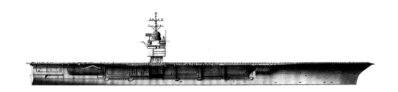

Nuclear-powered aircraft carriers had been suggested as far back as 1946, but cost delayed development of the project. *Enterprise* had a range of 643,720 kilometres (400,000 miles) at 20 knots. When completed in 1961 she was the largest vessel in the world, and was the second nuclear-powered warship to enter service. Her stowage capacity was huge, including 12,240,000 litres (2,720,000 gallons) of aviation fuel and 2560 tonnes (2520 tons) of aviation ordnance. She was refitted between 1979 and 1982 and given a revised island structure. *Enterprise* carries offensive tactical nuclear ordnance that includes 10kT B61, 20kT B57, 100kT B61, 330kT B61 and 900kT air-delivered gravity bombs, 10kT depth bombs; 1.4mT B43 and 1.1mT strategic nuclear weapons can also be carried as required. Her air group is similar in size and configuration to that of the Nimitz-class carriers.

Country of origin:	USA
Crew:	3325 crew, 1891 air group and 71 marines
Weight:	91,033 tonnes (89,600 tons)
Dimensions:	335.2m x 76.8m x 10.9m (1,100ft x 252ft x 36ft)
Range:	643,720km (400,000nm) at 20 knots
Armour:	Classified
Armament:	Surface-to-air missiles, 90 aircraft
Powerplant:	Quadruple screw geared turbines, steam supplied by eight nuclear reactors
Performance:	32 knots

Erin

Built as the *Reshadieh* for the Turkish Navy, *Erin* was taken over by the Royal Navy prior to her completion in 1914. She went on to serve with the Grand Fleet for the duration of World War I. Her reduced coal capacity, which was 1,148 tonnes (1,130 tons) less than that of a contemporary British battleship of the King George V class, did not detract from her performance which was considered to be good. Although shorter and wider than contemporary British battleships, nevertheless she carried the offensive power of an Iron Duke class vessel. Her main distinguishing features were two narrow funnels and a tripod mast with legs stepped forward. She was designed by Sir Richard Thurston and her turbines were by Parsons (Vickers). She was refitted in 1917, placed in reserve in 1919 and scrapped in 1921.

Country of origin:	Great Britain
Crew:	1070
Weight:	25,654 tonnes (25,250 tons)
Dimensions:	170.5m x 27.9m x 8.6m (559ft 5in x 91ft 6in x 28ft 3in)
Range:	9540km (5300nm) at 12 knots
Armour:	305mm – 102mm (12in – 4in) belt, 254mm – 75mm (10in – 3in) barbettes, 203mm – 102mm (8in – 4in) bulkheads
Armament:	10 343mm (13.5in) guns
Powerplant:	Quadruple screw turbines
Performance:	21 knots

Erzherzog Albrecht

Erzherzog Albrecht was the Austro-Hungarian Navy's first iron-hulled warship. She was designed with offensive power in mind and her speed reduced to allow for better protection. Launched in 1872, she served until 1908, when she was renamed *Feuerspeier* and became a tender to a gunnery training ship. In 1920 she was handed over to Italy as a war reparation and became the *Buttafuaco Custoza*. She was scrapped in 1946. The *Erzherzog Albrecht*, named after Archduke Albert, Duke of Teschen (1817–1895), field marshal of the Austrian Army, was one of 34 Austro-Hungarian warships required to be surrendered to the Allies under the terms of the armistice agreement. Fifteen submarines completed between 1910 and 1918 also had to be turned over, and all other vessels disarmed. These terms effectively reduced Austria to utter impotence.

Country of origin:	Austria
Crew:	540
Weight:	6075 tonnes (5980 tons)
Dimensions:	89.6m x 17m x 6.7m (294ft 3in x 56ft 3in x 22ft)
Range:	4289km (2320nm) at 10 knots
Armour:	203mm (8in) belt, 178mm (7in) casemate
Armament:	Eight 240mm (9.5in) guns
Powerplant:	Single screw, two-cylinder horizontal engine
Performance:	12.8 knots

Erzherzog Karl

Erzherzog Karl was one of three units that formed the last of the pre-dreadnought type built for the Austrian Navy. She served in the Adriatic in World War I, and was taken over by Yugoslavia in 1919. In 1920 she was handed over to France as part of Austria's war reparations and scrapped. She is known for being the first warship to have her secondary guns housed in electrically powered turrets. The *Erzherzog Karl* and her sister ships, *Erzherzog Ferdinand Max* and *Erzherzog Friedrich*, were good vessels for their size but obsolescent by the time they were completed in 1906–10. The *Erzherzog Karl* was named after Archduke Charles, Duke of Teschen (1771–1847), field marshal and commander of the Austrian forces against Napoleon. The *Friedrich* was ceded to Britain, the *Ferdinand Max* to France.

Country of origin:	Austria
Crew:	700
Weight:	10,640 tonnes (10,472 tons)
Dimensions:	126.2m x 21.7m x 7.5m (414ft 2in x 71ft 6in x 24ft 8in)
Range:	7412km (4000nm) at 10 knots
Armour:	210mm (8.4in) belt, 240mm (9.6in) turrets
Armament:	12 190mm (7.5in), four 240mm (9.45in) guns
Powerplant:	Twin screw, triple expansion engines
Performance:	20.5 knots

España

España and her two sisters combined dreadnought armament with pre-dreadnought dimensions. In 1923 *España* ran aground in fog off the Moroccan coast and could not be salvaged. *Alfonso XIII*, one of *España*'s sisters, took her name in 1931, but was sunk in 1937 when she hit a mine during the Spanish Civil War. Ironically the mine had been laid by the Nationalists – her own side. The Espana class of small battleships were built in Spain with British technical assistance. They had four twin turrets, a single funnel and two tripod masts. The completion of one of them, *Jaime I*, was held up by World War I and she was not completed until 1921. This vessel saw more action than the others in the Spanish Civil War; she was sunk by an explosion at Cartagena in June 1937, with over 300 dead.

Country of origin:	Spain
Crew:	845
Weight:	15,991 tonnes (15,740 tons)
Dimensions:	140m x 24m x 7.8m (459ft x 78ft 9in x 25ft 7in)
Range:	9000km (5000nm) at 10 knots
Armour:	203mm – 75mm (8in – 3in) belt, plus 75mm (3in) battery, 203mm (8in) on turrets
Armament:	20 102mm (4in), eight 305mm (12in) guns
Powerplant:	Quadruple screw turbines
Performance:	19.5 knots

Essex

By the end of the 1930s, the increased needs of the navy for air cover led to an explosion in the size of aircraft carriers, and a larger hull was introduced to stow the aviation fuel required for the 91 aircraft now carried. There were 24 vessels in the Essex class, their designs based around an enlargement of the earlier Yorktown class carriers. *Essex* was laid down in April 1941 and entered service in 1942. She was removed from the effective list in 1969 and scrapped in 1973. *Essex*'s battle honours in World War II included raids on Marcus and Wake Islands, the Gilbert Islands and Kwajalein (1943); raids on Truk and the Marianas, Saipan, Guam, Tinian, Palau and the Battle of the Philippine Sea (1944); raids on Luzon, the China coast, the Ryukus, Iwo Jima, Okinawa and Japan (1945). In November 1944 the carrier was damaged by a kamikaze hit at Leyte, and again in April 1945 off Okinawa.

Country of origin:	USA
Crew:	2687
Weight:	35,438 tonnes (34,880 tons)
Dimensions:	265.7m x 29.2m x 8.3m (871ft 9in x 96ft x 27ft 6in)
Range:	27,000km (15,000nm) at 12 knots
Armour:	102mm – 62.5mm (4in – 2.5in) belt and hangar deck
Armament:	12 127mm (5in) guns, 91 aircraft
Powerplant:	Quadruple screw turbines
Performance:	32.7 knots

Europa

Europa started life as the British merchant ship *Manila*, with a gross displacement of only 4200 tonnes (4134 tons). In 1898 her name was changed to *Salacia*. In 1911 she was sold to Germany. She then took the Italian flag under the name *Quarto*. In 1915 she was finally purchased by the Italian Navy and converted to a seaplane carrier, becoming the first Italian ship to operate fixed-wing aircraft. *Europa* emerged with two large aircraft hangars, one ahead and one aft of the low superstructure. There was a large davit mounted on the bow, which acted as a winch for launching and retrieving the aircraft. She could carry eight seaplanes, and normally operated a group of six fighters and two reconnaissance aircraft. She was based at Brindisi from October 1915 until January 1916, then transferred to Velona until 1918. She survived World War I, but was scrapped in 1920.

Country of origin:	Italy
Crew:	394
Weight:	8945 tonnes (8805 tons)
Dimensions:	123m x 14m x 7.6m (403ft 10in x 46ft x 25ft)
Range:	10,747km (5800nm) at 10 knots
Armour:	Belt 100mm (4in), hangars 50mm (2in)
Armament:	Two 30mm (1.2in) anti-aircraft guns, eight seaplanes
Powerplant:	Single screw, vertical triple expansion engines
Performance:	12 knots

Feth-I-Bulend

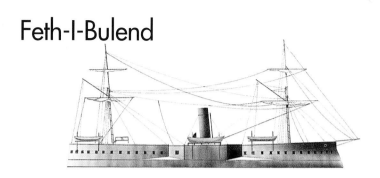

In a bid to support the backward Turkish Empire against Russian expansionist policies, Britain gave considerable aid to the Turkish in their efforts to build a powerful and modern naval fleet. In the 1860s and 1870s, so many modern ironclad warships were built on behalf of Turkey by both Britain and France that the Ottoman Empire became the world's third largest naval fleet. Much of this development occurred under the administration of a British naval officer, Hobart Pasha. Vessels of this era included *Feth-I-Bulend*, an iron-hulled, central battery ship built at Blackwall in London. *Feth-I-Bulend* was laid down in 1868 and completed in 1872. She was reconstructed between 1903 and 1907. In 1912, during the Balkans war, *Feth-I-Bulend* was sunk by the Greek torpedo vessel *No. 11*.

Country of origin:	Turkey
Crew:	220
Weight:	2805 tonnes (2761 tons)
Dimensions:	72m x 12m x 5.5m (236ft 3in x 39ft 4in x 18ft)
Range:	1927km (1040nm) at 10 knots
Armour:	229mm – 152mm (9in – 6in) waterline belt
Armament:	Four 229mm (9in) guns
Powerplant:	Single screw, horizontal compound engines
Performance:	13 knots

Flandre

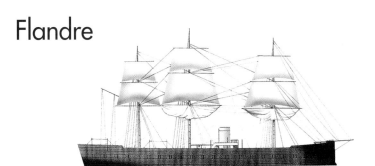

*F*landre and her nine sisters of the Provence class were authorised in 1860, and became the largest single group of French battleships ever built. They were originally envisaged as iron ships, but, because of the massive resources put into building armoured floating batteries for the Crimean War, nine of the ten in fact had wooden hulls. The exception was *Heroine*, which was built of iron. *Flandre* and her nine sister vessels (*Gauloise, Guyenne, Heroine, Magnanime, Provence, Revanche, Savoie, Surveillante* and *Valeureuse*) were designed by the celebrated engineer Dupuy de Lome. *Flandre* took part in the blockade of Prussia during the war of 1870. The ships were closely modelled on *La Gloire* but had thicker armour. All but four of their guns were carried on the broadside on the main deck. *Flandre* was stricken in 1886.

Country of origin:	France
Crew:	594
Weight:	5791 tonnes (5700 tons)
Dimensions:	80m x 17m x 8.2m (262ft 5in x 55ft 9in x 26ft 10in)
Range:	4465km (2410nm) at 10 knots
Armour:	152mm – 107.5mm (6in – 4.3in) iron belt
Armament:	22 152mm (6in), 10 55-pounder guns
Powerplant:	Single screw, horizontal compound engines
Performance:	13.9 knots

Flandre

*F*landre was laid down in October 1913 as one of a class of five units built in response to the increased gun calibres being used by other countries. It was decided to fit the 340mm (13.4in) guns in three quadruple turrets, which were in reality two twin mounts placed side by side in a single well-armoured barbette. Work halted on the class in 1914 and they were launched to clear the docks. Four were scrapped in 1924–25; one of the class, *Béarn*, was completed as an aircraft carrier. Impounded by the Americans at Martinique after going aground, she was towed to Puerto Rico. In 1943–44 she was refitted at New Orleans, rearmed, had her flight deck shortened, and was reclassified as an aircraft transport. Handed over to the Free French Navy, she saw service in the Far East in 1945–46, supporting the French reoccupation of Indo-China.

Country of origin:	France
Crew:	1200
Weight:	25,230 tonnes (24,833 tons)
Dimensions:	176.4m x 27m x 8.7m (578ft 9in x 88ft 7in x 28ft 6in)
Range:	11,700km (6500nm) at 12 knots
Armour:	300mm (11.8in) belt, 340mm – 250mm (13.26in – 9.75in) turrets
Armament:	12 340mm (13.4in), 24 140mm (5.5in) guns
Powerplant:	Quadruple screws - two for turbines and two for vertical triple expansion engines
Performance:	21 knots

Florida

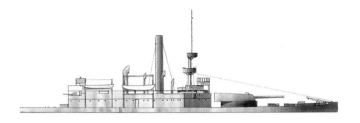

Launched in 1901, *Florida* was one of the Arkansas class of four that were the last of the big-gun monitors built for the US Navy. The maximum thickness of the belt armour was at the 37.5mm (1.5in) armoured-deck level only, tapering to 127mm (5in) at the lower edge and at the ends. The 305mm (12in) guns were in a single turret forward. Four 102mm (4in) guns were also carried, two at the rear of the superstructure and two under the bridge. All vessels of the class at some time served as submarine tenders. In 1908 she was renamed *Tallahassee* and was successively employed as an experimental ordnance ship and submarine tender. During World War I she served in the Panama Canal Zone, the Virgin Islands and Bermuda, and from 1920 to 1922 she was used as a Reserve training ship. She was sold and broken up in 1922, but her sister, *Wyoming* was not sold until 1939.

Country of origin:	USA
Crew:	270
Weight:	3277 tonnes (3225 tons)
Dimensions:	77.75m x 15.25m x 3.8m (255ft x 50ft x 12ft 6in)
Range:	3113km (1680nm) at 10 knots
Armour:	279mm – 127mm (11in – 5in) belt, 279mm – 229mm (11in – 9in) barbettes and turrets
Armament:	Two 306mm (12in) and four 102mm (4in) guns
Powerplant:	Twin screw, vertical triple expansion engines
Performance:	12.5 knots

Foch

Laid down in 1957 and completed in 1963, *Foch* is the second of the Clémenceau class carriers. She underwent a refit between 1981 and 1982 which enabled her to carry tactical nuclear weapons, and in 1984 received a satellite communications system. Further improvements have included the introduction of a point-defence missile system in place of 100mm (3.9in) guns, a new catapult mechanism and a laser landing system for her flight deck. Her missile system was improved again in 1996. Despite these upgrades, *Foch* has failed to retain a full air group. Since 1975 she has shared one with her sister *Clémenceau* and spends part of her time as a helicopter carrier. Her strike component consists of the Super Etendard attack aircraft, which can be armed with AN52 15kT tactical nuclear bombs. She is due to remain in service until 2003.

Country of origin:	France
Crew:	1338 (as aircraft carrier), 984 (as helicopter carrier)
Weight:	32,255 tonnes (32, 780 tons)
Dimensions:	265m x 31.7m x 8.6m (870ft x 104ft x 28ft)
Range:	13,500km (7500nm) at 12 knots
Armour:	Classified
Armament:	Eight 100mm (3.9in) guns, Crotale and Sadral surface-to-air missile systems, 40 aircraft
Powerplant:	Two shaft, geared steam turbines
Performance:	32 knots

Formidabile

Built in French yards, the vessels *Formidabile* and *Terribile* were originally designed as 30-gun floating batteries, but became instead ocean-going broadside ironclads with 20 guns. In addition, they were rearmed with eight 203mm (8in) guns. They had the distinction of being the first Italian ironclads. These two vessels were originally built for the Sardinian Navy prior to the unification of Italy. *Formidabile* was laid down at La Seyne in 1860 and launched in 1861. On 17 July 1866 she was damaged by shore batteries at Porto San Giorgio, Lissa, with the loss of three of her crew. She subsequently took part in the liberation of Rome in 1870, and from 1887 she served as a gunnery and torpedo school ship at La Spezia. *Formidabile* was removed from the effective list in 1903.

Country of origin:	Italy
Crew:	371
Weight:	2769 tonnes (2725 tons)
Dimensions:	65.8m x 13.6m x 5.4m (215ft 10in x 44ft 7in x 17ft 9in)
Range:	2340km (1300nm) at 10 knots
Armour:	85mm (3.4in) belt, 102mm (4in) citadel
Armament:	16 164mm (6.5in), four 203mm (8in) 72-pounder guns
Powerplant:	Single screw, single expansion engines
Performance:	10 knots

Formidable

From 1877 to 1879, France laid down seven barbette ships, of which *Formidable* was the last. *Formidable* had her three 371mm (14.6in) guns in single barbettes on the centreline, with the secondary battery on the main deck. The steel belt ran the full length of the vessel, but only 305mm (12in) of it was above water. *Formidable* was a member of the Baudin class, the other vessel being *Amiral Baudin*. The ships were reconstructed in 1897–98 when the amidships barbette was removed and replaced by a casemate; the mainmast was altered and new boilers were fitted. *Formidable* had an undistinguished career; in 1895 she went aground in Hyeres during exercises. Placed in reserve in 1903, she served as a base ship at Landevennec and was deleted from the navy list in 1911.

Country of origin:	France
Crew:	650
Weight:	11,908 tonnes (11,720 tons)
Dimensions:	101.4m x 21.3m x 8.5m (332ft 8in x 70ft x 27ft 9in)
Range:	5559km (3000nm) at 10 knots
Armour:	559mm – 356mm (22in – 14in) belt, 405mm (16in) barbettes
Armament:	Three 371mm (14.6in), four 160mm (6.3in), 10 140mm (5.5in) guns
Powerplant:	Twin screw, vertical compound engines
Performance:	16 knots

Formidable

The 1936 Royal Navy programme called for the construction of two 23,368-tonne (23,000-ton) carriers, and at first plans were drawn up based on *Ark Royal*. With the realisation that war in Europe was coming ever closer, and that such carriers would be subject to constant air attack, armour protection and defensive armament was seen as important. The aircraft hangar was set in an armoured box intended to be proof against 227kg (500lb) bombs and 152mm (6in) gunfire. *Formidable* was completed in Belfast in 1940. She received serious damage from air attack while transporting aircraft to Malta in 1941. After being repaired, she went on to serve in the Pacific and survived several kamikaze attacks. British fleet carriers had armoured flight decks, unlike their US counterparts, and were consequently far less vulnerable to air attack. She was scrapped in 1953.

Country of origin:	Great Britain
Crew:	1997
Weight:	28,661 tonnes (28,210 tons)
Dimensions:	226.7m x 29.1m x 8.5m (743ft 9in x 95ft 9in x 28ft)
Range:	20,383km (11,000nm) at 14 knots
Armour:	112mm (4.5in) belt, hangars and bulkheads
Armament:	16 112mm (4.5in) guns, 36 aircraft
Powerplant:	Triple screw turbines
Performance:	30.5 knots

Forrestal

*F*orrestal and her three sisters of the Forrestal class were authorised in 1951. Large size was needed to operate fast combat jets, which needed more fuel than their piston-engined predecessors. Designed with an angled flight deck and four steam catapults, *Forrestal* had space for around 3.4 million litres (750,000 gallons) of aviation fuel and 1670 tonnes (1650 tons) of aviation ordnance. She served with the Atlantic Fleet until 1965, when she underwent a refit before being transferred to the Pacific Fleet for operations off Vietnam. In July 1967 she was severely damaged by fire and explosion when fire broke out on the flight deck as aircraft were being readied for operations, touching off bombs and ammunition and killing 132 crew. *Forrestal* underwent a major refit between 1983–85. She is scheduled for frontline service until the turn of the century.

Country of origin:	USA
Crew:	2764 crew, 1912 air crew
Weight:	80,516 tonnes (79,248 tons)
Dimensions:	309.4m x 73.2m x 11.3m (1,015ft x 240ft x 37ft)
Range:	21,600km (12,000nm) at 10 knots
Armour:	Classified
Armament:	Eight 127mm (5in) guns, 90 aircraft
Powerplant:	Quadruple screw turbines
Performance:	33 knots

Francesco Caracciolo

Work started on *Francesco Caracciolo* and three sister units of the Caraciola class in 1914, but was halted in 1916 so that materials and labour could be devoted to building destroyers, submarines and light craft. Work recommenced in October 1919, but after the launch, the hull was sold in October 1920 to the Navigazione Generale Italiana which intended to convert her into a merchant ship. Lack of funds stopped this and a plan to turn her into an aircraft carrier was also dropped, and she was scrapped in 1921. The three sister ships were less advanced when work was halted and they were scrapped on the stocks. *Francesco Caracciolo*'s design gave her four widely spaced turrets, with the 152mm (6in) guns in two groups near the centre of the vessel. The other vessels in this class were the *Cristoforo Colombo*, *Francesco Morosini*, and *Marcantonio Colonnal*.

Country of origin:	Italy
Crew:	1200
Weight:	34,544 tonnes (34,000 tons)
Dimensions:	212m x 29.6m x 9.5m (695ft 6in x 97ft x 31ft 2in)
Range:	14,824km (8000nm) at 10 knots
Armour:	300mm (11.8in) on side, 400mm (16in) on turrets
Armament:	Eight 380mm (15in), 12 152mm (6in) guns
Powerplant:	Quadruple screw turbines
Performance:	28 knots

Francesco Morosini

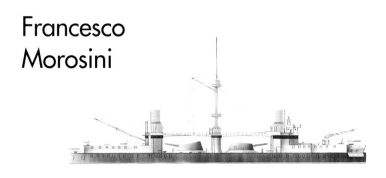

Francesco Morosini was authorised under the 1880 programme, laid down in 1881 at the Naval Arsenal, Venice, and completed in April 1889. Her design, and that of her two sisters of the Ruggiero di Lauria class, was based on the turret ship *Duilio*, but included improvements, such as a raised forecastle and breechloading guns. *Francesco Morosini* was sunk as a target in September 1909. The ship was named after the Doge of Venice (1608–1694), a noted naval and military commander. His leadership had a profound effect on his times, when the Italian states were menaced by the Turks. The latter besieged Vienna in 1683 and drove out the Emperor Leopold I. The Turks were defeated and driven across the frontier by John Sobieski of Poland and the Duke of Lorraine, while the Venetians forced them to relinquish Greece.

Country of origin:	Italy
Crew:	509
Weight:	11,914 tonnes (11,726 tons)
Dimensions:	105.9m x 19.8m x 8.7m (347ft 5in x 65ft x 28ft 6in)
Range:	5040km (2800nm) at 10 knots
Armour:	451mm (17.5in) thick belt amidships
Armament:	Four 425mm (17in), two 152mm (6in) guns
Powerplant:	Twin screw compound engines
Performance:	16 knots

Friedrich der Grosse

Prior to the formation of the German Empire in 1871, Prussia maintained only a small navy for coastal defence. Her first ironclads were built in Britain and another had originally been built for the Confederacy. There were exceptions, however. *Friedrich der Grosse* was laid down in 1859 at the Royal Naval Dockyard, Kiel, as one of a class of three turret ships. She was completed in November 1877. The two turrets were carried amidships behind 2m (7ft) bulwarks that were lowered in battle. Her sister *Grosser Kurfurst* was accidentally rammed and sunk 26 days after commissioning. *Friedrich der Grosse* and *Preussen* were modernised in 1889-90. Both vessels served as guard ships until the end of the 1890s and later became coal hulks. *Friedrich der Grosse* was sold for scrap in 1919.

Country of origin:	Germany
Crew:	500
Weight:	7718 tonnes (7596 tons)
Dimensions:	96.6m x 16.2m x 7.2m (316ft 10in x 53ft x 23ft 6in)
Range:	4632km (2500nm) at 10 knots
Armour:	102mm – 229mm (4in – 9in) belt, 203mm (8in) turrets and citadel
Armament:	Four 259mm (10.2in) guns
Powerplant:	Single screw, horizontal compound engine
Performance:	14 knots

Friedrich Carl

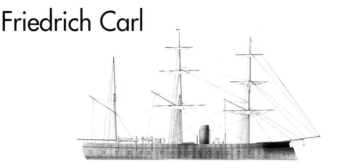

The ship-rigged central-battery vessel *Friedrich Carl* was the first battleship which was specifically ordered for the German Navy; the vessel was designed and built in Toulon. During the 1870 war with France, *Friedrich Carl* was stationed in the Jade. In 1873 she took part in the naval blockade of Cartagena, Spain, which was then in a state of civil war, and was responsible for the seizure of the insurgent sloop *Vigilanta* in July. A few weeks later, together with the British battleship *Swiftsure*, *Friedrich Carl* also accepted the surrender of the insurgent battleship *Vitoria*, which was returned to the Spanish government in September after its crew were put ashore at Escombera. In 1892, after a refit, *Friedrich Carl* became a torpedo school ship. She was renamed *Neptun* and sold in 1905.

Country of origin:	Germany
Crew:	531
Weight:	7043 tonnes (6932 tons)
Dimensions:	94.1m x 16.6m x 8m (308ft 10in x 54ft 6in x 26ft 3in)
Range:	4095km (2210nm) at 10 knots
Armour:	127mm – 112mm (5in – 4.5in) belt and battery
Armament:	16 210mm (8.25in) guns
Powerplant:	Single screw, horizontal single expansion engine
Performance:	13.6 knots

Frithjof

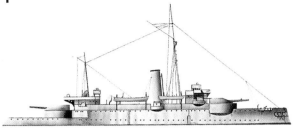

***F**rithjof* was one of a class of eight vessels of the Siegfried class, designed for coastal defence in the Baltic Sea. The main guns were carried in three turrets – two forward side by side on a raised barbette, with the third aft on the centreline. The 86mm (3.4in) secondary weapons were carried, all behind shields, at the corners of the superstructure and in the waist on sponsons. The class underwent a rebuild between 1900 and 1904, which included reboilering, the vessels receiving two funnels. In 1915 she was used for coastal defence and in the following year she became an accommodation ship at Danzig. The ships of her class were all named after heroes of Teutonic mythology – *Siegfried*, *Beowulf*, *Hagen*, *Heimdall* and *Hildebrand*. *Frithjof* was sold in 1919, becoming a cargo ship, and was broken up in 1930.

Country of origin:	Germany
Crew:	276
Weight:	3750 tonnes (3691 tons)
Dimensions:	78.9m x 14.9m x 5.8m (258ft 10in x 48ft 11in x 19ft)
Range:	2760km (1490nm) at 10 knots
Armour:	241mm – 178mm (9.5in – 7in) belt, 203mm (8in) on turrets
Armament:	Three 239mm (9.4in) guns
Powerplant:	Twin screw, triple expansion engines
Performance:	14.5 knots

Fuji

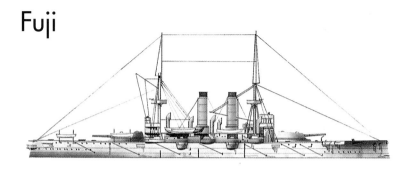

In the early 1890s, Japan anticipated war with China, and placed an order with Britain for two modern battleships. *Fuji*, and her sister *Yashima*, were improved versions of the Royal Sovereign class, although they carried lighter but equally effective 304mm (12in) guns instead of the 344mm (13.5in) weapons of the British ships. Their main armament was placed fore and aft of the vessel, while four of the 152mm (6in) guns were mounted in casements on the main deck. These were the first modern battleships in the Japanese Navy. They were completed too late for the 1894–95 Sino-Japanese war, but took part in the 1904–05 Russo-Japanese conflict. *Yashima* was sunk by a Russian mine in May 1904, but *Fuji* survived the war. She fought in the Battle of the Yellow Sea in August 1904 and sunk the Russian battleship *Borodino* at the Battle of Tsushima in 1905. She was stricken in 1923.

Country of origin:	Japan
Crew:	637
Weight:	12,737 tonnes (12,533 tons)
Dimensions:	125.3m x 22.3m x 8.1m (411ft x 73ft x 26ft 7in)
Range:	7412km (4000nm) at 10 knots
Armour:	457mm – 356mm (18in – 14in) main belt, 102mm (4in) upper belt, 356mm – 229mm (14in – 9in) on barbettes
Armament:	Four 254mm (10in), eight 152mm (6in) guns
Powerplant:	Twin screw, vertical triple expanion engines
Performance:	18 knots

Fulminant

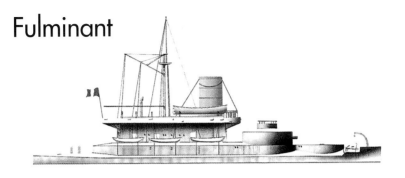

The *Fulminant* was a powerful, single-turreted, coastal defence ship, with the main armament concentrated in the large (10.5m [34ft 6in] diameter) turret forward. The superstructure aft was narrow and supported a wide flying bridge intended to be narrow enough for the widely spaced guns in the turret to fire directly aft. Her hull was built mainly of steel. *Fulminant* was laid down in 1875 as one of the Tonnere class monitors. She was completed in 1882, employed as a torpedo depot ship during the 1890s and finally stricken in 1908. By this time the French Navy had degenerated into a fifth-ranking force, and while the French Admiralty strove to build modern dreadnoughts the Anglo-French Entente of 1904 had relieved France of the responsibility of defending the Channel, eliminating the need for vessels of this type.

Country of origin:	France
Crew:	220
Weight:	5663 tonnes (5574 tons)
Dimensions:	75.5m x 17.5m x 6.5m (248ft x 57ft 9in x 21ft 4in)
Range:	3113km (1680nm) at 10 knots
Armour:	330mm – 254mm (13in – 10in) belt, 330mm (13in) breastwork, and 330mm – 305mm (13in – 12in) on turrets
Armament:	Two 274mm (10.8in) guns
Powerplant:	Single screw, horizontal compound engines
Performance:	13.7 knots

Furieux

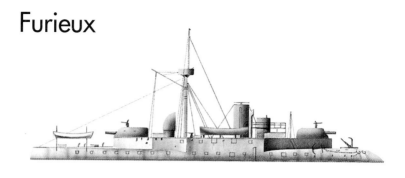

Built in Cherbourg and launched in 1883, France's powerful coastal defence force was made up of second-class battleships such as *Furieux*. These would not only deter assaults on the French coast but would act as a second line of defence after both French and enemy forces had sustained heavy losses in a major battle. *Furieux* was completed in 1887 and was rebuilt in 1902-4 with two 238mm (9.4in) guns and an extra mast. She eventually became a depot ship and was stricken in 1913. She was an improved Tonnere type with larger guns in barbettes fore and aft, heavier armour and a turtleback forecastle. The basic design was modified after the keel was laid down. Like *Fulminant*, she ceased to be significant after the 'entente cordiale' of 1904 eliminated what had long been seen as a potential threat from Britain.

Country of origin:	France
Crew:	235
Weight:	6020 tonnes (5925 tons)
Dimensions:	72.5m x 17.8m x 7.1m (238ft x 58ft 6in x 23ft)
Range:	2779km (1500nm) at 10 knots
Armour:	457mm – 330mm (18in – 13in) thick waterline belt, 457mm (18in) on barbettes
Armament:	Two 340mm (13.4in) guns
Powerplant:	Twin screw, vertical compound engines
Performance:	13 knots

Furious

The origin of one of the best-known British aircraft carriers of World War II dates back to pre-1914 when Jack Fisher, then First Sea Lord, planned for a fleet of fast, powerful cruisers with shallow draught to operate in the Baltic. *Furious* was one of three such vessels built. Launched in 1916, she was converted to a carrier in 1917 to increase the Grand Fleet's aircraft support. Originally her flight deck and hangar were built over her forward gun positions. After undergoing a more complete rebuild, she served with the Home and Mediterranean fleets in World War II. Together with HMS *Eagle*, she was an invaluable asset in the early months of the Mediterranean war, flying off fighter aircraft to Malta. Her aircraft attacked *Tirpitz* in 1944 and she was taken out of operational service the same year. She was scrapped in 1948.

Country of origin:	Great Britain
Crew:	1218
Weight:	22,758 tonnes (22,400 tons)
Dimensions:	239.6m x 27.4m x 7.3m (786ft 4in x 90ft x 24ft)
Range:	5929km (3200nm) at 19 knots
Armour:	75mm (3in) belt
Armament:	Six 102mm (4in) guns, 36 aircraft
Powerplant:	Quadruple screw turbines
Performance:	30 knots

Fuso

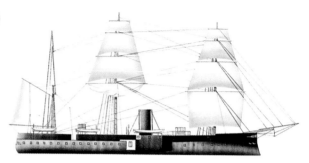

In 1875, Japan ordered three armoured vessels. Two were armoured broadside cruisers; the other was a powerful central battery ironclad named *Fuso*. All were designed by Sir Edward Reed, one of the world's leading naval architects. Rebuilt in 1894, just before the war with China, *Fuso* emerged with eight 152mm (6in) guns and two military masts, and fought at the Battle of the Yalu where she was damaged. She suffered further damage in 1897, when she was beached after colliding with the cruiser *Matsushima* in a gale. She was salvaged and repaired in the following year. She was the mother of the modern Japanese Navy and the first ironclad to be built in Japan; prior to her construction, Japan's only ironclad vessel was the former Confederate ram *Stonewall*. She was reclassified as a coastal defence ship in 1903 and broken up in 1910.

Country of origin:	Japan
Crew:	250
Weight:	3777 tonnes (3837 tons)
Dimensions:	67m x 14.6m x 5.6m (220ft x 48ft x 18ft 3in)
Range:	8100km (4500nm)
Armour:	102mm – 229mm (4 – 9in) thick waterline belt, 203mm (8in) on the central battery
Armament:	Four 236mm (9in) guns
Powerplant:	Twin screw, compound horizontal, surface-condensing engines
Performance:	13 knots

Fuso

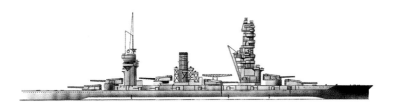

With the laying down of this vessel in March 1912 in a home yard, Japan confirmed her position as a leading naval power in the Pacific. Up until then, all Japanese battleships had been built in British yards. Although *Fuso* and her sister *Yamarisho* were less heavily armoured than contemporary US battleships, they carried a heavier armament and were two knots faster. As originally completed in 1915, *Fuso* had two funnels, with the first between the bridge and third turret. In an extensive refit in the 1930s, this was removed and replaced by a massive bridge structure. Underwater protection was greatly improved and new machinery fitted. *Fuso* served in the Aleutians and at Leyte during World War II, and it was during the Battle of Leyte Gulf that she and the *Yamashiro* were sunk by gunfire and torpedoes from US battleships in October 1944.

Country of origin:	Japan
Crew:	1193
Weight:	36,474 tonnes (35,900 tons)
Dimensions:	205m x 28.7m x 8.6m (672ft 6in x 94ft x 28ft)
Range:	14,400km (8000nm)
Armour:	305mm – 102mm (12in – 4in) belt, 305mm – 120mm (12in – 4.7mm) on turrets, 203mm (8in) on barbettes
Armament:	12 356mm (14in), 16 152mm (6in) guns
Powerplant:	Quadruple screw turbines
Performance:	23 knots

Gambier Bay

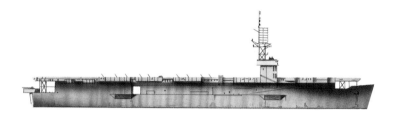

*G*ambier Bay was one of a 50-strong group of light escort carriers, completed from the unfinished hulls of a standard type of merchant ship mass-produced by Henry J. Kaiser in 1942. All 50 vessels were completed in under one year. The class was designed to carry an air group of nine fighters, nine bombers and nine torpedo bombers. The first mission for *Gambier Bay* was in early 1944, when she ferried aircraft to USS *Enterprise* and then supported US forces off Saipan, in the Marianas, and later at Leyte. She was sunk by gunfire during action off Samar in October 1944. Her loss occurred during one of the most epic sea-fights of the war, when the lightly armed escort carrier groups supporting the invasion of the Philippines fought off the main Japanese battle fleet in a surface action. The survivors of the class were all laid up at the end of the war.

Country of origin:	USA
Crew:	860
Weight:	11,074 tonnes (10,900 ton)
Dimensions:	156.1m x 32.9m x 6.3m (512ft 3in x 108ft x 20ft 9in)
Range:	18,360km (10,200nm) at 12 knots
Armour:	50mm (2in) belt
Armament:	One 127mm (5in), 16 40mm (1.6in) guns, 27 aircraft
Powerplant:	Twin screw, reciprocating engines
Performance:	19 knots

Gangut

Designed at a time when the battle line was likely to be in line abreast , instead of a line ahead, *Gangut* had her single 305mm (12in) gun mounted forward in a centreline turret on the foredeck. The four 229mm (9in) guns were concentrated in a battery amidships, protected by 127mm (5in) armour. Two 152mm (6in) guns were placed forward on the same level alongside the turret, but these could only fire straight ahead. Two more 152mm (6in) guns were positioned right aft and these also lacked broadside fire. Laid down in 1889, *Gangut* was completed in 1894. Whilst returning from gunnery practice in 1897, she struck an uncharted rock off Transund harbour and sank. In her short career she had served with the Baltic Fleet, where conditions were suited to vessels of her size. Russia made very little use of large battleships in these confined waters, as they would have presented easy targets.

Country of origin:	Russia
Crew:	521
Weight:	6697 tonnes (6592 tons)
Dimensions:	88.3m x 18.9m x 6.4m (289ft 8in x 62ft x 21ft)
Range:	4632km (2500nm) at 10 knots
Armour:	400mm – 254mm (16in – 10in) belt, 229mm – 178mm (9in – 7in) on barbette, 127mm (5in) on battery
Armament:	One 305mm (12in), four 229mm (9in) and four 152mm (6in) guns
Powerplant:	Twin screw, vertical compound engines
Performance:	14.7 knots

Gangut

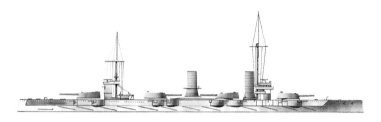

Launched in 1911, *Gangut* and her three sisters were Russia's first dreadnoughts. The contract was won by Blohm and Voss, Hamburg, but the Russian government refused funds unless they were built in Russia. As Russian industry could not produce enough high tensile steel, an ingenious construction method was used, based upon the Italian *Dante Alighieri*. Building time was lengthy, and *Gangut* was not ready until 1914, by which time she was largely obsolete. Her main guns, however, were the largest then at sea. She was renamed *Oktyabrskaya Revolutsia* in 1919. In the 'Winter War' against Finland (1939–40) she was used to bombard Finnish shore positions. In September 1941, while taking part in the defence of Leningrad, she was severely damaged by six bombs during a Stuka attack, and was again hit by four bombs in April 1942. She was scrapped in 1956–59.

Country of origin:	Russia
Crew:	1126
Weight:	26,264 tonnes (25,850 tons)
Dimensions:	182.9m x 26.9m x 8.3m (600ft x 88ft 3in x 27ft 3in)
Range:	7412km (4000nm) at 16 knots
Armour:	226mm – 102mm (8.9in – 4in) belt , 203mm – 127mm (8in – 5in) on turrets, and 203mm (8in) on barbettes
Armament:	12 305mm (12in), 16 120mm (4.7in) guns
Powerplant:	Quadruple screw turbines
Performance:	23 knots

General Admiral Apraksin

Launched in 1896, *General Admiral Apraksin* was one of three in a class of coastal defence ships intended for service in the Baltic, to counter the threat from Sweden. The 1.8m (6ft) deep armour belt ran for 53.6m (176ft) of the length of the vessel, or just over half way, with 203mm – 153mm (8in – 6in) thick bulkheads at each end. In February 1905 she sailed for the Far East as part of the 3rd Pacific Squadron, and on 28 May she surrendered to the Japanese in the aftermath of Tsushima – one of the most complete naval victories of all time, in which the Japanese sank six battleships and captured two for the loss of three destroyers. Of eleven assorted Russian cruisers and armoured ships, only three escaped to be interned in neutral ports. *General Admiral Apraksin* was taken into Japanese service as the *Okinoshima*. She was scrapped in 1926.

Country of origin:	Russia
Crew:	404
Weight:	4192 tonnes (4126 tons)
Dimensions:	84.6m x 15.8m x 5.2m (277ft 6in x 51ft 10in x 17ft)
Range:	4818km (2600nm) at 10 knots
Armour:	254mm – 102mm (10in – 4in) belt, 203mm (8in) on turrets
Armament:	Three 254mm (10in), four 120mm (4.7in) guns
Powerplant:	Twin screw, triple expansion engines
Performance:	16.2 knots

General Stirling Price

Originally launched in 1856, the steamboat *Laurent Millaudon* was taken over by the Confederate Navy in 1862 and renamed *General Stirling Price*. She was captured by Union forces in the same year and was used in numerous attacks. She was sold at the end of the war in 1865. In addition to vessels impressed for service and converted for naval use, 28 ships either served with, or were laid down on behalf of, the Confederate Navy in 1861–1865. Of these, 25 were ironclad rams, two (*Mississippi* and *North Carolina*) were turret ships, and one (*Virginia*, formerly *Merrimac*) was a casemate ironclad. Three of the vessels were unnamed; one was destroyed incomplete to prevent capture, one was sold to Prussia and renamed *Prinz Adalbert*, and the other, constructed in Britain under the cover name *Santa Maria*, was sold to Denmark.

Country of origin:	Confederate States of America
Crew:	50
Weight:	643 tonnes (633 tons)
Dimensions:	55.5m x 9.1m x 2.8m (182ft x 30ft x 9ft 3in)
Range:	1112km (600nm) at 10 knots
Armour:	–
Armament:	One 32-pounder rifled gun
Powerplant:	Side wheel-paddles
Performance:	12 knots

George Washington

George Washington is one of eight Nimitz class supercarriers built to date. She was laid down in August 1986, 17 years after *Nimitz*, the first of the class. *George Washington* carries extensive damage-control systems, including 63mm- (2.5in-) thick armour over parts of the hull, plus box protection over the magazines and machinery spaces. Aviation equipment includes four lifts and four steam catapults, and over 2540 tonnes (2500 tons) of aviation ordnance. The life of the nuclear reactors is 15 years. *George Washington*'s air wing, like that of all Nimitz class carriers, comprises 90–95 aircraft, with two squadrons of Grumman F-14 Tomcats forming the interceptor element. The big carriers form the nucleus of a US fleet's Battle Force, the principal task force. Nimitz-class carriers and their associated warships have supported United Nations peacekeeping operations around the world.

Country of origin:	USA
Crew:	5621 crew and air group
Weight:	92,950 tonnes (91,487 tons)
Dimensions:	332.9m x 40.8m x 11.3m (1,092ft 2in x 133ft 10in x 37ft)
Range:	Unlimited
Armour:	63mm (2.5in) on hull and magazines
Armament:	Four Vulcan 20mm guns plus three Sparrow surface-to-air missile launchers
Powerplant:	Quadruple screw turbines, two water-cooled nuclear reactors
Performance:	30 knots+

Georgia

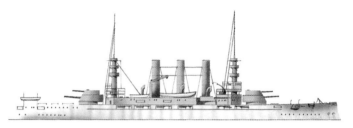

Georgia and her four sisters of the Virginia class were a major development in US battleship design. They were well-protected and carried the heaviest possible armament on a relatively modest displacement. To reduce the risk of fire damage, wood was eliminated wherever possible. Launched in 1904, *Georgia* was given cage masts in 1909–10, and was later reboilered. In 1906–07 she served with the Atlantic Fleet, and in 1907 she was damaged by a powder explosion in one of her 8in turrets while in Cape Cod Bay. She supported US action in Mexico in 1914 and worked with the Atlantic Fleet throughout World War I; in 1919 she made five voyages as a troop transport, bringing US personnel home from Europe, and was then transferred to the Pacific Fleet, in which she served from 1919 to 1920. She was sold in 1923.

Country of origin:	USA
Crew:	812
Weight:	16,351 tonnes (16,094 tons)
Dimensions:	134.5m x 23.2m x 7.2m (441ft 3in x 76ft 2 in x 23ft 9in)
Range:	9117km (4920nm) at 10 knots
Armour:	279mm – 152mm (11in – 6in) belt, 305mm – 152mm (12in – 6in) on barbettes and turrets
Armament:	12 152mm (6in), eight 203mm (8in), four 305mm (12in) guns turrets
Powerplant:	Twin screw, vertical triple expansion engines
Performance:	19.2 knots

Giulio Cesare

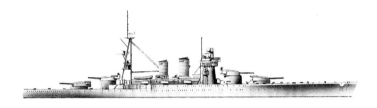

Designed in 1908 by Engineer-General Masdea, *Giulio Cesare* and her two
sisters were the first large group of Italian dreadnoughts. *Giulio Cesare* was
completely rebuilt between 1933 and 1937, and emerged from this lengthy
transformation with improved protection, new machinery and revised armament.
She served in the Adriatic during World War I and saw early action against the
British Mediterranean Fleet in World War II, being hit by the battleship *Warspite*
in the Ionian Sea in July 1940. She was damaged by a near miss in an air raid
on Naples in January 1941, and in December took part in the Battle of Sirte.
In September 1943 she sailed for Malta to surrender to the Allies. At the end of
World War II the ship was handed over to the Soviet Union and was re-named
Novorossisk. She served in the Black Sea until 1955.

Country of origin:	Italy
Crew:	1235
Weight:	29,496 tonnes (29,032 tons)
Dimensions:	186.4m x 28m x 9m (611ft 6in x 92ft x 30ft)
Range:	8640km (4800nm) at 10 knots
Armour:	254mm (10in) on sides and turrets
Armament:	12 120mm (4.7in), 10 320mm (12.6in) guns
Powerplant:	Quadruple screw turbines
Performance:	28.2 knots

Giuseppe Miraglia

In 1923 the ex-liner *Citta di Messina* was renamed *Giuseppe Miraglia* and re-construction work began to convert her into a seaplane carrier with full servicing facilities. She was used extensively for catapult launching experiments, and during World War II she served as an aircraft transport and carried out training duties. In 1943 she was surrendered to the Allies at Malta. In all, 43 Italian warships and 33 submarines surrendered to the Allies under the terms of the armistice in September 1943. *Giuseppe Miraglia* sailed from the Adriatic together with the battleship *Giulio Cesare*, the destroyer *Riboty* and the torpedo boat *Sagittario*. Not all the vessels reached Allied harbours; the battleship *Roma* was sunk by radio-controlled bombs and the destroyers *Da Noli* and *Vivaldi* were sunk by mines and gunfire.

Country of origin:	Italy
Crew:	180
Weight:	5486 tonnes (5400 tons)
Dimensions:	115m x 15m x 5.2m (377ft 4in x 49ft 3in x 17ft)
Range:	7412km (4000nm) at 14 knots
Armour:	50mm (2in) belt
Armament:	Four 102mm (4in) guns, 20 aircraft
Powerplant:	Twin screw turbines
Performance:	21.5 knots

Glatton

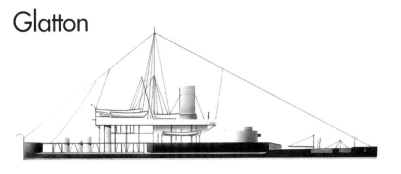

Designed by Sir Edward Reed, and launched in March 1871, *Glatton* was intended to combine harbour defence with a sea-going offensive role. The raised breastwork structure amidships protected the base of the turret and funnel. A light flying bridge housed the ship's boats, and a deck also ran from the breastwork to a small raised poop aft. *Glatton* only went to sea once, in 1887. She was designed at a time when the wind of change was sweeping through the Royal Navy. In 1873, a radical new vessel, *Devastation,* was built without masts or rigging and with guns that could fire in any direction, and in time this became the design that prevailed over others, such as *Glatton*, which was described by at least one critic as the 'acme of uselessness.' She spent her entire career based at Portsmouth.

Country of origin:	Great Britain
Crew:	600
Weight:	4990 tonnes (4912 tons)
Dimensions:	74.6m x 16.4m x 5.7m (245ft x 54ft x 19ft)
Range:	3706km (2000nm) at 10 knots
Armour:	304mm – 245mm (11.9in – 9.6in) belt, 355mm – 304mm (13.9 – 11.9in) on turrets
Armament:	Two 305mm (12in) guns
Powerplant:	Twin screw engines
Performance:	12 knots

Glatton

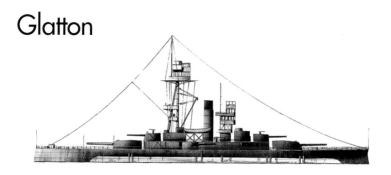

Glatton was one of two coast defence ships ordered by Norway in 1913 and laid down in Britain later that year. In November 1914 both vessels were bought by the Royal Navy for service in World War I, and modified to take standard British shells. Due to more pressing building work, *Glatton* was not completed until 1918. In that year she was assigned to the Dover patrol, which was intended to prevent German U-boats passing through the English Channel from their North Sea bases. German destroyers from Ostend and Zeebrugge attempted to break down the patrols by sudden raids, but they were repulsed in fierce night actions. Thirteen U-boats were destroyed in the Dover area in 1918. *Glatton* had been on station for only a short time when she was wrecked by an internal explosion on 16 September 1918 with the loss of 77 crew.

Country of origin:	Great Britain
Crew:	305
Weight:	5831 tonnes (5740 tons)
Dimensions:	94.5m x 22.4m x 5m (310ft x 73ft 6in x 16ft 5in)
Range:	5003km (2700nm) at 11 knots
Armour:	178mm – 75mm (7in – 3in) belt, 203mm (8in) on turrets, 203mm – 152mm (8in - 6in) on barbettes
Armament:	Four 152mm (6in), two 233mm (9.2in) guns
Powerplant:	Twin screw, triple expansion engines
Performance:	12 knots

Gloire

Designed by Dupuy de Lome, *Gloire* was the first armoured ship of-the-line (in other words, the first modern battleship) in the world. She was constructed with a wooden hull and armour plating to the upper deck because French manufacturers were unable to provide sufficient plating and armour in time to construct an iron hull. The battleship's design was based on the steam frigate *Napoleon* in that it had a full-length battery along the hull. Plans showed 68-pounder, smoothbore guns, although the battleship was fitted with rifled versions of the same weapon and was later rearmed with modern guns. Her barquentine rig was later changed to full ship rig. *Gloire* was launched in 1859 and discarded in 1879, being broken up four years later. Other ships in her class included *Invincible* and *Normandie*.

Country of origin:	France
Crew:	570
Weight:	5720 tonnes (5630 tons)
Dimensions:	77.8m x 17m x 8.4m (255ft 6in x 55ft 9in x 27ft 10in)
Range:	7412km (4000nm) at 8 knots
Armour:	120mm – 107.5mm (4.7in – 4.3in) wrought iron belt
Armament:	36 162.5mm (6.4in) guns
Powerplant:	Single screw, horizontal return engines
Performance:	13 knots

Glorious

One of the Courageous class of cruisers, *Glorious*, her sister *Courageous*, and near sister *Furious* combined maximum firepower with speed. Completed in 1917, *Glorious* was laid up in 1919, but along with her sister ships she was converted into an aircraft carrier during the 1920s. In the afternoon of 8 June 1940, *Glorious* and her escorts were intercepted by *Scharnhorst* and *Gneisenau*, out on a sortie against the Allied troop transports west of Harstad, Norway. The carrier was caught completely unaware; for reasons that were never explained, none of her reconnaissance Swordfish aircraft were airborne. Desperate attempts were made to arm and launch them as the enemy battlecruisers came in sight, but she was overwhelmed and was sunk before this could be accomplished. Her escorting destroyers, *Ardent* and *Acasta*, were also sunk.

Country of origin:	Great Britain
Crew:	842
Weight:	23,327 tonnes (22,960 tons)
Dimensions:	239.5m x 24.7m x 6.7m (786ft x 81ft x 22ft 3in)
Range:	5929km (3200nm) at 19 knots
Armour:	76mm – 51mm (3in – 2in) belt, 228mm – 178mm (9in – 7in) on turrets
Armament:	18 102mm (4in), four 380mm (15in) guns
Powerplant:	Quadruple screw, turbines
Performance:	33 knots

Gneisenau

Both launched in 1936, *Gneisenau* and her sister *Scharnhorst* were completed with straight stems, but the bows were later lengthened. Both vessels served in World War II, attacking British commerce and sinking the British aircraft carrier *Glorious*. Both ships received damage from air attacks in 1941 while in Brest harbour, and in February 1942, together with the cruiser *Prinz Eugen*, they broke out and made an epic dash across the English Channel, for the north German ports. *Gneisenau* reached Kiel without incident only to be damaged in an RAF bombing raid two weeks later, after which she was moved to Gdynia (Gdansk). She was decommissioned in July 1942 and her turrets were removed for coastal defence. A planned refit was abandoned in 1943 and her hulk was sunk as a blockship at Gdynia in March 1945. Salved by the Russians, she was broken up in 1947–51.

Country of origin:	Germany
Crew:	1840
Weight:	39,522 tonnes (38,900 tons)
Dimensions:	226m x 30m x 9m (741ft 6in x 98ft 5in x 30ft)
Range:	16,306km (8800nm) at 18 knots
Armour:	343mm – 168mm (13.75in – 6.75in) belt, 356mm – 152mm (14in – 6in) on turrets
Armament:	14 104mm (4.1in), 12 150mm (5.9in), nine 279mm (11in) guns
Powerplant:	Triple screw turbines, with diesels for cruising
Performance:	32 knots

Goeben

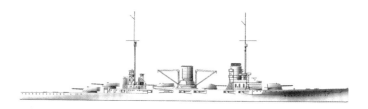

*G*oeben was one of two ships in the Moltke class that formed the second group of battlecruisers built for the rapidly expanding German Imperial Navy before World War I. With the outbreak of war, *Goeben* and her sister ship *Breslau* were pursued across the Mediterranean by British ships *Indomitable* and *Indefatigable*, but they easily outran the British and put into the Turkish port of Constantinople. Both ships were transferred to the Turkish Navy, and *Goeben* was renamed *Yavuz Sultan Selim* on 16 August 1914. In November 1914 she was seriously damaged in action with Russian battleships off Samsoun; in December she struck two mines on the approaches to the Bosphorus; and she was again damaged by Russian warships in May 1915. In January 1918 she sank the British monitors *Raglan* and *M28* at Mudros, and was again damaged by mines afterwards. She was broken up in 1954.

Country of origin:	Germany
Crew:	1053
Weight:	25,704 tonnes (25,300 tons)
Dimensions:	186.5m x 29.5m x 9m (611ft 10in x 96ft 9in x 29ft 6in)
Range:	7634km (4120nm) at 14 knots
Armour:	270mm – 100mm (10.7in – 4in) belt, 229mm – 60mm (9in – 2.4in) on turrets
Armament:	12 150mm (5.9in), 10 280mm (11in) guns
Powerplant:	Quadruple screw turbines
Performance:	28 knots

Golden Hind

The *Golden Hind* was originally named *Pelican*. The vessel was highly typical of the small, fast warships of her period. She was of the French pattern, built along Venetian lines, with her poop and forecastle raised significantly above her tiny main deck. Her fore and main masts carried a full rig of square sails, while there was a lateen sail on the mizzen mast. She was made famous as the flagship of Sir Francis Drake's epic voyage of global circumnavigation in 1577–80. This expedition entered the Pacific Ocean in September 1578, but here began the worst ordeal of the whole voyage. A series of savage storms lashed the tiny ships, and one sank. Eventually Drake in *Pelican* voyaged as far north as the present-day location of San Francisco. Drake's reputation as a navigator and fighter was undoubtedly justified, but his arrogance often put him at odds with his superiors.

Country of origin:	England
Crew:	70
Weight:	102 tonnes (100 tons)
Dimensions:	31m x 6m x 2.7m (102ft x 20ft x 9ft)
Range:	Dependent on weather, victualling etc.
Armour:	None
Armament:	18 guns
Powerplant:	–
Performance:	3 knots approx.

Gorgon

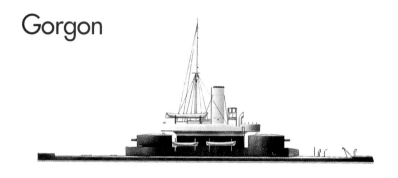

The threat of war with France in 1870, with its consequent threat to British coastlines, led to the hasty construction of a group of shallow-draught coastal defence vessels. However, as the threat of war receded, building was slowed down and *Gorgon* did not enter service until 1874. *Gorgon* had a fine armament-to-displacement ratio. To improve her poor seakeeping qualities, between 1886 and 1889 the breastwork was extended. *Gorgon* spent most of her career as a tender at Devonport in use with the Particular Service Squadron, the Royal Navy's general duties unit. Other ships in *Gorgon*'s class were *Cyclops*, *Hecate* and *Hydra*. Following a refit, she was sold for scrap in 1903. The need to build 'panic' vessels such as *Gorgon* disappeared with the signing of the Anglo-French Entente shortly after the turn of the century. She was scrapped in 1903.

Country of origin:	Great Britain
Crew:	150
Weight:	3535 tonnes (3480 tons)
Dimensions:	68.5m x 13.7m x 4.9m (225ft x 45ft x 16ft 4in)
Range:	5559km (3000nm) at 10 knots
Armour:	203mm – 152mm (8in – 6in) on hull, 228mm – 203mm (9in – 8in) on breastwork, 254mm – 228mm (10in – 9in) on turrets
Armament:	Four 254mm (10in) guns
Powerplant:	Twin screw, horizontal direct acting engines
Performance:	11 knots

Graf Spee

*G**raf Spee* was to have been an improved version of the powerful *Hindenburg* battlecruiser launched in 1917. The main armament of *Graf Spee* was updated, the weapons being positioned in four twin turrets, two superfiring fore and aft. The secondary armament was concentrated on the upper deck in a long battery that was a continuation of the raised foredeck. The Germans hoped to complete all four vessels in the class by 1918, but although *Graf Spee* was launched in 1917 she was never completed and was scrapped in 1921–23. Other vessels in her class were the *Mackensen*, *Prinz Eitel Friedrich* and *Furst Bismarck*; work on all of these was suspended in 1917 and the last two were never launched. By this time the German Fleet was virtually inactive, except in the Baltic, and materials intended for new-build warships were urgently needed in other sectors of the war industry.

Country of origin:	Germany
Crew:	1186
Weight:	36,576 tonnes (36,000 tons)
Dimensions:	223m x 30.4m x 8.4m (731ft 8in x 99ft 9in x 27ft 7in)
Range:	14,400km (8000nm) at 10 knots
Armour:	300mm – 102mm (11.8in – 4in) belt and turrets
Armament:	12 150mm (5.9in), eight 350mm (13.8in) guns
Powerplant:	Quadruple screw turbines
Performance:	28 knots

Graf Zeppelin

After World War I Germany was denied any opportunity of developing a carrier force as a result of restrictions imposed upon them in 1919. By 1933 Wilhelm Hadelar had prepared a basic design for a full deck carrier able to operate 40 aircraft, but lack of construction experience delayed the project. In 1935 work began, but *Graf Zeppelin*'s completion was delayed to make way for the U-boat programme. The incomplete carrier was scuttled a few months before the end of World War II. She was raised by the Soviet Union, but sank on her way to Leningrad. *Graf Zeppelin* was originally intended to carry an air group of 12 Ju87D dive-bombers and 30 Me109F fighters; this was later amended to 28 Ju87Ds and 12 Me109s. Half of a sister ship was also completed; it was speculated that this vessel would be named *Peter Strasser*, after the commander of the German Naval Airship Division in World War I.

Country of origin:	Germany
Crew:	1760 (estimated)
Weight:	28,540 tonnes (28,090 tons)
Dimensions:	262.5m x 31.5m x 8.5m (861ft 3in x 103ft 4in x 27ft 10in)
Range:	14,842km (8000nm) at 19 knots
Armour:	89mm (3.5in) belt, 37.5mm (1.5in) on flight deck
Armament:	12 104mm (4.1in), 16 150mm (5.9in) guns, 43 aircraft
Powerplant:	Quadruple screw turbines
Performance:	35 knots

Grosser Kurfürst

Turbines were used in German battleships for the first time on *Grosser Kurfürst* and her three sisters. The ships were greatly improved versions of *Helgoland*, and had superfiring guns aft, allowing the broadside to be increased from six to ten 305mm (12in) guns. Vessels of this class were contemporaries of the first British 343mm (13.5in) gunned battleships with similar displacement, but where the British had adopted the heavier guns and had only moderate protection, *Grosser Kurfürst* and her sisters retained the 305mm (12in) guns and used more armour. Launched in 1913, *Grosser Kurfürst* saw action at the Battle of Jutland, taking eight hits. She surrendered at the end of World War I, and was scuttled with the rest of the German fleet in 1919. She was raised and scrapped in 1934. Her sister ships were *König*, *Kronprinz* and *Markgraf*. Of these, only *König* was not raised after being scuttled.

Country of origin:	Germany
Crew:	1136
Weight:	28,598 tonnes (28,148 tons)
Dimensions:	175.7m x 29.5m x 8.3m (576ft 5in x 96ft 9in x 27ft 3in)
Range:	12,240km (6800nm) at 10 knots
Armour:	350mm – 80mm (14in – 3.2in) belt, 300mm – 80mm (11.8in – 3.2in) on turrets
Armament:	Eight 86mm (3.4in) and 14 150mm (5.9in) guns
Powerplant:	Triple screw turbines
Performance:	21 knots

Guam

Guam and her sister ship *Alaska*, were built to combat the fast raiders of the German *Scharnhorst* type believed in 1940 to be under construction for the Imperial Japanese Navy. *Guam* was an enlarged version of the cruiser *Baltimore*, with three triple turrets housing specially designed 305mm (12in) guns and upgraded armour. Completed in 1944, she was flush-decked, with a single funnel flanked by the cranes for the two catapults which launched the scout planes. Range at 15 knots was 22,800km (12,000 miles). In March 1945 she was part of a covering force of warships operating in support of US carriers making a series of air strikes on the Japanese island of Kyushu, and in April–June she again supported naval task forces attacking Okinawa. Her last operations, in August 1945, were against shipping in the East China Sea. *Guam* was scrapped in 1961.

Country of origin:	USA
Crew:	1517
Weight:	34,801 tonnes (34,253 tons)
Dimensions:	246m x 27.6m x 9.6m (807ft 5in x 90ft 9in x 31ft 9in)
Range:	22,800km (12,000nm) at 15 knots
Armour:	229mm – 127mm (9in – 5in) belt, 305mm – 203mm (12in – 8in) on turrets
Armament:	12 127mm (5in), nine 305mm (12in) guns
Powerplant:	Quadruple screw turbines
Performance:	33 knots

Habsburg

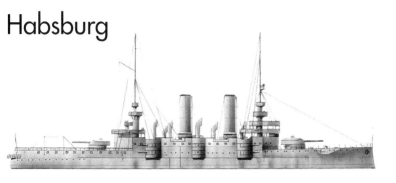

Habsburg was one of a trio of vessels that were the first true Austrian ocean-going battleships since the launching of *Tegetthoff* in 1878. Launched in 1900, she later underwent a reconstruction, having her top superstructure removed in 1910–11. By now Austria was starting to build new ships at a faster rate, but lack of funds hindered development. During the period before World War I, however, the navy had two staunch supporters, the heir to the throne – Archduke Franz Ferdinand – and the navy commander, Admiral Montecuccoli. It was the latter who ordered Austria's first and only class of Dreadnought in 1911; construction was begun even before the government had actually approved it. After World War I, all three of *Habsburg*'s class (the others being *Arpad* and *Babenberg*) were handed over to Britain and scrapped in 1921.

Country of origin:	Austria
Crew:	638
Weight:	8964 tonnes (8823 tons)
Dimensions:	114.5m x 19.8m x 7.4m (376ft x 65ft 2in x 24ft 6in)
Range:	6670km (3600nm) at 10 knots
Armour:	203mm – 50mm (8in – 2in) belt, 203mm – 152mm (8in – 6in) on barbettes and turrets
Armament:	12 150mm (5.9in), three 240mm (9.4in) guns
Powerplant:	Twin screw, vertical triple expansion engines
Performance:	19.6 knots

Hansa

Hansa was the first battleship to be built in Germany. She was laid down at the Danzig dockyard in 1868 and took seven years to complete, by which time her iron hull had badly corroded. The 210mm (8.25in) guns were carried in a two-tier casemate, with two guns on each side in the lower level, and four firing from corner positions in the upper level. Classed as an armoured corvette, *Hansa* was a small central battery ship built for foreign service. She was the first German-designed armoured vessel, and she had a wooden hull. In 1878–80 she served in South American waters as a trade protection vessel, the Germans having substantial commercial interests in Latin America, and for eight years after that she was used as a guard ship at Kiel. *Hansa* became a training hulk in 1888 and was scrapped in 1906.

Country of origin:	Germany
Crew:	399
Weight:	4403 tonnes (4334 tons)
Dimensions:	73.4m x 14.1m x 6.7m (241ft x 46ft 3in x 22ft 3in)
Range:	2465km (1330nm) at 10 knots
Armour:	152mm – 114mm (6in – 4.5in) belt, 114mm (4.5in) on central battery
Armament:	Eight 210mm (8.25in) guns
Powerplant:	Single screw, horizontal single expansion engines
Performance:	12.5 knots

Haruna

Haruna was one of the first dreadnought-type warships to be laid down in a Japanese yard, and her sister *Kongo* was the last major Japanese warship to be built abroad. The four ships in *Haruna*'s class originally had three funnels and light military masts. In 1927–28 *Haruna* underwent a major refit and was reclassified as a battleship. The fore funnel was removed, and the second enlarged and heightened. Sixteen new boilers were installed, bulges were fitted and the armour thickened, increasing the total weight from 6606 tonnes (6502 tons) to 10,478 tonnes (10,313 tons). In December 1941 she formed part of the distant covering force for the Japanese landings in Malaya and the Philippines and then took part in every major action of the Pacific War. *Haruna* was sunk by US aircraft in July 1945. She was raised and broken up in 1946.

Country of origin:	Japan
Crew:	1221
Weight:	32,715 tonnes (32,200 tons)
Dimensions:	214.5m x 28m x 8.4m (703ft 9in x 91ft 10in x 27ft 6in)
Range:	14,400km (8000nm) at 12 knots
Armour:	203mm – 76mm (8in – 3in) belt, 228mm (9in) on turrets
Armament:	16 152mm (6in), eight 355mm (14in) guns
Powerplant:	Quadruple screw turbines
Performance:	27.5 knots

Helgoland

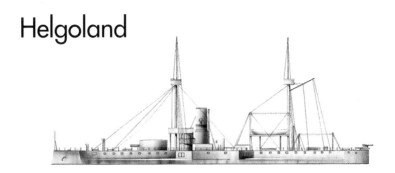

For many years, *Helgoland* was Denmark's largest warship. The battery housing the four 260mm (10.2in) guns was situated amidships, with the sides of the hull on each side of the battery recessed to allow for end-on fire. A single turret forward housed the 304mm (12in) gun. Two 127mm (5in) guns were also carried, one fore and one aft. A small outfit of sails could be carried on the two masts. Designated as a coast defence torpedo ram, she was named after the Danish naval victory over the combined forces of Prussia and Austria off Heligoland on 9 May 1864. Laid down at Copenhagen in 1876, she was completed in 1879 and underwent a refit in 1884. Denmark maintained a fleet of small coastal defence ships and also guarded its neutrality throughout the later European conflicts until 1940. *Helgoland* was removed from the effective list in about 1907.

Country of origin:	Denmark
Crew:	331
Weight:	5417 tonnes (5332 tons)
Dimensions:	79m x 18m x 5.8m (259ft 7in x 59ft x 19ft 4in)
Range:	2594km (1400nm) at 9 knots
Armour:	304mm – 203mm (12in – 8in) belt, 254mm (10in) on turret and central battery
Armament:	One 304mm (12in), four 260mm (10.2in) guns
Powerplant:	Twin screws
Performance:	13.7 knots

Helgoland

L aunched in 1909, *Helgoland* was the last three-funnelled German battleship, and the first to adopt the 304mm (12in) gun as a main armament. All ships in her class served in World War I, two being damaged at the Battle of Jutland in 1916. *Helgoland* herself was hit by one shell. After this decisive battle, the German High Seas Fleet never again contested possession of the North Sea. It sortied on three further occasions, twice in 1916 and once in 1918. None resulted in action, and the low level of activity resulted in disillusionment and, ultimately, open rebellion. The crew of *Helgoland*, in command with most of their compatriots, mutinied in 1918. This turn of events might have been avoided if the High Seas Fleet had embarked on an all-out war against Allied commerce. *Helgoland* was broken up in 1924.

Country of origin:	Germany
Crew:	1113
Weight:	24,700 tonnes (24,312 tons)
Dimensions:	166.4m x 28.5m x 8.3m (546ft x 93ft 6in x 27ft 6in)
Range:	6670km (3600nm) at 18 knots
Armour:	300mm – 102mm (11.8in – 4in) belt, 280mm (11in) on turrets, 170mm – 75mm (6.7in – 3in) on casemates
Armament:	14 150mm (5.9in), 12 304mm (12in) guns
Powerplant:	Triple screw, triple expansion engines
Performance:	20.3 knots

Henri IV

*H*enri IV was unusual in that weight was saved by cutting down the aft hull leaving very little freeboard. The 270mm (10.8in) guns were carried one forward on the raised superstructure 8.5m (28ft) above the water, and one in the aft turret 4.8m (16ft) above the water. The belt was 2m (7ft) deep, with just over half the depth below the waterline. The decks were flat and armoured. She also had lateral armoured bulkheads. Total weight of armour was about 3556 tonnes (3500 tons). In 1907 she was damaged off Algiers in a collision with the destroyer *Dard*, which lost its bow. In March 1915 she was sent to the Dardanelles, where a French naval squadron was operating under the orders of Admiral Carden. She subsequently took part in the bombardment of Turkish forts, and in May she covered the landing of General Bailloud's Algerian Division. *Henri IV* was stricken in 1921.

Country of origin:	France
Crew:	464
Weight:	8948 tonnes (8807 tons)
Dimensions:	108m x 22.2m x 6.9m (354ft 4in x 73ft x 23ft)
Range:	11,118km (600nm) at 10 knots
Armour:	254mm (10in) steel plate
Armament:	Seven 140mm (5.5in), two 274mm (10.8in) guns
Powerplant:	Triple screw, triple expansion engines
Performance:	17 knots

Henri Grâce à Dieu

Henri Grâce à Dieu was commissioned by King Henry VIII as a replacement for the 609-tonne (600-ton) *Regent*, which was lost in action in 1512. Upon completion, the new ship was the largest warship in the world, with only the Portuguese *Santa Catarina Do Monte Sinai* coming anywhere near her in size. *Henri Grâce à Dieu* was built at Deptford on the River Thames. She was carrack-built with a very high forecastle and poop. She had four masts and carried a large spread of heavily ornate golden sails. Square sails were carried on the fore and main masts, with lateen sails on the two mizzen masts. She was rebuilt between 1536 and 1539, and accidentally destroyed by fire in 1553. During the first years of his reign Henry VIII built 24 ships. His most important innovation was the heavy gun, mounted on the lower deck and firing through ports in the ship's side.

Country of origin:	England
Crew:	150
Weight:	1016 tonnes (1000 tons) approx
Dimensions:	Unknown
Range:	Unknown
Armour:	None
Armament:	21 heavy bronze guns, 130 iron guns, 100 hand guns
Powerplant:	–
Performance:	4 knots

Hercules

*H*ercules was a 'one-off' design developed from the *Bellerophon*, but with better armour and weight distribution, which made her much steadier in bad weather. She had a pointed ram and no poop, the upper line of the hull being a complete sweep. She was launched in 1868. On Christmas Day 1872 she was damaged in a collision with the ironclad *Northumberland* at Funchal, Madeira. After a refit she served in the Mediterranean from 1875 to 1877. In 1878 she was in service with the Particular Service Squadron. She was re-engined and reconstructed in 1892–93. Placed in reserve, she became a depot ship at Gibraltar in 1905. In 1909 she was renamed *Calcutta* and assigned as a training ship at Portsmouth in 1914; in 1915 she was again renamed, this time as *Fisgard II*. She was broken up in 1932 at Preston, Lancashire.

Country of origin:	Great Britain
Crew:	638
Weight:	8971 tonnes (8830 tons)
Dimensions:	99m x 18m x 7.6m (324ft 10in x 59ft x 25ft)
Range:	4002km (2160nm) at 10 knots
Armour:	229mm – 152mm (9in – 6in) belt, 203mm (8in) on battery
Armament:	Four 178mm (7in), two 229mm (9in), eight 254mm (10in) muzzle-loading guns
Powerplant:	Single screw, horizontal truck engines
Performance:	14.7 knots

Hermes

*H**ermes* was the first true purpose-designed aircraft carrier to be ordered by any navy. She was laid down in 1917, but was not completed until 1924, and was thus beaten into service by the Japanese carrier *Hosho*. Her hull had a cruiser form, with the main deck providing the strength. Above this was a 122m (400ft) hangar deck, surmounted by the flight deck. Her bridge, funnel, command centre and masts were all grouped in a large island on the starboard side of the flight deck. Her 150mm (5.9in) guns were set in the hull, while the smaller weapons were mounted on the starboard edge of the flight deck. She could not carry many aircraft, and in 1940 her air wing comprised only 12 fighters. She was sunk by Japanese carrier aircraft off Ceylon on 9 April 1942, together with the Australian destroyer *Vampire*, the corvette *Hollyhock* and two tankers, during an enemy sortie towards Ceylon.

Country of origin:	Great Britain
Crew:	664
Weight:	13,208 tonnes (13,000 tons)
Dimensions:	182.9m x 21.4m x 6.5m (600ft x 70ft 2in x 21ft 6in)
Range:	7412kt (4000nm) at 15 knots
Armour:	75mm (3in) belt, 25mm (1in) deck
Armament:	Three 102mm (4in), six 140mm (5.5in) guns
Powerplant:	Twin screw turbines
Performance:	25 knots

Hermes

In 1943 designs were drawn up for a class of eight carriers, with machinery twice as powerful as that installed in the earlier *Colossus* class. Armour was to be improved, and a stronger flight deck was planned to handle the new, heavier aircraft then entering service. Eventually, only four ships were laid down, and the Admiralty decided to scrap these while they were still on the stocks at the end of World War II. However, due to the inability of many existing carriers to handle the new jet aircraft, construction was continued. After several design changes, *Hermes* was completed in 1959. During a scheduled refit in 1979 she was given a 12-degree ski ramp to operate the British Aerospace Sea Harrier FSR.1 V/STOL strike aircraft, two squadrons of six being embarked. In 1982 she served as flagship during the Falklands War. She was put on reserve in 1984, and later sold to India.

Country of origin:	Great Britain
Crew:	1830 and 270 air group
Weight:	25,290 tonnes (24,892 tons)
Dimensions:	224.6m x 30.4m x 8.2m (737ft x 100ft x 27ft)
Range:	7412km (4000nm) at 15 knots
Armour:	40mm (1.6in) over magazines, 19mm (0.74in) on flight deck
Armament:	32 40mm (1.6in) guns
Powerplant:	Twin screw turbines
Performance:	29.5 knots

Hood

After the Battle of Jutland in 1916, in which three of Britain's battlecruisers blew up, designs were put in hand for a better-protected vessel. *Hood* was to have been the first of four such ships, but was the only one completed. Her engines developed 144,000hp, and range was 7600km (4000 miles) at 10 knots. Despite being designed to avoid the fate of her predecessors, whilst engaging the German battleship *Bismarck* and the cruiser *Prinz Eugen* on 21 May 1941, her upper armour was breached by a shell which reached her magazine, blowing her in two. There were only three survivors; 1338 were lost. The sinking of *Hood* was keenly felt by the British people, who held her in great affection. She had 'shown the flag' for Britain several times, most notably in 1923, when she embarked on a world cruise. Her assailant, *Bismarck*, survived her by just three days before she too was sunk.

Country of origin:	Great Britain
Crew:	1477
Weight:	45,923 tonnes (45,200 tons)
Dimensions:	262m x 31.7m x 8.7m (860ft x 104ft x 28ft 6in)
Range:	7200km (4000nm) at 10 knots
Armour:	305mm – 127mm (12in – 5in) belt and barbettes
Armament:	12 140mm (5.5 in), eight 381mm (15in) guns
Powerplant:	Quadruple screw turbines
Performance:	32 knots

Huascar

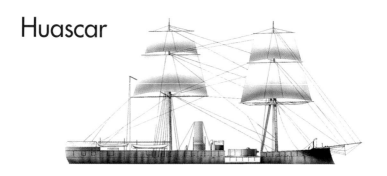

Huascar was built at Birkenhead, England, for the Peruvian Navy. Her 254mm (10in) main armament was mounted in a single, heavily protected Coles turret, mounted low on the main deck aft of the foremast but in front of the light bridge. The freeboard at this point was only 1.52m (5ft), and when the ship was not in action, hinged metal bulwarks were raised to give the deck some protection. She fought her first action in May 1877 against two British warships, after her crew mutinied. She was one of only two effective Peruvian warships in the 1879 war with Chile. In October 1879, she was caught by two Chilean ironclads, and surrendered after a hard fight. She was then rebuilt and used by Chile, being commissioned into the Chilean Navy after repairs at Valparaiso. She fought on the Congressional side in the civil war, in several naval actions. *Huascar* is preserved as a museum ship.

Country of origin:	Peru
Crew:	170
Weight:	2062 tonnes (2030 tons)
Dimensions:	60.9m x 10.6m x 5.5m (200ft x 35ft x 18ft)
Range:	3335km (1800nm) at 10 knots
Armour:	127mm – 102mm (5in – 4in) belt, 203mm (8in) on turret face, 152mm (6in) on turret sides
Armament:	Two 254mm (10in), two 40-pounder guns
Powerplant:	Single screw, single expansion engine
Performance:	12.3 knots

Hydra

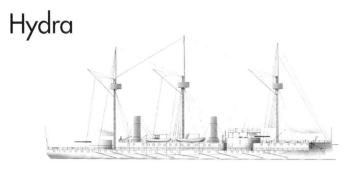

Built in 1889, *Hydra* was of an unusual design, with two of its 274mm (10.8in) guns mounted in the top storey of a two-tier battery situated forward. The lower tier housed four of the 150mm (5.9in) guns, and the fifth was positioned under the bridge. *Hydra* was refitted in 1900 and given two military masts. In 1912 she was in action against Turkish warships in the Balkan wars. Although Greece is a nation with a long seafaring tradition, at this time she had only a small navy whose main purpose was defence against the Turks. Until the advent of the *Hydra*, the principal vessels were two small ironclads . It was not until 1900 that steps were taken to increase the size of the navy, providing Greece with a large enough force to defeat the Turks in the war of 1912. Under the command of Admiral Condouriotis the Greeks gained mastery of the Aegean and were able to seize the Aegean islands.

Country of origin:	Greece
Crew:	440
Weight:	4885 tonnes (4808 tons)
Dimensions:	102m x 15.8m x 5.4m (334ft 8in x 51ft 10in x 18ft)
Range:	5559km (3000nm) at 10 knots
Armour:	305mm – 102mm (12in – 4in) belt, 356mm – 305mm (14in – 12in) on battery, 305mm (12in) on barbette
Armament:	Five 150mm (5.9in), three 274mm (10.8in) guns
Powerplant:	Twin screw, vertical triple expansion engines
Performance:	17 knots

Ibuki

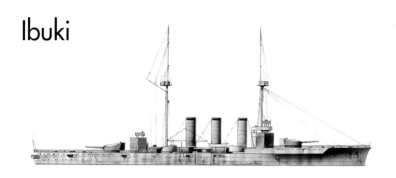

Ibuki was the first Japanese warship to be fitted with turbine engines. Laid down in May 1907, she was quickly built, but her launch was delayed due to other construction work already in hand. The delay enabled her design to be modified, prior to completion, to include the installation of turbine machinery, which developed 24,000hp. Coal supply was 2032 tonnes (2000 tons), plus 221 tonnes (218 tons) of oil fuel. *Ibuki* served as an escort for Australian troops on their way to the Dardanelles during the early part of World War I, and also took part in the search for the German cruiser *Emden*, which was engaged in commerce raiding in the Indian Ocean. *Emden* took 21 Allied ships and also destroyed a small Russian cruiser and a French destroyer, as well as destroying a signal station, before being sunk by the cruiser HMAS *Sydney*. *Ibuki* was scrapped in 1924.

Country of origin:	Japan
Crew:	844
Weight:	15,844 tonnes (15,595 tons)
Dimensions:	148m x 23m x 8m (465ft x 75ft 4in x 26ft 1in)
Range:	6485km (3500nm) at 15 knots
Armour:	178mm – 102mm (7in – 4in) on belt, barbettes and turrets
Armament:	Four 305mm (12in), eight 203mm (8in) guns
Powerplant:	Twin screw turbines
Performance:	21 knots

Idaho

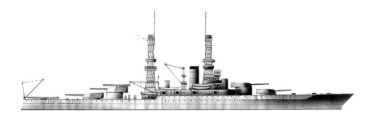

Idaho was one of a trio of battleships of the New Mexico class that introduced a new 356mm (14in) gun which could be elevated independently; with previous guns, all weapons in a turret had been locked into the same elevation. The main guns were housed in triple turrets. Originally 22 127mm (5in) guns were planned. The number was reduced to 14, allowing extra armour in some areas. *Idaho* was extensively rebuilt in 1930–31. From 1919 to 1941 she served with the Pacific Fleet, being transferred to the Atlantic Fleet for a brief period before returning to the Pacific. She subsequently fought actions off Attu, the Gilbert Islands, Kwajalein, Saipan, Guam, Palau, Iwo Jima and Okinawa, running aground off the latter island in June 1945. By 1943 she had had all her 127mm (5in) guns removed. *Idaho* was stricken in 1947; her sister ships were *New Mexico* and *Mississippi*.

Country of origin:	USA
Crew:	1084
Weight:	33,528 tonnes (33,000 tons)
Dimensions:	190.2m x 29.7m x 9.1m (624ft x 97ft 6in x 29ft 10in)
Range:	14,400km (8000nm) at 10 knots
Armour:	343mm – 203mm (13.5in – 8in) belt, 254mm – 229mm (10in – 9in) on sides, 450mm (18in) on turrets
Armament:	12 356mm (14in), 14 127mm (5in) guns
Powerplant:	Quadruple screw turbines
Performance:	21 knots

Imperator Pavel I

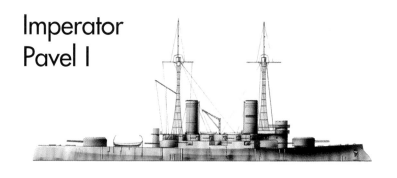

Imperator Pavel I was laid down in April 1904, but construction was delayed to incorporate lessons learned in the Russo-Japanese War of 1904–05. The hull was completely armoured and was flush-decked. The superstructure housed six of the 203mm (8in) guns and all the 120mm (4.7in) guns, with twin 203mm (8in) turrets mounted on the upper deck at each corner of the superstructure. The 304mm (12in) guns were in turrets. She saw action in the Baltic during World War I and was renamed *Respublika* after the successful Russian revolution in 1917. She was scrapped in 1923. The Baltic, where this vessel spent its operational service, was the scene of a number of fierce naval actions during World War I, as the Russians attempted to contest German domination of the Baltic states. Most actions were fought against warships of the German 3rd High Sea Squadron.

Country of origin:	Russia
Crew:	933
Weight:	17,678 tonnes (17,400 tons)
Dimensions:	140.2m x 24.4m x 8.2m (460ft x 80ft x 27ft)
Range:	11,118km (6000nm) at 12 knots
Armour:	127 – 216mm (5 – 8.5in) thick belt, 102 203mm (4 – 8in) on main turrets and 127 – 165mm (5 – 6.5in) on battery
Armament:	Four 305mm (12in), 14 203mm (8in) and 12 119mm (4.7in) guns
Powerplant:	Twin screw, vertical triple expansion engines
Performance:	17.5 knots

Independence

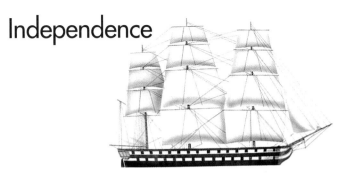

Independence was one of three 74-gun sailing line-of-battle ships that were modelled upon an earlier class of 1799, although the plans for *Independence* were never submitted to the Navy Department. When she was ready for sea it was found that the sills of the lower gunports were only 1.2m (3ft 10in) above the waterline when the full war complement and stores for six months were on board. In 1836 it was decided to cut her three-decks down to two to improve performance. After this, *Independence* became a very successful vessel and a smart sailer, thanks to the retention of the earlier rig of a 74-gun ship; she also became the largest frigate in the US Navy. *Independence* was finally broken up in 1914. Originally intended for convoy protection, the first frigates were modest in size, but became much bigger in the 18th and 19th centuries – mounting 50–60 guns on two decks.

Country of origin:	USA
Crew:	250
Weight:	2293 tonnes (2257 tons)
Dimensions:	57.9m x 15.2m (190ft x 50ft)
Range:	3706km (2000nm) at 6 knots
Armour:	None
Armament:	30 long 32-pounder, 33 medium 32-pounder guns, 24 32-pounder carronades
Powerplant:	
Performance:	8 knots

Independence

During 1942 the US Navy lost four aircraft carriers, and for a time had only *Enterprise* in the Pacific. The first of the large Essex-class carriers were not expected to enter service until the following year, so plans were put in hand to convert some of the 39 light cruisers of the Cleveland class then under construction. Emergency work was carried out on nine of the vessels and they all entered service in 1943. *Independence* had 45 aircraft, but she had room to 'ferry' up to 100. Her World War II battle honours included raids on the Gilbert Islands, Palau, Leyte, Luzon, Taiwan, Okinawa, the China coast, the Ryukus and the Japanese Home Islands. During the invasion of the Gilbert Islands in November 1943 the carrier was severely damaged by an aerial torpedo off Tarawa. She was used as a target in the Bikini atomic bomb tests, and was finally sunk as a target ship in 1951.

Country of origin:	USA
Crew:	1569
Weight:	14,980 tonnes (14,751 tons)
Dimensions:	189.78m x 33.3m x 7.4m (622ft 6in x 109ft 2in x 24ft 3in)
Range:	23,400km (13,000nm) at 12 knots
Armour:	127mm (5in) belt and bulkheads, armour deck 50mm (2in)
Armament:	Two 40mm (1.5in), 22 20mm (0.78in) guns, 30 aircraft
Powerplant:	Quadruple screw turbines
Performance:	31.6 knots

Independencia

Launched in 1865, *Independencia* and her sister ship *Huascar* were the only major armoured vessels built for Peru, and their loss in the war with Chile in 1879 was disastrous for that country. Early in the war both *Independencia* and *Huascar* went to Iquique to raise the blockade by two small Chilean gunboats, and was blown up to prevent capture after running aground in action with the Chilean gunboat *Covadonga* off Iquique. She was one of two armoured vessels built for Peru in the 1860s, in addition to two monitors that were purchased from the USA. The other armoured vessel, *Huascar* (q.v.) made history when she was seized by mutineers and then engaged the British cruiser *Shah* in 1877. During the war in the Pacific, from which Chile emerged victorious, Peru lost its ironclad ships.

Country of origin:	Peru
Crew:	250
Weight:	3556 tonnes (3500 tons)
Dimensions:	65.5m x 13.6m x 6.7m (215ft x 44ft 9in x 22ft)
Range:	2594km (1400nm) at 10 knots
Armour:	114mm belt (4.5in), 114mm (4.5in) over battery
Armament:	Two 178mm (7in), twelve 70-pounder muzzle-loading guns
Powerplant:	Single screw, horizontal compound engines
Performance:	12 knots

Indiana

Indiana was one of a class of four units of the South Dakota class that were the last US battleships designed within the weight limits of the 1922 London Treaty. Completed in 1942, all *Indiana*'s secondary 127mm (5in) guns were concentrated on two levels in twin turrets amidships, and her single funnel was faired into the rear of the bridge. The class carried over 100 40mm (1.5in) and 20mm (0.78in) anti-aircraft guns. *Indiana* saw extensive service in the Pacific during World War II. She saw action in the Southwest Pacific, the Gilbert Islands, Kwajalein, the Philippine Sea, Saipan, Guam, Palau, Iwo Jima and Okinawa. In February 1944 she was damaged in collision with the battleship *Washington* off Kwajalein; in June that year she was hit by a suicide aircraft off Saipan; and in June 1945 she was further damaged by a typhoon off Okinawa. She was sold in 1963

Country of origin:	USA
Crew:	1793
Weight:	45,231 tonnes (44,519 tons)
Dimensions:	207.2m x 32.9m x 10.6m (680ft x 108ft x 35ft)
Range:	27,000km (15,000nm) at 12 knots
Armour:	309mm (12.2in) belt, 457mm (18in) facings on turrets
Armament:	20 127mm (5in), nine 406mm (16in) guns
Powerplant:	Quadruple screw turbines
Performance:	27.5 knots

Indianola

Indianola had one of the shortest careers of any Union ironclad of the American Civil War. She was ordered by the US Army for service on the Mississippi, and was taken over by the US Navy in early 1863. Despite the fact that she was not yet finished, *Indianola* was rushed into service to help defend Cincinnati against a strong Confederate force. However, on 24 February 1863 she was attacked by the Confederate ram *Queen of the West* and two other vessels and was grounded. The Confederates tried to raise *Indianola* but when a strong Union force appeared, they blew her up before retreating. The value of the Union's gunboats was illustrated in the Battle of Shiloh, April 1862, when *Lexington* and *Tyler*, gave supporting fire to General Grant's left flank, sending eight-inch shells crashing into the Confederate lines throughout the night of 6/7 April while Grant waited for vital reinforcements.

Country of origin:	USA
Crew:	50
Weight:	520 tonnes (511 tons)
Dimensions:	53m x 15m x 1.5m (175ft x 52ft x 5ft)
Range:	Not known
Armour:	75mm (3in) sides
Armament:	Two 228mm (9in), two 280mm (11in) guns
Powerplant:	Twin screws, paddlewheels
Performance:	6 knots

Inflexible

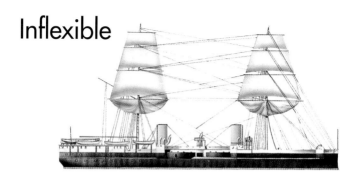

Designed by Nathaniel Barnaby, *Inflexible* was one of the most powerful
vessels of her time. Laid down in 1881 in direct response to the giant Italian
battleships *Duilio* and *Dandolo*, and to French moves towards arming their new
ships with large guns. As completed in 1874, *Inflexible* had the heaviest muzzle-
loading rifled guns of any vessel in the Royal Navy – and the thickest armour.
The 81-tonne (80-ton) guns were positioned in turrets at opposite corners of the
citadel. As they were too long to be reloaded in the turrets, the guns were designed
to depress into an armoured glacis for reloading on the main deck. In 1881 she
was assigned to the Mediterranean Fleet, and in 1882 she was damaged by shellfire
during the bombardment of Alexandria following anti-foreign riots there. This
led to conflict between the British and Egyptians. She was scrapped in 1903.

Country of origin:	Great Britain
Crew:	440
Weight:	12,070 tonnes (11,880 tons)
Dimensions:	104.8m x 22.8m x 7.7m (344ft x 75ft x 25ft 6in)
Range:	6300km (3400nm) at 10 knots
Armour:	600mm – 400mm (24in – 16in) citadel, 425mm – 400mm (17in – 16in) on turrets
Armament:	Four 406mm (16in) guns
Powerplant:	Twin screw, compound engines
Performance:	14.7 knots

Inflexible

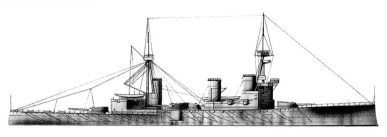

In 1904 the powerful Japanese *Tsukuba* and *Ibuki* classes convinced the British Admiralty of the need for a vessel combining the speed of a cruiser with the firepower of a battleship. The answer was *Inflexible* and her sisters of the Invincible class. *Inflexible* was launched in 1907 and completed in 1908. In May 1911 she suffered a damaged bow in collision with the battleship *Bellerophon* in the English Channel. Early in World War I she took part in the naval action off the Falklands and the hunt for the German cruiser *Goeben*; in 1915 she was one of the vessels covering the Dardanelles landings, and while carrying out a bombardment operation in March she was severely damaged by shore batteries and a mine. She was at Jutland in 1916 but received no damage, unlike her sister *Invincible* which was blown up by German shell fire. *Inflexible* and *Indomitable* were sold for scrap in 1922.

Country of origin:	Great Britain
Crew:	784
Weight:	20,320 tonnes (20,000 tons)
Dimensions:	172.8m x 23.9m x 8m (567ft x 78ft 6in x 26ft 10in)
Range:	5562km (3090nm) at 10 knots
Armour:	152mm – 102mm (6in – 4in) belt, 178mm (7in) on turrets
Armament:	16 102mm (4in), eight 305mm (12in) guns
Powerplant:	Quadruple screw turbines
Performance:	25.5 knots

Invincible

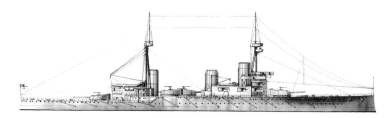

Completed in 1908, *Invincible* was the world's first battlecruiser, and so was the first of an entirely new type of warship. It sacrificed armoured protection for speed, range and battleship-sized armament, and could outrun and outfight its prey – the armoured cruiser. However, as the disastrous loss of *Invincible* and two other battlecruisers at Jutland was to show, when up against a battleship's firepower, the lack of armour, particularly around the magazines, was a fatal flaw. Despite being refitted with more armour as a result of the this débâcle, events had proved the obsolescence of this type of vessel and development was stopped. *Invincible* blew up and sank with the loss of 1026 lives, including Rear-Admiral H.L.A. Hood. The battlecruiser *Queen Mary* suffered the same fate at Jutland, exploding with the loss of 1266 lives after a direct hit from the battlecruiser *Derfflinger*.

Country of origin:	Great Britain
Crew:	784
Weight:	20,421 tonnes (20,100 tons)
Dimensions:	175.5m x 23.9m x 7.7m (576ft x 78.5ft x 25.5ft)
Range:	5559km (3000nm) at 25 knots
Armour:	152mm (6in) belt, 178mm (7in) on barbettes and bulkheads
Armament:	Eight 305mm (12in), 16 102mm (4in) guns
Powerplant:	Four shaft geared turbines
Performance:	25 knots

Iowa

Designs for the Iowa class of fast battleships were started in 1936 in response to rumours that the Japanese were laying down battleships of 46,736 tonnes (46,000 tons). *Iowa* was laid down in 1940 and commissioned in 1943. The class including the *New Jersey* and *Missouri*, had greater displacement than the previous South Dakota class, and had more power and protection. The *Iowa* class served as escort for carriers in World War II, being the only battleships fast enough to keep up with carrier groups. She was used to bombard shore positions during the Korean War. The last of the Iowas, *Kentucky*, was not launched until 1950. They were the fastest battleships ever built, with a high length to beam ratio; the armour belt was inside the hull. Two of the class, *Illinois* and *Kentucky*, were not completed. *Iowa* was damaged by gunfire from shore batteries on Mili Island in March 1944.

Country of origin:	USA
Crew:	1921
Weight:	56,601 tonnes (55,710 tons)
Dimensions:	270.4m x 33.5m x 11.6m (887ft 2in x 108ft 3in x 38ft)
Range:	27,000km (15,000nm) at 12 knots
Armour:	302mm – 152mm (12.1 – 6.1in) belt, 152mm (6in) on deck, 492mm – 290mm (19.7in – 11.6in) on turrets
Armament:	Nine 406mm (16in), 20 127mm (5in) guns
Powerplant:	Quadruple screw turbines
Performance:	32.5 knots

Iron Duke

Launched in 1912, *Iron Duke* was the British flagship at the Battle of Jutland in 1916, and was one of the longest serving pre-World War I dreadnought battleships. She was a member of a class of four vessels that formed the third group of super-dreadnoughts. They were all armed with 343mm (13.5in) guns, and were the first major capital ships to revert to 152mm (6in) guns for anti-torpedo boat defence. Minor changes were later made to the secondary armament. The rest of her class was scrapped to comply with the Washington Treaty in the 1920s, but *Iron Duke* herself became a training ship in 1931, and was a depot ship at Scapa Flow between 1939–45. On 17 October 1939 she was attacked by four Junkers Ju88 dive-bombers of I/KG30 while at anchor in Scapa Flow and had to be beached after sustaining damage from near-misses. She was finally scrapped in 1946.

Country of origin:	Great Britain
Crew:	1022
Weight:	30,866 tonnes (30,380 tons)
Dimensions:	189.8m x 27.4m x 9m (622ft 9in x 90ft x 29ft 6in)
Range:	14,000km (7780nm) at 10 knots
Armour:	304mm – 102mm belt (12 – 4in), 228mm (9in) middle belt, 152mm – 51mm (2in – 6in) on battery
Armament:	12 152mm (6in), 10 342mm (13.5in) guns
Powerplant:	Quadruple screw turbines
Performance:	21.6 knots

Ise

Launched in 1916, *Ise* was an improved version of the previous Fuso class, and carried two twin superfiring guns amidships. She was extensively modernised between World Wars I and II, and by 1937 had been lengthened aft by 7.6m (25ft). Following the large loss of Japanese aircraft carriers at Midway in June 1942, *Ise* was converted to a hybrid battleship-carrier in 1943 when a hangar and flight deck were built on her quarter deck. Because of a lack of space, her complement of 22 seaplanes were launched by catapult but had to be retrieved by crane. She took part in the battles of Midway and Leyte Gulf, and was deactivated after being damaged by mines laid by American aircraft. She was sunk at Kure in July 1945 in a two-day series of air strikes that also destroyed the battleships *Hyuga* and *Haruna* and the aircraft carrier *Amagi*. She was raised and scrapped in 1946.

Country of origin:	Japan
Crew:	1376 as battleship, 1463 as carrier
Weight:	32,576 tonnes (32,063 tons) as battleship
Dimensions:	208.2m x 28.6m x 8.8m (683ft x 94ft x 29ft)
Range:	7412km (4000nm) at 15 knots
Armour:	304mm – 229mm (12in – 9in) belt, 304mm (12in)
Armament:	12 356mm (14in), 20 140mm (5.5in) guns
Powerplant:	Quadruple screw turbines
Performance:	23 knots

Italia

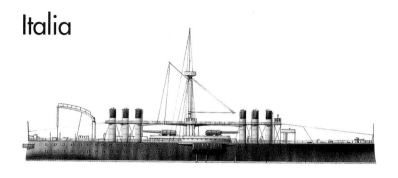

At the time of her completion in 1880, *Italia* and her sister *Lepanto* were among the fastest vessels afloat. This was partially due to the lack of side armour, these ships having no armoured belt. Instead they had a thick armoured deck which curved down to the waterline, and which was supplemented by an extensive honeycomb of watertight compartments. Their 104-tonne (102-ton) main guns were mounted in pairs on turntables, which were placed on a huge single oval-shaped armoured barbette. Ammunition had to be trundled up from below the armoured deck, and each gun could only fire one shell every five minutes. In the event technology overtook these vessels, and by the time they entered service the quick-firing gun and improved high-explosive shell had rendered them obsolete. *Italia* was transferred to harbour duties in 1914, and was scrapped in 1921.

Country of origin:	Italy
Crew:	701
Weight:	15,904 tonnes (15,654 tons)
Dimensions:	124.7m x 22.5m x 8.7m (409ft 2in x 73ft 10in x 28ft 6in)
Range:	9000km (5000nm) at 10 knots
Armour:	102mm- (4in-) thick deck, 482mm (19in) on citadel
Armament:	Four 431mm (17in) guns
Powerplant:	Twin screw, vertical compound engines
Performance:	17.8 knots

Iwo Jima

Iwo Jima – first of a class of seven – and was the world's first ship designed to carry and operate helicopters. She can also carry a Marine battalion of 2000 troops, plus their artillery and support vehicles. The flight deck allows for the simultaneous take-off of up to seven helicopters, and *Iwo Jima* has hangar facilities for up to 20 helicopters. The two lifts are situated at the very edges of the deck, so as not to reduce the flight-deck area. Storage capacity is provided for 1430 litres (6500 gallons) of petrol for the vehicles, plus over 88,000 litres (400,000 gallons) for the helicopter force. In 1970 a Sea Sparrow missile launcher was installed, followed by a second three years later. Iwo Jima and her six sisters have extensive medical facilities, including operating theatres and a large hospital. Other vessels in the class are *Guadalcanal, Guam, Inchon, Okinawa, Tripoli* and *New Orleans*.

Country of origin:	USA
Crew:	667, plus 2000 troops
Weight:	18,330 tonnes (18,042 tons)
Dimensions:	183.6m x 25.7m x 8m (602ft 8in x 84ft x 26ft)
Range:	11,118km (6000nm) at 18 knots
Armour:	100mm (2in) flight deck, 200mm (4in) belt
Armament:	Four 76mm (3in) guns
Powerplant:	Single screw turbines
Performance:	23.5 knots

Jauréguiberry

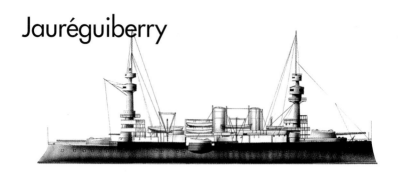

*J*auréguiberry was designed by Lagane as an enlarged version of his successful small battleship *Capitan Prat*, launched in 1890. After initial problems with her boilers, *Jauréguiberry* became a good steamer and was able to maintain high speed for long periods. Though in poor condition, she saw service in the early months of World War I. At the time of the warship's launch France was still obsessed with the view that Great Britain was her traditional enemy, and so was developing her fleet in a manner that threatened British trade and also aimed to offset the size of the Royal Navy by innovative technology. British policy of the day was to maintain a so-called 'two-power standard', which kept the Royal Navy equal in numbers to any two foreign navies and consequently saw large numbers of battleships built in the years up to 1906. *Jauréguiberry* was hulked in 1920 and scrapped in 1934.

Country of origin:	France
Crew:	631
Weight:	11,823 tonnes (11,637 tons)
Dimensions:	108.5m x 22m x 8.4m (356ft x 72ft 8in x 27ft 8in)
Range:	6485km (3500nm) at 10 knots
Armour:	450mm – 254mm (18in – 10in) belt, 380mm (15in) on turrets
Armament:	Two 305mm (12in), two 270mm (10.8in), eight 140mm (5.5in) guns
Powerplant:	Twin screw, vertical triple expansion engines
Performance:	17.7 knots

Javary

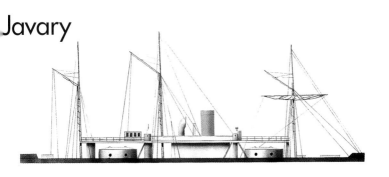

Upon completion in 1874, the armoured turret ships, *Javary* and her sister *Solimoes* were the most powerful vessels in the Brazilian Navy. During the Brazilian revolution of 1893, *Javary* sank as a result of leaks in the hull which were caused by the constant firing of her guns during her bombardment of government shore fortifications. *Javary,* and the other turret ship, *Aquibadan,* (which blew up and sank near Rio de Janeiro in 1906) remained the backbone of Brazil's navy for many years, but the increase in the size of the Argentine Navy compelled Brazil to commission the building of two dreadnoughts in British yards in 1907. As a result, Brazil possessed dreadnoughts before such larger powers as France, Italy and Russia. During World War I Brazil offered to send its dreadnoughts to join the British Grand Fleet, but the offer was turned down.

Country of origin:	Brazil
Crew:	135
Weight:	3699 tonnes (3641 tons)
Dimensions:	73m x 17m x 3.4m (240ft x 57ft x 11ft 5in)
Range:	1260km (680nm) at 10 knots
Armour:	305mm (12in) belt, 305mm – 279mm (12in – 11in) on turret
Armament:	Four 254mm (10 in) muzzle-loaders
Powerplant:	Twin screw, compound double cylinder engines
Performance:	11 knots

Jeanne D'Arc

Originally to be named *La Résolue*, this ship was authorised in 1957 as a training cruiser to replace the pre-World War I *Jeanne D'Arc*. Due to the cancellation of a large carrier, *La Résolue* underwent major design changes, emerging in 1964 as *Jeanne D'Arc*, a combination of cruiser, helicopter carrier and assault ship. Her superstructure is situated forward, with the aft of the vessel being a helicopter deck below which is housed the narrow hangar. In her role as a troop carrier, *Jeanne D'Arc* can transport 700 men and eight large helicopters. In 1975 Exocet missiles were fitted, giving her a full anti-ship role. In peacetime she reverts to a training role, providing facilities for up to 198 cadets. The ship has a modular type action information and operations room with a computerised tactical data handling system, and a combined command and control centre for amphibious warfare operations.

Country of origin:	France
Crew:	627, plus 198 cadets
Weight:	13,208 tonnes (13,000 tons)
Dimensions:	180m x 25.9m x 6.2m (590ft 6in x 85ft x 20ft 4in)
Range:	10,800km (6000nm) at 12 knots
Armour:	Classified
Armament:	Four 100mm (3.9in) guns, Exocet missiles, 4 – 8 helicopters
Powerplant:	Twin screw turbines
Performance:	26.5 knots

Kaiser

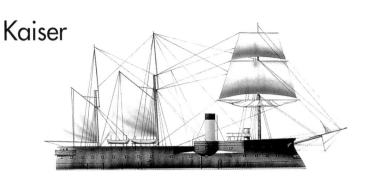

Austria was primarily a land power with only a short coastline along the Adriatic. As a result, the navy was always subordinated to the army. A constant shortage of money meant that in general the navy had to rely on ships that were less powerful than those of other leading fleets, and which were usually obsolescent by the time they were completed. *Kaiser* was a typical example of this penny-pinching policy. She was originally a wooden-hulled two-decker battleship. She took part in the Battle of Lissa in 1866, when she suffered severe damage. Due to lack of funds for new construction, the damaged vessel was converted into an ironclad central battery ship in 1869. She was rebuilt in iron from the waterline up, and in 1874 rejoined the fleet. She was rearmed in 1882, and again in 1885. *Kaiser* served as a barrack hulk from 1902–1918 and was scrapped in 1920.

Country of origin:	Austria
Crew:	471
Weight:	5811 tonnes (5720 tons)
Dimensions:	77.7m x 17.7m x 7.3m (255ft x 58ft 3in x 24ft 2in)
Range:	2779km (1500nm) at 10 knots
Armour:	152mm – 102mm (6in – 4in) wrought iron belt, 127mm (5in) casemates
Armament:	10 228mm (9in) muzzle-loaders, as rearmed in 1882
Powerplant:	Single screw, horizontal compound engines
Performance:	11.5 knots

Kaiser

L aunched in 1911 and completed in 1912, *Kaiser* was the first of a new type
of German dreadnought that was to set the style for following vessels and
eventually develop into *Bismarck* and *Tirpitz* of World War II. There were five
units in the Kaiser class. All had superfiring turrets aft and diagonally offset wing
turrets. Machinery developed 31,000hp, coal supply was 3000 tonnes (2953 tons),
and range at 12 knots was nearly 15,200km (8000 miles). *Kaiser* was in action at
the Battle of Jutland, and all vessels in the class were interned at Scapa Flow and
scuttled in 1919. From 1929–1937 the class was salvaged and broken up. *Kaiser*
was originally laid down as *Ersatz Hildebrand*. Other vessels in her class were
Friedrich der Grosse, *Kaiserin*, *König Albert* and *Prinzregent Luitpold*. They
were the first German battleships to be equipped with turbines.

Country of origin:	Germany
Crew:	1278 (at Jutland)
Weight:	26,998 tonnes (26,573 tons)
Dimensions:	172.4m x 29m x 8.3m (565ft 8in x 95ft 2in x 27ft 3in)
Range:	15,200km (8000nm) at 12 knots
Armour:	350mm – 80mm (14in – 3.2in) belt and turrets
Armament:	10 304mm (12in), 14 150mm (5.9in) guns
Powerplant:	Triple screw turbines
Performance:	23.5 knots

Kaiser Friedrich III

K̲aiser Friedrich III was laid down in 1895 and completed in 1898. Six of her 152mm (6in) guns were in single turrets high on the superstructure, with the remainder in casemates. The 86.3mm (3.4in) guns were carried singly behind shields on the upper deck. She set a pattern for German pre-dreadnoughts of the period with their light main armament and triple screws. *Kaiser Friedrich III*'s total armour weight was 3860 tonnes (3800 tons). She was fleet flagship in 1906, and was reconstructed between 1907–10. By 1916, however, she was hulked as being obsolete and was eventually scrapped in 1920. Other vessels in her class, all named after German emperors, were *Kaiser Barbarossa*, *Kaiser Wilhelm der Grosse*, *Kaiser Wilhelm II* and *Kaiser Karl der Grosse*. All except the last were modernised; new funnels and casemates were fitted, and pole masts replaced military masts.

Country of origin:	Germany
Crew:	651
Weight:	11,784 tonnes (11,599 tons)
Dimensions:	125.3m x 20.4m x 8.2m (411ft x 67ft x 27ft)
Range:	4170km (2250nm) at 12 knots
Armour:	305mm – 152mm (12in – 6in) belt, 254mm (10in) on main turrets, 152mm (6in) on secondary turrets and casemates
Armament:	Four 238mm (9.4in), 18 152mm (6in), 12 86.3mm (3.4in) guns
Powerplant:	Triple screw, triple expansion engines
Performance:	17 knots

Kaiser Max

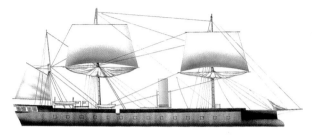

Kaiser Max was one in a three-unit class of ironclads which were built for the Austrian Navy. They were modified versions of the preceding class, with uprated engines, more guns and sternchasers. Within a few years *Kaiser Max*'s hull was found to be rotten. Her machinery was removed and put into an iron casemate ship of the same name which proved eventually to be three times as expensive as building a new ship. The hull was scrapped in 1878. Other vessels in the class were *Juan de Austria*, *Kaiser Max* and *Prinz Eugen*. All were poor sea boats, and the lack of funds had a damaging effect on their construction programme. *Juan de Austria*, for example, fought in the battle of Lissa with her armour incomplete. Because of factors such as this, the Austrian Navy's victory over the Italians was a remarkable feat.

Country of origin:	Austria
Crew:	400
Weight:	3645 tonnes (3588 tons)
Dimensions:	70.2m x 12.8m x 6.3m (230ft 7in x 42ft 2in x 20ft 9in)
Range:	3706km (2000nm) at 10 knots
Armour:	110mm (4.3in) belt
Armament:	14 14-pounder, 16 48-pounder guns
Powerplant:	Single screw, horizontal compound engine
Performance:	11.4 knots

Kalamazoo

Kalamazoo was one of a class of four units that, with the exception of *Dunderberg*, were the largest warships in the US Navy at the time. Named after a river in Michigan, *Kalamazoo* was a double-turreted monitor with two massive funnels and a single, large, armoured ventilating trunk. Her hull was plated with 152mm (6in) armour with a 762mm (30in) thick wooden backing. The deck armour was 75mm (3in) thick, laid on top of a 152mm- (6in-) thick wooden deck, with another 75mm (3in) of wood laid on top of the armour plating. As a result, the hulls and decks were very strong, but as they were made from unseasoned wood they rapidly deteriorated. *Kalamazoo* was laid down in 1863, but after the end of the American Civil War, construction work on all ships in the class was slow. All four units had been broken up by 1884 without having been launched.

Country of origin:	USA
Crew:	–
Weight:	5690 tonnes (5600 tons)
Dimensions:	105m x 17m x 5.3m (345ft 5in x 56ft 8in x 17ft 6in)
Range:	Unknown
Armour:	152mm – 75mm (6in – 3in) iron sides, 380mm (15in) turrets
Armament:	Four 380mm (15in) guns
Powerplant:	Twin screw, horizontal direct acting engines
Performance:	11 knots

Keokuk

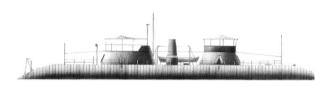

Built in New York, *Keokuk* was one of the designs submitted to the ironclad design board of 1861, in an attempt to produce a vessel able to combat the powerful Confederate ironclads then under construction. One of the other designs was the famous *Monitor*. *Keokuk* had an armoured pilot house in the middle of two fixed gun houses. The guns inside were traversable, firing out of three gun ports lying at 90 degree angles. During action off Charleston in 1863, *Keokuk* was hit 90 times and sank in shallow water. The Confederates salvaged her 279mm (11in) guns and left her hull as a wreck. The Confederate Navy was created by Congress on 16 March 1861, though the initial strength was small: four captains, four commanders, 30 lieutenants, five surgeons, five assistant surgeons, six paymasters and two chief engineers, plus other ranks.

Country of origin:	USA
Crew:	Unknown
Weight:	687 tonnes (677 tons)
Dimensions:	48.6m x 10.9m x 2.6m (159ft 6in x 36ft x 8ft 6in)
Range:	Unknown
Armour:	102mm (4in) thick strips, 25mm (1in) apart, with the intervening spaces filled with wood
Armament:	Two 280mm (11in) muzzle-loading smoothbore guns
Powerplant:	Twin screw, condensing engines
Performance:	9 knots

Kearsage

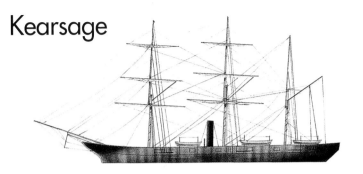

Kearsage was built for the Union under the war programme of 1861. She was commissioned in 1862, and was immediately sent to European waters to locate and destroy the Confederate commerce raider *Sumter*, which had already destroyed a number of Union merchant vessels. In her most famous action, in June 1864, she tracked down the Confederate raider *Alabama* to the French port of Cherbourg, where the extremely successful rebel ship was awaiting repairs. Lying offshore, the *Kearsage* attacked as the *Alabama* met the challenge and sailed out into international waters. In just over an hour the Confederate ship, which had taken 65 Union vessels, was reduced to a sinking wreck by the *Kearsage*. In 1894 *Kearsage* ran aground off Nicaragua, was looted by the local populace and became a total loss.

Country of origin:	USA
Crew:	212
Weight:	1511 tonnes (1488 tons)
Dimensions:	60.6m x 10.3m x 4.7m (198ft 11in x 33ft 10in x 15ft 6in)
Range:	–
Armour:	–
Armament:	One 105mm (4.2in) muzzle-loading rifle, two 279mm (11in) smoothbores, six 32-pounder smoothbores
Powerplant:	Single shaft engine
Performance:	12 knots

Kiev

*K*iev was the first Soviet aircraft carrier to be built with a full flight deck and a purpose-built hull. She was laid down in September 1970 in the Black Sea Nikolayev Dockyard. She was completed in May 1975. The flight deck is angled, with most of the armament carried forward, comprising a full range of anti-ship, anti-air and anti-submarine missiles. Twenty-four of the lethal SS-N-12 Shaddock type missiles are carried. The large bridge structure is set on *Kiev*'s starboard side, and houses an array of radar equipment. Designated a 'through-deck cruiser' by the Russians, the ship sailed from the Black Sea in the summer of 1976, passed through the Mediterranean and joined the Soviet Northern Fleet. *Kiev* carries an air group of Yakovlev Yak-38 Forger VTOL fighter-bombers and anti-submarine helicopters. Other vessels in the Kiev class are *Minsk*, *Novorossiysk* and *Baku*.

Country of origin:	Soviet Union
Crew:	1700
Weight:	38,608 tonnes (38,000 tons)
Dimensions:	273m x 47.2m x 8.2m (895ft 8in x 154ft 10in x 27ft)
Range:	24,300km (13,500nm) at 10 knots
Armour:	100mm (4in) flight deck, 50mm (2in) belt
Armament:	Four 76.2mm (3in) guns, plus up to 136 missiles
Powerplant:	Quadruple screw turbines
Performance:	32 knots

King Edward VII

King Edward VII has the historical distinction of being the first British battleship built in the 20th century. She was laid down in 1902, completed three years later, and was first in a class of eight. Known throughout the service for her eccentric steering, she also suffered in having a mixed secondary armament which prevented her employing large enough weapons in high enough numbers. *King Edward VII* hit a German mine off northern Scotland in 1916 and sank after a 12-hour struggle. Other ships in this class were *Africa, Britannia, Commonwealth, Dominion, Hibernia, Hindustan* and *New Zealand.* In 1912 *Hibernia* was fitted with a flying-off platform, and on 9 May 1912 Lt C.R. Samson became the first pilot in the world to take off in an aircraft from a ship under way, flying a Short seaplane off the platform as *Hibernia* steamed into wing at 10kt.

Country of origin:	Great Britain
Crew:	777
Weight:	17,566 tonnes (17,290 tons)
Dimensions:	138.3m x 23.8m x 7.72m (453ft 9in x 78ft x 25ft 8in)
Range:	12,970km (7000nm) at 10 knots
Armour:	229mm – 203mm (9in – 8in) belt, 305mm (12in) on barbettes, 304mm – 203mm (12in – 8in) on gun houses
Armament:	Four 304mm (12in), four 230mm (9.2in) guns
Powerplant:	Twin shaft vertical triple expansion engine
Performance:	18.5 knots

Kirishima

Launched in 1913 as a Kongo class battlecruiser, *Kirishima* underwent reconstruction between 1927–1930 and, like the rest of the class, was reclassified as a battleship. Further rebuilding between 1934–1936 completely altered her aft, added over 393 tonnes (400 tons) of armour to her barbettes and increased her anti-aircraft armament. In December 1941 she was part of the escort to the carriers whose aircraft attacked Pearl Harbor; she subsequently covered Japanese landings at Rabaul and in the Dutch East Indies, and on 1 March 1942 she sank the destroyer USS *Edsall* south of Java. During the second Battle of Guadalcanal in November 1942, she fell victim to the accurate radar-directed gunfire of USS *Washington*. At night over a range of 7677m (8400yds) she was hit by nine 400mm (16in) and 40 127mm (5in) shells and had to be scuttled.

Country of origin:	Japan
Crew:	1437 (after 1936 re-fit)
Weight:	32,491 tonnes (31,980 tons) as battleship
Dimensions:	219.6m x 222.1m x 9.7m (720ft 6in x 738ft 7in x 31ft 11in)
Range:	14,824km (8000nm) at 14 knots
Armour:	203mm – 75mm (8in – 3in), 254mm (10in) on barbettes, 229mm (9in) on turrets
Armament:	Eight 356mm (14in), 14 152mm (6in), eight 127mm (5in) guns
Powerplant:	Four shaft turbines
Performance:	30.4 knots

Kniaz Pozharski

Completed in 1870, *Kniaz Pozharski* was the first Russian ironclad to serve in the Pacific. She was laid down in 1864 as part of Russia's rapidly growing fleet, but unlike her sister vessels, she was the only one of her type to be designed as a cruising ironclad. She had a good spread of sail for extended patrolling and a steady gun platform. She was modernised in 1884–86. Two 152mm (6in) guns were mounted fore-and-aft on the upper deck, and 203mm (8in) guns replaced the 229mm (9in) weapons on the battery deck. After service in the Pacific she transferred to the Baltic Fleet in 1880, and after a refit she became a training ship before being reclassified a first-class cruiser in 1892. She again assumed a training role in 1906. She was named after Prince Dmitri Mikhailovich Pozharski (1578–1642), who waged a successful campaign against the Poles. She was broken up in 1907.

Country of origin:	Russia
Crew:	455
Weight:	5220 tonnes (5138 tons)
Dimensions:	83m x 15m x 7.4m (272ft 4in x 49ft 3in x 24ft 6in)
Range:	6002km (3250nm) at 10 knots
Armour:	112mm (4.5in) wrought iron on belt and battery
Armament:	Eight 203mm (8in), two 152mm (6in) guns and 2.4m (8ft) bow ram
Powerplant:	Single screw, horizontal direct-acting engines
Performance:	11.7 knots

Kniaz Suvarov

Launched in 1902 and completed in September 1904, *Kniaz Suvarov* was the Russian flagship at the Battle of Tsushima in May 1905, and was sunk by Japanese torpedoes. She was one of five vessels of the Borodino class. Her sister ships, *Borodino* and *Alexander,* were also sunk at Tsushima, while *Orel* surrendered to Japanese forces, later being renamed *Iwami*. The remaining ship in the class, *Slavia*, was not completed in time to join her ill-fated sisters. While en route to their fatal rendezvous, the Russian ships created a major diplomatic incident by opening fire on some British trawlers (which the crews mistook for Japanese torpedo boats!) in the North Sea. Gibraltar was put on a war footing and 28 British warships stood ready to intercept and destroy the Russian Pacific Squadron for several hours before the situation was defused.

Country of origin:	Russia
Crew:	835
Weight:	13,730 tonnes (13,513 tons)
Dimensions:	121m x 23m x 7.9m (397ft x 76ft 2in x 26ft 2in)
Range:	12,274km (6624nm) at 10 knots
Armour:	190mm – 152mm (7.5in – 6in) belt, 254mm – 102mm (10in – 4in) on turrets
Armament:	12 152mm (6in), four 304mm (12in), 20 11-pounder guns
Powerplant:	Twin screw, vertical triple expansion engines
Performance:	17.5 knots

Kongo

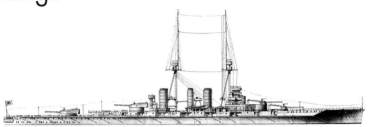

Completed in 1912, *Kongo* and her sisters, *Hiei, Haruna* and *Kirishima,* were inspired by the design and performance of British battlecruisers, *Kongo* herself being built in a British yard. Following the lessons of World War I and the naval treaties of the 1930s, the class was rebuilt with greater deck armour and anti-torpedo bulges. The development of fast carrier groups also led to further remodelling, including an improvement of machinery which took the speed of the class up to 30 knots. All four vessels were sunk during World War II. *Kongo* was torpedoed by the US submarine *Sealion* in November 1944. Of the others, *Hiei* and *Kirishima* were both sunk in the battle for Guadalcanal, the former receiving 50 shell hits, one bomb hit from a B-17, and two torpedo hits from aircraft operating from the USS *Enterprise. Haruna* was sunk by US aircraft at Kure in July 1945.

Country of origin:	Japan
Crew:	1221
Weight:	27,940 tonnes (27,500 tons)
Dimensions:	214.7m x 28m x 8.4m (704ft x 92ft x 27ft 7in)
Range:	14, 824km (8000nm) at 14 knots
Armour:	203mm (8in) belt, 254mm (10in) on barbettes
Armament:	Eight 356mm (14in), 16 152mm (6in) guns
Powerplant:	Four shaft geared turbines
Performance:	27.5 knots

König Wilhelm

*K*önig Wilhelm was an armoured frigate originally laid down in Britain for the Turkish Navy in 1865, but bought by Germany prior to completion in 1869. In 1878 she collided with and sank *Grosser Kurfürst*. She then underwent extensive repairs and was reboilered, given a stronger ram and extra smaller guns. She emerged rerated as a heavy cruiser, her ship rig reduced to two military masts. She was then the most powerful ship in the Imperial German Navy and its flag ship. In 1897 she was redesignated armoured cruiser, and in 1904 relegated to harbour service as a boys' school ship at Kiel, most of her armament being removed. Her original name was *Fatikh*; she was renamed *Wilhelm I* on her purchase by Prussia, but received her final name in 1867. She was stricken and scrapped in 1921.

Country of origin:	Germany
Crew:	730
Weight:	10,933 tonnes (10,761 tons)
Dimensions:	112m x 18.3m x 8.5m (368ft x 60ft x 28ft)
Range:	2408km (1300nm) at 10 knots
Armour:	304mm – 152mm (12in – 6in) wrought iron belt, 203mm – 152mm (8in – 6in) on battery
Armament:	18 238mm (9.4in), five 210mm (8.3in) guns
Powerplant:	Single screw, horizontal single expansion engine
Performance:	14.7 knots

Kreml

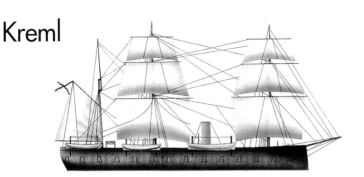

*K*reml was one of five vessels of the Pervenetz class that formed the basis of the Russian ironclad fleet. She had two near-sisters, one of which, *Pervenetz*, was designed by George Mackrow and built in Britain. *Kreml* was laid down in 1864 and completed in 1866. Schooner-rigged, she was an iron-hulled broadside ironclad. Her engines, taken from a Russian wooden screw ship, developed 1630hp. She eventually became a gunnery training ship before being scrapped in 1905. Like Austria, Russia was primarily a military power in the mid-19th century, with its naval arm subordinate to the army. However, two wooden vessels were converted to ironclads as early as 1861, and Russia's first armoured warship, *Pervenietz* (the name means 'Firstborn') was ordered and built in Britain, along with a sister ship, *Nye Tron Menya* ('Touch-me-not').

Country of origin:	Russia
Crew:	395
Weight:	4064 tonnes (4000 tons)
Dimensions:	67.6m x 16m x 5.9m (221ft 9in x 53ft x 19ft 6in)
Range:	2780km (1500nm) at 10 knots
Armour:	112mm (4.5in) wrought iron on side, 140mm (5.5in) on battery
Armament:	Eight 203mm (8in), six 152mm (6in), eight 86mm (3.4in) guns
Powerplant:	Single screw, horizontal direct acting engine
Performance:	9 knots

Kurfürst Friedrich Wilhelm

Kurfürst Friedrich Wilhelm of the Brandenburg class was one of four powerful pre-dreadnoughts that formed the basis of the German Navy in the early 1900s. Laid down in 1890 and completed in 1893, she was one of the first German warships to be fitted with wireless telegraph. Her main armament was installed in three twin turrets on the centreline; an amidships turret with guns of shorter calibre had a restricted field of fire. She was sold to Turkey in 1910, becoming *Heireddin Barbarossa*. In Turkish service she took part in the bombardment of Varna in 1912, and in December that year she was damaged in action with a Greek naval squadron off the Dardanelles. She was again damaged in the same area a week later, and on 8 August 1915 she was torpedoed and sunk by the British submarine *E11* in the Dardanelles with the loss of 253 lives.

Country of origin:	Germany
Crew:	568
Weight:	10,210 tonnes (10,050 tons)
Dimensions:	115.7m x 19.5m x 7.9m (379ft 7in x 64ft x 26ft)
Range:	8338km (4500nm) at 10 knots
Armour:	406mm – 304mm (16in – 12in) belt, 304mm (12in) on barbettes, 127mm (5in) on gun houses
Armament:	Six 280mm (11in), six 105mm (4.1in), eight 88mm (3.4in) guns
Powerplant:	Twin screw, triple expansion engines
Performance:	14 knots

Leonardo Da Vinci

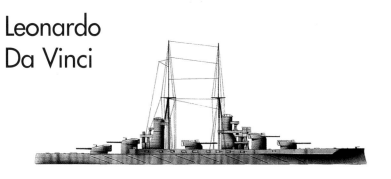

Leonardo da Vinci and her two sisters were an improvement on the previous Dante Alighieri class, having 13 big guns mounted in five centreline turrets, with superfiring twin turrets fore and aft. Instead of carrying the secondary armament in twin turrets, the battery was concentrated amidships in casemates. Machinery developed 31,000hp, and range at 10 knots was 8640km (4800 miles). *Leonardo da Vinci* was completed in 1914, and spent her war service in the Adriatic. On 2 August 1916 she caught fire, blew up and capsized at Taranto. The explosion, which was caused either by unstable cordite or Austrian sabotage, left 249 dead. In September 1919 she was refloated upside down and was righted in January 1921. However, she was not repaired and was broken up in 1923. Her two sister ships were *Conte de Cavour* and *Giulio Cesare*.

Country of origin:	Italy
Crew:	1235
Weight:	25,250 tonnes (25,086 tons)
Dimensions:	176m x 28m x 9.3m (577ft 9in x 91ft 10in x 30ft 10in)
Range:	8640km (4800nm) at 10 knots
Armour:	248mm – 127mm (9.8in – 5in) belt, 280mm (11in) on turrets, 127mm – 110mm (5in – 4.3in) on secondary battery
Armament:	13 304mm (12in), 18 120mm (4.7in) guns
Powerplant:	Quadruple screw turbines
Performance:	21.6 knots

Lepanto

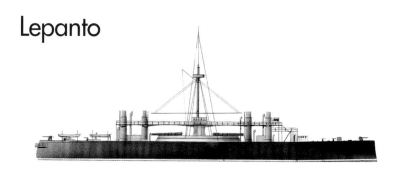

Upon completion in 1887, Benedetto Brin's *Lepanto* was the fastest capital ship in the world and, together with her sister *Italia*, was also one of the largest and most powerful. Her four funnels were linked by a narrow flying bridge, the front of which was connected to a tiny conning bridge. She could carry large numbers of troops in times of emergency. By the time she and her sister entered service, though, great strides had been made in the development of quick-firing guns and high-explosive shells. These fine ships, with their inadequate armour and slow rate of fire (one shot every five minutes from each gun), were soon incapable of meeting a modern battleship face to face. Later, *Lepanto* had more quick-firing light guns fitted to her maindeck. After first-line service, she served as a gunnery training ship, a depot ship at Spezia, and finally a guardship at Derna. She was stricken in 1914.

Country of origin:	Italy
Crew:	701
Weight:	16,154 tonnes (15,900 tons)
Dimensions:	124.7m x 22.3m x 9.6m (409ft 1in x 73ft 2in x 31ft 6in)
Range:	15,660km (8700nm) at 10 knots
Armour:	483mm (19in) on central citadel
Armament:	Four 431mm (17in), eight 152mm (6in) guns
Powerplant:	Twin screw, vertical compound engines
Performance:	18.4 knots

Lexington

*L*exington was the first fleet aircraft carrier completed for the US Navy. She was laid down in 1921 as a battlecruiser, but work was stopped as a result of the 1922 Washington Naval Treaty. Her design was then changed to that of an aircraft carrier, though her cruiser-type hull form was retained. A 137m x 21m (450ft x 70ft) hangar was installed and for many years she remained the largest aircraft carrier afloat. In May 1942 she was operating as part of Task Force 11, one of three Allied naval task forces which combined to thwart a Japanese landing at Port Moresby, New Guinea, in the Battle of the Coral Sea. On the morning of 8 May the opposing carrier forces sighted one another and flew off their aircraft (90 Japanese and 78 American) to attack. *Lexington* (Capt F.C. Sherman) was hit by two torpedoes and three bombs and was abandoned, being sunk later by the destroyer USS *Phelps*.

Country of origin:	USA
Crew:	2327
Weight:	48,463 tonnes (47,700 tons)
Dimensions:	270.6m x 32.2m x 9.9m (88ft x 105ft 8in x 32ft 6in)
Range:	18,900km (10,500nm) at 10 knots
Armour:	178mm – 127mm (7in – 5in) belt, 31mm (1.2in) on armoured deck
Armament:	Eight 203mm (8in), 12 127mm (5in) guns, 80 aircraft
Powerplant:	Quadruple screw turbo electric drive
Performance:	33.2 knots

Lion

The Lion class of ship were the first battlecruisers to surpass battleships in terms of size. Launched in 1910 and completed in 1912, *Lion* had eight 343mm (13.5in) guns, and these were mounted in twin turrets, two forward with one superfiring, one aft and one amidships (the latter having a restricted arc of fire) between the second and third funnels. During World War I *Lion* was the flagship of the Grand Fleet's Battlecruiser Fleet (commanded by Admiral Sir David Beatty). On 24 January 1915 *Lion* received a total of 21 shell hits during the Battle of Dogger Bank, and during the Battle of Jutland in 1916 she narrowly escaped destruction when she was severely damaged by twelve shells, with the loss of 99 of her crew. She was eventually sold and broken up at Blyth, Northumberland, in 1924.

Country of origin:	Great Britain
Crew:	997
Weight:	30,154 tonnes (29,680 tons)
Dimensions:	213.3m x 27m x 8.7m (700ft x 88ft 6in x 28ft 10in)
Range:	10,098km (5610nm) at 10 knots
Armour:	127 – 228mm (5 – 9in) main belt, 102 – 152mm (4 – 6in) upper belt, 102 – 228mm (4 – 9in) on turrets
Armament:	16 102mm (4.2in), eight 343mm (13.5in) guns
Powerplant:	Quadruple screw turbines
Performance:	27 knots

Littorio

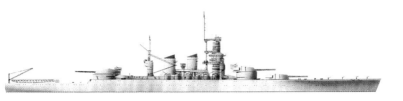

Littorio was one of the last battleships to be built for the Italian Navy. Completed in 1940, she was also the first Italian battleship to be commissioned after World War I. Her impressive outline was all the more striking due to the raised height of the aft turret, which was designed to avoid blast damage to the two fighter planes carried on the poop deck. On 12 November 1940 she was severely damaged by three torpedoes dropped by Swordfish aircraft during the Royal Navy's attack on Taranto, and she received further damage in June 1942 when she was torpedoed by British aircraft during an attack on a Malta convoy. In 1943 she was renamed *Italia*, and after the Italian surrender she was damaged by a German radio-controlled bomb. She was interned on the Suez Canal's Great Bitter Lake until February 1946. Stricken in 1948, she was broken up in 1960.

Country of origin:	Italy
Crew:	1950
Weight:	46,698 tonnes (45,963 tons)
Dimensions:	237.8m x 32.9m x 9.6m (780ft 2in x 108ft x 31ft 6in)
Range:	8487km (4580nm) at 16 knots
Armour:	280mm – 70mm (10.9in – 2.7in), 350mm – 280mm (13.6in – 10.9in) on barbettes, 350mm – 200mm (12in – 7.8in) on turrets
Armament:	Nine 380mm (15in), 12 152mm (6in), four 120mm (4.7in) 11 89mm (3.5in) guns
Powerplant:	Quadruple screw turbines
Performance:	28 knots

Lord Nelson

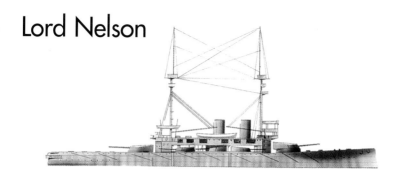

*L*ord Nelson and her sister *Agamemnon* were the last pre-dreadnoughts built for the Royal Navy. *Lord Nelson* was completed in October 1908. The 305mm (12in) guns were in twin turrets, with the 233mm (9.2in) guns in a mix of twin and single turrets on the broadside. The main belt ran her full length, supplemented by an upper belt which ran to the base of the 'Y' turret. She was further protected by a number of solid bulkheads, the first to be fitted to a British battleship. She saw extensive service during World War I, a notable action being the bombardment of the Narrows at the Dardanelles on 7 March 1915. *Lord Nelson* and *Agamemnon* had engaged Turkish forts with direct gunfire at a range of 12,000 – 14,000 yd, putting two forts out of action. The British ships were covered by the French battleships *Gaulois, Charlemagne, Bouvet* and *Suffren*. *Lord Nelson* was broken up in 1920.

Country of origin:	Great Britain
Crew:	900
Weight:	17,945 tonnes (17,663 tons)
Dimensions:	135m x 24m x 7.9m (443ft 6in x 79ft 6in x 26ft)
Range:	17,010km (9180nm) at 10 knots
Armour:	304mm – 203mm (12in – 8in) belt, 203mm – 178mm (8in – 7in) on turrets
Armament:	Four 304mm (12in), ten 233mm (9.2in) guns
Powerplant:	Twin screw, triple expansion engines
Performance:	18.7 knots

Los Andes

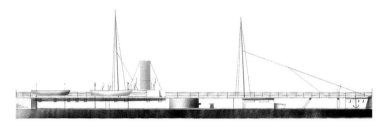

L os Andes was a low freeboard turret ship of the El Plata class, and one of the first capital ships to be built for the Argentine Navy, her sister being *El Plata*. A light superstructure carried a flying bridge extending fore and aft, and was narrow enough to allow firing directly ahead from both turret guns. She had one funnel abaft the turret, and two light pole masts were carried. On her initial journey from her British builders she spread only a single fore sail. *Los Andes* entered service in 1875. A permanent Argentine navy had only been established three years earlier, with the purchase of several small vessels, including these two armoured monitors. In the 1890s, a border dispute with Chile led to great expansion of the Argentine fleet. Four armoured cruisers were ordered from Italy, though only two were delivered, the dispute having been settled. *Los Andes* was scrapped in 1929.

Country of origin:	Argentina
Crew:	200
Weight:	1703 tonnes (1677 tons)
Dimensions:	56.4m x 15.7m x 3.2m (185ft 4in x 51ft 7in x 10ft 6in)
Range:	5336km (2880nm) at 10 knots
Armour:	152mm (6in), 229mm – 203mm (9in – 8in) on turret
Armament:	Two 228mm (9in) guns
Powerplant:	Twin screw, compound engines
Performance:	9.5 knots

Louisiana

L *ouisiana* was one of three powerful ironclads intended for the defence of the lower Mississippi. Lack of suitable materials meant that a lot of unseasoned 'green' wood was used in her construction, and she leaked so badly that water was knee deep on the gun deck during action. In action during April 1862, she put up a fierce defence against overwhelming odds, but when the Union fleet pushed past her to New Orleans, *Louisiana* was set on fire by her commander and left to explode. Federal advances into Tennessee and the Mississippi Valley during the first half of 1862 owed much to the Union Navy's Western Flotilla. In March and April 1862 the Flotilla contributed largely to the fall of two Confederate strongpoints on the Mississippi. In May, the Federals beat off an attack by the Confederate River Defense Fleet, which was destroyed at Memphis in June 1862.

Country of origin:	Confederate States of America
Crew:	150
Weight:	1422 tonnes (1400 tons)
Dimensions:	80m x 18.8m (260ft x 62ft)
Range:	1853km (1000nm) at 6 knots
Armour:	102mm (4in) on casemate, plus wooden backing
Armament:	Two 178mm (7in), four 203mm (8in), three 228mm (9in), seven 32-pounder guns
Powerplant:	Twin screw, paddlewheels
Performance:	8 knots

Lutfi Djelil

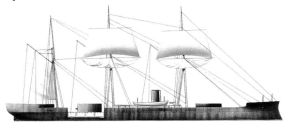

Lutfi Djelil was ordered by Egypt, but she was claimed by Turkey in 1869 while she was still on the stocks in France. She had twin turrets, the larger fore turret housing the two 203mm (8in) guns and the aft turret housing the 178mm (7in) guns. Both turrets were manually operated, needing 24 crew to rotate them. Hinged bulwarks amidships were lowered to protect the crew during action. She also had an armoured ram in her bow. In May 1877 during the Russo-Turkish War, *Lutfi Djelil* was off Braila when rounds from the Russian shore batteries pierced her magazine and blew her up. The Turkish Navy did little during the war with Russia in 1877–78, losing *Lutfi Djelil* and another ironclad to inferior Russian forces. Three capital ships being built in Britain were seized under the British neutrality laws and completed for the Royal Navy. From then on, Turkey's large navy became steadily more antiquated.

Country of origin:	Turkey
Crew:	130
Weight:	2580 tonnes (2550 tons)
Dimensions:	62m x 14m x 4.2m (203ft 4in x 46ft x 13ft 9in)
Range:	2779km (1500nm) at 10 knots
Armour:	140mm (5.5in) iron belt, 75mm (3in) on side, 140mm (5.5in) on turret
Armament:	Two 203mm (8in), two 178mm (7in), muzzle-loading guns
Powerplant:	Twin screw, compound engines
Performance:	12 knots

Magenta

Launched in 1861, *Magenta* and her sister *Solferno* were the only two-decker, broadside ironclads to be built. The armour was concentrated amidships where the guns were housed on main and upper decks, with shotproof transverse bulkheads. The two-tier placing gave the upper-deck guns increased elevation and range, as well as lightening the ends of the vessel. *Magenta* was an imposing-looking ship, with a pronounced tumble-home to the hull and a prominent ram. On 31 October 1875 she blew up as a result of a fire that started in the wardroom galley. *Magenta*'s sister vessel, *Solferino* – named after the French and Sardinian naval victory over Austria in June 1859 – remained in first-line service for ten years before being placed in reserve in 1871 and broken up in 1884. She was the only French ironclad with a figurehead, a golden eagle.

Country of origin:	France
Crew:	674
Weight:	6832 tonnes (6715 tons)
Dimensions:	86m x 57.7m x 8.4m (282ft x 56ft 8in x 27ft 8in)
Range:	2913km (1840nm) at 10 knots
Armour:	120mm (4.7in) belt
Armament:	Two 223mm (8.8in) howitzers, 34 162mm (6.4in) and 16 55-pounder guns
Powerplant:	Single screw, horizontal return connecting rod engine
Performance:	13 knots

Maine

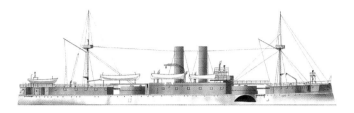

Launched in 1889, initial designs for *Maine* showed a three-masted sail rig, but this was abandoned and she entered service in 1895 with two military masts instead. In January 1898 she was sent to Havana, Cuba, to protect US interests there, but in February she was sunk by an explosion in her forward magazine. This was thought to be the result of Spanish sabotage, and war began between the USA and Spain the following month. The wreck was raised in 1912 and evidence suggested that a coal bunker fire had been the cause of the tragedy. The war with Spain gained the USA a number of territories. Cuba was occupied until 1902, after which America was guaranteed political control and commercial dominance; Hawaii was annexed; and the Philippines, although at first seen as a major prize, cost over 4000 American lives in suppressing a rebellion that lasted three years.

Country of origin:	USA
Crew:	374
Weight:	6789 tonnes (7180 tons)
Dimensions:	98.9m x 17.4m x 6.9m (318ft x 57ft x 21ft 6in)
Range:	6670km (3600nm) at 10 knots
Armour:	304mm – 152mm (12in – 6in) belt, 304mm (12in) on barbettes, 203mm (8in) on turrets
Armament:	Four 254mm (10in), six 152mm (6in) guns
Powerplant:	Twin screw, triple expansion engines
Performance:	16.4 knots

Majestic

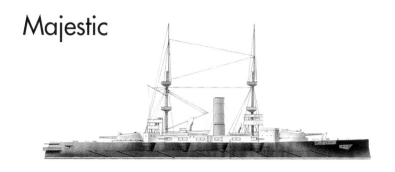

Completed in 1895, *Majestic*, together with her eight sisters, proved to be the best battleships of the 1890s, and set the pattern for all battleship design until the coming of *Dreadnought* in 1905. Designer Sir William White used improved armour, allowing for adequate protection at less cost in weight. The armoured hull curved down to meet the lower edge of the belt, so increasing internal protection. In December 1904 she suffered a coal gas explosion while in the Channel, and in July 1912 she was damaged in a collision with her sister ship *Victorious* (the others were *Caesar*, *Hannibal*, *Illustrious*, *Jupiter*, *Magnificent*, *Mars* and *Prince George*). After escort duty and Channel patrols, she was sent to the Mediterranean. *Majestic* was sunk in the Dardanelles on 27 May 1915, after being struck by two torpedoes from the German submarine *U21*.

Country of origin:	Great Britain
Crew:	672
Weight:	16,317 tonnes (16,060 tons)
Dimensions:	128.3m x 22.8m x 8.2m (421ft x 75ft x 27ft)
Range:	14,082km (7600nm) at 10 knots
Armour:	228mm belt (9in), 355mm – 304mm (14in – 12in) bulkheads, 355mm (14in) on barbettes, 254mm (10in) on turrets
Armament:	Four 304mm (12in), 12 152mm (6in) guns
Powerplant:	Twin screw, triple expansion engines
Performance:	17 knots

Masséna

Completed in 1898, *Masséna* was the first French warship to be constructed with triple screws. The ship itself had a long, sleek hull, a pronounced tumble-home and a prominent bow ram. Her 304mm (12in) guns were housed in single turrets, one high up on the bows and the other placed right aft, at main deck level. The 270mm (10.8in) guns were mounted singly on each side of the ship, and were on deep barbettes which protruded outwards from the hull so that the guns could fire in line with the keel. *Masséna* was hulked in 1913 and on 9 November 1915 was subsequently sunk as a breakwater at Seddulbahir in the Dardanelles. The ship was similar in construction to another French ship *Charles Martel*, which was laid down a year earlier, discarded in 1915 and then broken up in 1922.

Country of origin:	France
Crew:	667
Weight:	11,922 tonnes (11,735 tons)
Dimensions:	112.6m x 20.2m x 8.8m (369ft 7in x 66ft 6in x 29ft)
Range:	8524km (4600nm) at 10 knots
Armour:	450mm – 254mm (18in – 10in) belt, 356mm (14in) on turrets
Armament:	Two 304mm (12in), two 274mm (10.8in), 140mm (5.5in), eight 100mm (3.9in) guns
Powerplant:	Triple screw, triple expansion engines
Performance:	17 knots

Messina

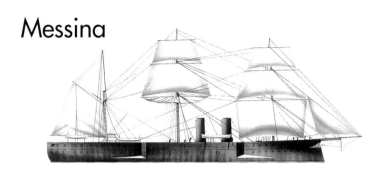

Although Inspector Engineer Mattei designed *Messina* as a wooden-hulled frigate, she was converted into a broadside ironclad before her completion in 1867. Built at the Castellammare naval dockyard, she formed part of the second group of ironclads (the Principe di Carignano class) built for the Italians, and the first built in Italy. In about 1870 her armament was changed to eight 164mm (6.5in), four 203mm (8in) and two 254mm (10in) guns. In September 1870 she took part in the liberation of Rome, an event that was marred when she went aground in the mouth of the River Tiber. Her class leader, *Principe de Carignano,* was also converted to an armoured vessel after construction had started, and the third ship, *Conte Verde* was laid down as an ironclad, but with incomplete protection was removed from the effective list in 1880.

Country of origin:	Italy
Crew:	572
Weight:	4382 tonnes (4313 tons)
Dimensions:	75.8m x 15m x 7.3m (248ft 8in x 49ft 6in x 24ft)
Range:	2160km (1200nm) at 8 knots
Armour:	114mm (4.5in) belt
Armament:	16 164mm (6.5in), four 78-pounder guns
Powerplant:	Single screw, single expansion six-cylinder engine
Performance:	10.4 knots

Michigan

Completed in 1910, *Michigan* was designed before, but built after, the epoch-making *Dreadnought*. One of the South Carolina class, her design introduced the concept of all-big-guns on the centreline. Most of the 76mm (3in) guns were concentrated in a box battery amidships, with the rest on the upper deck. Cage masts greatly reduced the target area offered to enemy gunners and were a characteristic of US dreadnoughts. As the turbine was still in the development stage, triple expansion engines were installed instead. *Michigan* served with the Atlantic Fleet between 1910 and 1916 and in 1917–18 was employed on convoy escort duty. In January 1918 she lost her cage foremast in a storm off Cape Hatteras, and in 1919 she made two voyages as a troop transport, bringing US servicemen home from Europe. She was decommissioned in 1922 and broken up at Philadelphia in 1924.

Country of origin:	USA
Crew:	869
Weight:	18,186 tonnes (17,900 tons)
Dimensions:	138.2m x 24.5m x 7.5m (453ft 5in x 80ft 4in x 24ft 7in)
Range:	9000km (5000nm) at 10 knots
Armour:	304mm – 229mm (12in – 9in) belt, 304mm – 203mm (12in – 8in) on turrets
Armament:	Eight 305mm (12in), 22 76mm (3in) guns
Powerplant:	Twin screw, vertical triple expansion engines
Performance:	18.5 knots

Mikasa

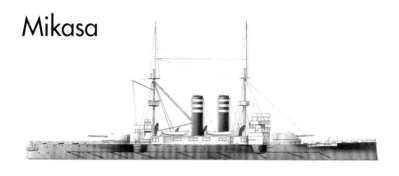

Completed in 1902, *Mikasa* was the last battleship built under the Japanese naval expansion programme of 1896, and was the flagship of Vice-Admiral Togo during the Russo-Japanese War of 1904–05. In February 1904 she was hit three times during the bombardment of Port Arthur, and in August she was again damaged by gunfire in the Battle of the Yellow Sea, receiving 22 hits. She took yet more serious damage at the Battle of Tsushinma on 27 May 1905, when she was hit 32 times. On 12 September that year she sank at her moorings at Sasebo after an ammunition explosion in her after magazine that left 114 crew dead, but was refloated and recommissioned in August 1906. In 1921 she was reclassified as a coastal defence ship. She retired in 1923 after running aground, and is now on permanent public display as the last surviving battleship of her period.

Country of origin:	Japan
Crew:	830
Weight:	15,422 tonnes (15,179 tons)
Dimensions:	131.7m x 23.2m x 8.2m (432ft x76ft 3in x 27ft 2in)
Range:	16,677km (9000nm) at 10 knots
Armour:	229mm – 102mm (9in – 4in) belt, 75mm – 50mm (3in – 2in) on deck, 356mm – 203mm (14in – 8in) on turrets
Armament:	Four 305mm (12in), 14 152mm (6in) guns
Powerplant:	Twin screw, vertical triple expansion engines
Performance:	18 knots

Minas Gerais

Minas Gerais was originally designed as a pre-dreadnought battleship in answer to the powerful vessels then being built for Chile. Her design was later modified and she became the first powerful dreadnought to be built for a minor navy. She was constructed in Britain and completed in 1910. She was extensively modernised in the USA in 1923, and again in Brazil from 1934 to 1937. *Minas Gerais* was scrapped in 1954. Brazil offered the services of both ships of this class (the other being *Sao Paulo*) for service with the British Grand Fleet in 1917, after the country revoked its neutrality and seized German ships in Brazilian ports, but the offer was declined because of fuel problems. Tentative plans for Brazilian warships to serve in European waters in 1918 under the command of Admiral Bonti did not materialise.

Country of origin:	Brazil
Crew:	900
Weight:	21,540 tonnes (21,200 tons)
Dimensions:	165.8m x 25.3m x 8.5m (544ft x 83ft x 27ft 10in)
Range:	18,000km (10,000nm) at 10 knots
Armour:	229mm (9in) belt, 304mm – 229mm (12in – 9in) on turrets
Armament:	12 304mm (12in), 22 120mm (4.7in) guns
Powerplant:	Twin screw, vertical triple reciprocating engines
Performance:	21 knots

Missouri

*M**issouri*** was the last Confederate ironclad to see active service during the American Civil War. She was laid down in December 1862 and was completed by the following September, for service on the rivers still under Confederate control. The vessel had a 40m (130ft) long casemate housing her mixed armament. The single 6.7m- (22ft-) diameter paddle wheel was situated aft in the casemate, which was plated with 114mm- (4.5in-) thick railroad iron laid at an angle to avoid having to cut it. The armour was laid in two interlocking layers, and extended 1.8m (6ft) below the waterline. *Missouri* served as a troop transport and minelayer until she was surrendered to Union forces in June 1865, two months after the official Confederate surrender. All the scattered Confederate forces, apart from an isolated command in the Indian Territory, had laid down their arms by May. *Missouri* was sold in 1865.

Country of origin:	Confederate States of America
Crew:	100
Weight:	399
Dimensions:	55.7m x 17m x 2.6m (183ft x 55ft 8in x 8ft 6in)
Range:	1853km (1000nm) at 5 knots
Armour:	102mm (4in) on casemate, plus wooden backing
Armament:	One 228mm (9in), one 280mm (11in), one 32-pounder guns
Powerplant:	Single paddle wheel, poppet valve engines
Performance:	6 knots

Moltke

Moltke was laid down in 1909 and completed in 1911, and like her sister *Goeben* was the successor to the battlecruiser *Von der Tann*, having two more 280mm (11.1in) guns in a second aft turret. *Moltke* served with Admiral Hipper's squadron in World War I and had a remarkable war, surviving two torpedo strikes from British submarines as well as 304mm (12in) shell hits at Jutland. She saw action at Dogger Bank and the Heligoland Bight and took part in the bombardment of English east coast towns. The bombardment of these 'soft' targets, which took place at intervals between November 1914 and the spring of 1916, caused much outrage among the British public, and added to the wealth of stories about German atrocities of the time. *Moltke* was torpedoed by the British submarine *E42* but survived. In 1919 she was scuttled with the rest of the German fleet. In 1927 she was raised and scrapped.

Country of origin:	Germany
Crew:	1355 (at Jutland)
Weight:	25,704 tonnes (25,300 tons)
Dimensions:	186.5m x 29.5m x 9m (611ft 11in x 96ft 10in x 26ft 11in)
Range:	7416km (4120nm) at 12 knots
Armour:	270mm – 102mm (10.7in – 4in) belt, 230mm – 30mm (8.9in – 1.1in) on barbettes, 230mm (8.9in) on turrets
Armament:	Ten 280mm (11.1in), 12 150mm (5.9in) guns
Powerplant:	Four shaft geared turbines
Performance:	28 knots

Monadnock

In 1862 four powerful, double-turreted monitors, the Miantonomoh class, were ordered by the US Navy. Like their predecessors, their production was rushed, and their unseasoned wooden hulls were prone to deterioration. Early plans specified a Coles turret, but this was dropped in favour of the Ericsson type, which was not so effective. *Monadnock* was commissioned in 1864, too late to serve in the American Civil War, and she was sent to the Pacific coast. The Miantonomoh class were good seaboats, and were very steady gun platforms even in bad weather. *Monadnock* was named after a mountain in New Hampshire; the other vessels in the class were the *Agamenticus* (a mountain in Maine), *Miantonomoh* (chief of the Narragansett Indians) and *Tonawanda*, (a township in New York.) All were decommissioned and scrapped at about the same time. *Monadnock* was scrapped in 1875.

Country of origin:	USA
Crew:	150
Weight:	3454 tonnes (3400 tons)
Dimensions:	78.8m x 16m x 3.9m (258ft 6in x 52ft 9in x 12ft 8in)
Range:	2316km (1250nm) at 8 knots
Armour:	254mm (10in) on turrets, 127mm (5in) on hull, 50mm (2in) on deck
Armament:	Four 380mm (15in) guns
Powerplant:	Twin screw, vibrating lever engines
Performance:	9 knots

Monarch

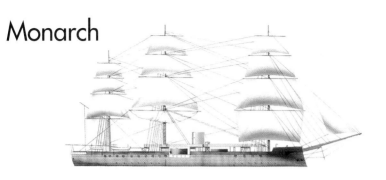

Monarch was the first large, ocean-going turret ship of the monitor type, and the first to carry 304mm (12in) guns. Completed in 1869, she had a forecastle and poop, and still carried a full sailing rig. Her engines developed 7842hp, and upon completion she was the fastest battleship in the world. Her twin turrets were surmounted by a flying bridge. In 1869–70 she made a voyage to the USA, and after her first refit in 1871 she was assigned to the Mediterranean Fleet. In 1882, during the Egyptian campaign, she bombarded Alexandria together with other Royal Navy warhips, an action that provoked the resignation of the Liberal politician John Bright from the British government. Two torpedo launchers were added in 1878, and she underwent a full modernisation in 1890–97 when she was re-engined. She became a depot ship in 1904, and was renamed *Simoom*. She was sold in 1906.

Country of origin:	Great Britain
Crew:	575
Weight:	8455 tonnes (8322 tons)
Dimensions:	100.5m x 17.5m x 7.3m (330ft x 57ft 6in x 24ft 2in)
Range:	3706km (2000nm) at 10 knots
Armour:	178mm – 114mm (7in – 4.5in) belt, 254mm – 203mm (10in – 8in) on turrets
Armament:	Four 304mm (12in), three 178mm (7in) muzzle-loading rifles
Powerplant:	Single screw, return connecting rod engines
Performance:	14.9 knots

Monarch

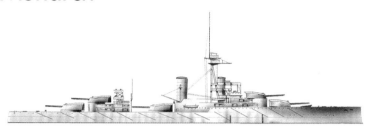

*M*onarch was one of four units that were the first vessels to carry 343mm (13.5in) guns since the days of the Royal Sovereign class of 1889. With a massive increase of 2540 tonnes (2500 tons) displacement over contemporary dreadnoughts, *Monarch* and her three sisters of the Orion class were called 'super-dreadnoughts'. They were the first capital ships of the dreadnought era to carry all the main guns on the centreline. Armour protection was thorough, the side armour rising to upper deck level 5m (17ft) above the waterline. All ships in the class served at Jutland in 1916. *Monarch* was sunk as a target in 1925. Of the other three, *Conqueror* (damaged in a collision with *Monarch* in December 1914) was broken up at Upnor, Kent in December 1922, as was *Orion*; and *Thunderer*, which ended her career as a seagoing cadet training ship, was broken up at Blyth in 1924.

Country of origin:	Great Britain
Crew:	752
Weight:	26,284 tonnes (25,870 tons)
Dimensions:	177m x 26.9m x 8.7m (580ft x 88ft 6in x 28ft 9in)
Range:	12,114km (6730nm) at 10 knots
Armour:	304mm – 203mm (12in – 8in) belt, 280mm (11in) on turrets
Armament:	10 343mm (13.5in), 16 102mm (4in) guns
Powerplant:	Quadruple screw turbines
Performance:	20.8 knots

Moreno

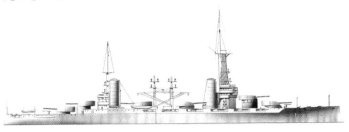

Rivalry between South American republics reached a new height around 1910, when Brazil ordered two powerful dreadnoughts from British yards. Argentina answered with a programme of three dreadnoughts, but owing to financial limitations only two were ordered, from US yards. *Moreno* and her sister *Rivadavia* were modernised in 1924–25. They were converted to run on oil, the lattice mast forward was shortened and the pole mast aft was replaced by a tripod. Displacement increased by 1016 tonnes (1000 tons). In 1937 *Moreno* went on a cruise to Europe, and after service in territorial waters in World War II she successively became a depot ship and a prison ship. Together with her sister ship, *Rivadavia* (which accompanied *Moreno* on her European cruise) she remained Argentina's largest warship until the 1950s. *Moreno* was sold in 1956.

Country of origin:	Argentina
Crew:	1130
Weight:	30,500 tonnes (30,000 tons)
Dimensions:	173.8m x 29.4m x 8.5m (270ft 3in x 96ft 9in x 27ft 10in)
Range:	19,800km (11,000nm) at 12 knots
Armour:	304mm – 254mm (12in – 10in) belt, 304mm (12in) on turrets
Armament:	12 304mm (12in), 12 152mm (6in), guns
Powerplant:	Three shaft geared turbines
Performance:	22.5 knots

Moskva

Moskva was the first helicopter carrier built for the Soviet Navy. She was laid down in 1962 and completed in 1967. She was designed to counteract the growing threat from the US nuclear-powered missile submarines that first entered service in 1960, and to undertake search and destroy missions. However, by the time *Moskva* and *Leningrad* had been completed at the Nikolayev South shipyard, they were incable of coping with both the numbers and capabilities of NATO submarines, so the building programme was terminated. Classed by the Russians as *PKR* (*Protivolodochnyy Kreyser*, or anti-submarine cruiser) the ships proved to be poor sea boats in heavy weather. *Moskva* has a massive central block which dominates the vessel and houses the major weapons systems and a huge sonar array. She is still on the active list, though her sister ship *Leningrad* was stricken in 1991.

Country of origin:	Soviet Union
Crew:	850
Weight:	14,800 tonnes (14,567 tons)
Dimensions:	191m x 34m x 7.6m (626ft 8in x 111ft 6in x 25ft)
Range:	8100km (4500nm) at 12 knots
Armour:	102mm (4in) deck, 51mm (2in) superstructure
Armament:	One twin SUW-N-1 launcher, two twin SA-N-3 missile launchers, 14 – 20 helicopters
Powerplant:	Twin screw turbines
Performance:	30 knots

Mount Whitney

America's Pacific battles during World War II convinced the US Navy and Marine Corps of the value of specialised amphibious assault forces. There was a core of experience in mounting amphibious operations, which was used to construct the Guam class assault ships. *Mount Whitney*, launched in 1969, and her sister ship *Blue Ridge*, use the same hull form and machinery as the Guam class, and have flat open decks to allow maximum antenna placement. There is a helicopter flight deck aft. These ships are crammed with communications equipment, while there are briefing areas, planning facilities and command spaces. They have space for 200 staff officers and 500 men. Their engines develop 22,000hp, and range at 16 knots is 25,650km (13,500 miles). They have limited self-defence weapons, and normally rely on an escorting task force for protection. They now serve as fleet flagships.

Country of origin:	USA
Crew:	720, plus 700 fleet staff
Weight:	19,598 tonnes (19,290 tons)
Dimensions:	189m x 25m x 8.2m (620ft 5in x 82ft x 27ft)
Range:	25,650km (13,500) at 16 knots
Armour:	Command centres protected by 51mm (2in) Kevlar
Armament:	Two 76mm (3in) guns, two 8-tube Sea Sparrow missile launchers (removed in 1992)
Powerplant:	Single screw turbines
Performance:	23 knots

Nagato

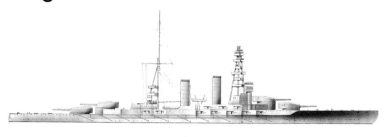

Nagato and her sister *Mutsu* heralded a new era in battleship design with the adoption of the 406mm (16in) gun. Completed in 1920, it had a range of some 40,233m (44,000yds), combining great accuracy with greater destructive power. A massive tripod foremast rose above a large bridge structure, and in the mid-1920s the first funnel was angled back to clear the bridge and mast of smoke fumes. New machinery requiring only one funnel was installed between 1934 and 1936, and the first funnel was then removed. As flagship of the Combined Fleet she saw action at Midway and in the Battle of the Philippine Sea. In October 1944 she received bomb damage at Leyte Gulf and was out of action for the remainder of the war at Yokosuka. In July 1946 *Nagato* was a target ship for the US nuclear tests at Bikini; severely damaged in the second test, her wreck sank on 29 July.

Country of origin:	Japan
Crew:	1333
Weight:	39,116 tonnes (38,500 tons)
Dimensions:	215.8m x 29m x 9m (708ft x 95ft 1in x 29ft 10in)
Range:	9900km (5500nm) at 10 knots
Armour:	304mm – 102mm (12in – 4in) belt, 304mm (12in) on barbettes and turrets
Armament:	Eight 406mm (16in), 20 140mm (5.5in) guns
Powerplant:	Quadruple screw turbines
Performance:	23 knots

Napoli

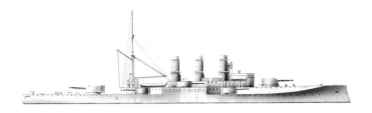

Napoli was designed by Vittorio Cuniberti, and evolved from a project to build an 8128-tonne (8000-ton) ship, protected with 152mm (6in) armour and armed with twelve 203mm (8in) guns that could achieve 22 knots. From this idea Cuniberti developed *Napoli*, a battleship that was faster than any afloat, as well as being far more powerful than any cruiser. Completed in 1907 as one of the Regina Elena class, she was a forerunner of the battlecruiser. Her 304mm (12in) guns were in turrets fore and aft, and the 203mm (8in) guns were in twin turrets, three on each beam. In 1911 she took part in naval operations at Tobruk, and in the bombardment of Benghazi; in 1912 she saw action in the Dardanelles and the Aegean Sea, being part of the covering force during the Italian occupation of Rhodes. In World War I she saw active service in the Adriatic. *Napoli* was removed from service in 1926.

Country of origin:	Italy
Crew:	764
Weight:	14,338 tonnes (14,112 tons)
Dimensions:	144.6m x 22.4m x 8.5m (474ft 5in x 73ft 6in x 27ft 10in)
Range:	18,000km (10,000nm) at 12 knots
Armour:	245mm (9.8in) on sides, 203mm (8in) on turrets
Armament:	Two 304mm (12in), 12 203mm (8in) guns
Powerplant:	Twin screw, vertical triple expansion engines
Performance:	22 knots

Nashville

Nashville was built at Montgomery, Alabama, and was completed at Mobile. While her casemate and pilot houses were armoured, her huge paddle wheel houses were not. She entered service in early 1865, forming part of the main Confederate defence force against Union forces in and around Mobile. When Mobile fell in 1865, *Nashville* headed up river to make a final stand, but she ran aground on 10 May 1865 and surrendered. Mobile was of particular strategic importance to the Confederates, being one terminus of the Mobile and Ohio railroad. This joined with the Memphis and Charleston Railroad, the Confederacy's only east-west cross-country link. Responsibility for guarding the coast between Mobile and Pensacola was assigned to General Braxton Bragg in the early part of the war; he commanded the Confederate II Corps in the Battle of Shiloh (April 1862).

Country of origin:	Confederate States of America
Crew:	80
Weight:	Unknown
Dimensions:	82m x 18.8m (30m over paddle houses) x 3.2m (271ft x 62ft 6in {95ft over paddle wheel houses} x 10ft 6in)
Range:	Unknown
Armour:	Three layers of 50mm (2in) plate
Armament:	Three 178mm (7in) guns, one 24-pounder howitzer
Powerplant:	Paddlewheels, twin side-lever engines
Performance:	6 knots

Nassau

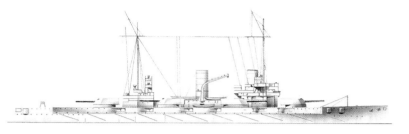

Nassau was laid down in 1906 as Germany's first dreadnought, though she was not commissioned until 1910. She was the first ship in the Nassau class, which also included *Westfalen*, *Posen* and *Rheinland*. Originally designed to carry only eight guns in her main armament, two extra double turrets were included in her construction which affected her performance, though she was still a steady gun platform. Present at the Battle of Jutland, during which she survived a collision with the British destroyer *Spitfire*, *Nassau* surrendered at the end of World War I and was scrapped in 1921. Of the other ships in her class, *Westfalen* survived being torpedoed by the British submarine *E23* in August 1916 and was broken up in 1924; *Posen* collided with the cruiser *Elbing* at Jutland and was stricken in 1919; and *Rheinland* went aground during landings in Finland in April 1918, and was stricken in 1919.

Country of origin:	Germany
Crew:	966
Weight:	20,533 tonnes (20,210 tons)
Dimensions:	146m x 27m x 8.5m (479ft 4in x 88ft 3in x 27ft 10in)
Range:	10,2609km (5700nm) at 10 knots
Armour:	293mm – 102mm (11.75in – 4in) belt, 304mm (12in) on turrets
Armament:	12 150mm (5.9in), 12 279mm (11in) guns
Powerplant:	Triple screw, vertical triple expansion engines
Performance:	20 knots

Navarin

Navarin was based upon the successful British Nile class battleship. She was laid down in 1889 in St Petersburg. She had a rectangular central superstructure which held the 152mm (6in) guns in broadside, protected by 127mm (5in) armour. Her main 304mm (12in) guns were mounted in two twin armoured turrets, fore and aft of the superstructure. She was well-protected, with her main belt covering the centre section in two strakes. There was also a 76mm (3in) thick armoured deck which rested on top of the main belt. *Navarin* took part in the Battle of Tsushima in May 1905, where the Russian fleet was destroyed by superior Japanese gunnery and ship handling. The next day, on 28 May 1905, she made a run for Vladivostock, but was torpedoed by Japanese destroyers. She sank with heavy loss of life. She was named after the Battle of Navarino, in which an Allied fleet defeated Turkey in 1827.

Country of origin:	Russia
Crew:	622
Weight:	10,370 tonnes (10,206 tons)
Dimensions:	109m x 20.4m x 8.3m (357ft 7in x 67ft x 27ft 6in)
Range:	5652km (3050nm) at 10 knots
Armour:	406mm – 203mm (16in – 8in) belt, 305mm (12in) on turrets, 127mm (5in) on battery
Armament:	Four 304mm (12in), eight 152mm (6in) guns
Powerplant:	Twin screw, vertical triple expansion engines
Performance:	15.5 knots

Nelson

Nelson and her sister ship *Rodney* were the first battleships to be completed within the limits of the Washington Treaty of 1922, which fixed the maximum displacement for each class of vessel. They were also the first British warships to carry 406mm (16in) guns. Completed in 1927, *Nelson*'s main armament was concentrated forward of the tower bridge in three triple turrets, saving on armour weight. More weight was saved by adopting less powerful machinery. The secondary battery was carried in twin turrets level with the main mast. The engine rooms were placed forward of the boiler rooms to keep the bridge structure clear of funnel smoke. She was out of action for nearly a year after being torpedoed by Italian aircraft while escorting the Malta convoy 'Halberd' on 27 September 1941, and was damaged by a German torpedo off Normandy in July 1944. Both ships were scrapped in 1948–49.

Country of origin:	Great Britain
Crew:	1361 (as flagship)
Weight:	38,608 tonnes (38,000 tons)
Dimensions:	216.8m x 32.4m x 9.6m (711ft x 106ft 4in x 31ft 6in)
Range:	30,574km (16,500nm) at 12 knots
Armour:	356mm – 330mm (14in – 13in) belt, 380mm – 350mm (15in – 12in) on barbettes, 406mm (16in) on turrets
Armament:	Nine 406mm (16in), 12 152mm (6in) guns
Powerplant:	Twin screw turbines
Performance:	23.5 knots

Nelson

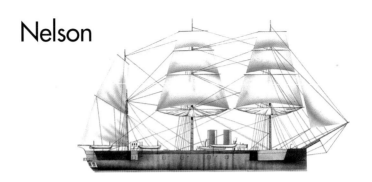

L aunched in 1876, *Nelson* was built in answer to the growing number of Russian armoured cruisers then in service or under construction. She and her sister *Northampton* were intended for overseas service, mainly in the Pacific where the lack of coaling stations meant long periods at sea under sail alone. From 1881 to 1885 *Nelson* served on the Australian station before returning to England for a refit; her sister ship, *Northampton*, was stationed off North America and the West Indies. She later became a seagoing training ship for boys and was sold and broken up at Morecambe in 1905. Both ships were classed as armoured frigates. *Nelson* carried 1168 tonnes (1150 tons) of coal herself, but also carried a barque rig of 2201 sq m (23,690 sq ft). She became a stokers' training ship in 1901 and was sold in 1910.

Country of origin:	Great Britain
Crew:	560
Weight:	7592km (7473 tons)
Dimensions:	85.3m x 18.3m x 7.6m (280ft x 60ft x 24ft)
Range:	9265km (5000nm) at 10 knots
Armour:	229mm – 152mm (9in – 6in) belt and bulkheads, 75mm – 50mm (3in – 2in) on deck
Armament:	Four 254mm (10in), eight 229mm (9in) muzzle-loading rifles
Powerplant:	Twin screw, three cylinder engine
Performance:	14 knots

Neptune

Neptune was originally *Independencia*, designed for the Brazilian Navy in 1872. She was taken over during a period when war between Britain and Russia seemed likely, and she was converted at Portsmouth for service in the Royal Navy. The 304mm (12in) guns were in twin turrets amidships, separated by a short superstructure that supported a flying bridge. The two 229mm (9in) guns were under the forecastle. Because the sails on the mainmast were so close to the funnels, the sails had to be replaced several times due to smoke rot. *Neptune* was broken up in 1903. She had an unfortunate start and finish to her career, becoming stuck in the mud during her launching ceremony on 30 July 1874 and remaining there until 10 September. In 1903, while being towed through Portsmouth harbour, she rammed HMS *Victory*, collided with the battleship *Hero* and narrowly missed several others.

Country of origin:	Great Britain
Crew:	541
Weight:	9276 tonnes (9130 tons)
Dimensions:	91.4m x 19.2m x 7.6m (300ft x 63ft x 25ft)
Range:	2742km (1480nm) at 10 knots
Armour:	304mm - 229mm (12in – 9in) belt, 254mm (10in) on citadel, 330mm – 279mm (13in – 11in) on turrets
Armament:	Four 304mm (12in), two 229mm (9in) guns
Powerplant:	Single screw, horizontal trunk engines
Performance:	14.2 knots

Nevada

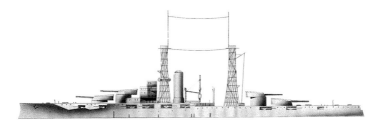

Nevada was one of the first battleships to be built on the 'all-or-nothing' principle, adopted by other navies after World War I, in which the thickest possible armour was applied to vital areas, leaving the rest virtually unprotected. She and her sister *Oklahoma* were second-generation dreadnoughts, and were the first US battleships to burn only oil fuel. Launched in 1914, and seeing service off Ireland in World War I, *Nevada* was badly damaged at Pearl Harbor in December 1941. After repairs, she served as one of the bombardment force of warships at the Normandy landings of June 1944, and off southern France in August before returning to the Pacific, where she was damaged by a kamikaze and shore batteries. In July 1946 she was a target vessel at Bikini, an experience she survived. She was sunk as a target by aircraft and gunfire off Hawaii in July 1948.

Country of origin:	USA
Crew:	1374 (during World War II)
Weight:	29,362 tonnes (28,900 tons)
Dimensions:	177.7m x 29m x 9.5m (583ft x 95ft 3in x 31ft)
Range:	18,530km (10,000nm) at 10 knots
Armour:	343mm – 203mm (13.5in – 8in) belt, 450mm – 229mm (18in – 9in) on turrets
Armament:	21 127mm (5in), 10 355mm (14in) guns
Powerplant:	Twin screw turbines
Performance:	20.5 knots

New Ironsides

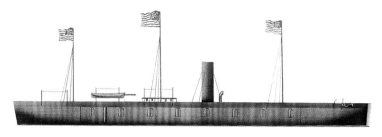

New Ironsides was one of three ironclads ordered in 1861. Launched in 1862 she was wooden-hulled, with iron plates covering her battery and located in a continuous belt below the waterline. Originally rigged as a barque, she served as the Union flagship, and although she saw constant action during the Civil War, her armour was never pierced. During that unhappy conflict she served successively with the South Atlantic and North Atlantic Blockading Squadrons. On 8 September 1863 she was hit 50 times during an attack on Fort Moultrie, and on 5 October she survived a spar torpedo attack by the Confederate topside boat *David* off Charleston without damage. Her crew became convinced that she was invulnerable, which she virtually was. She was destroyed by a fire in Philadelphia in 1865.

Country of origin:	USA
Crew:	449
Weight:	4277 tonnes (4210 tons)
Dimensions:	70m x 17.5m x 4.8m (232ft x 57ft 6in x 15ft 8in)
Range:	2780km (1500nm) at 10 knots
Armour:	112mm – 75mm (4.5in – 3in) belt, 112mm (4.5in) over battery
Armament:	14 280mm (11in), two 150-pounder and two 50-pounder guns
Powerplant:	Single screw, horizontal direct acting engines
Performance:	6.5 knots

New York

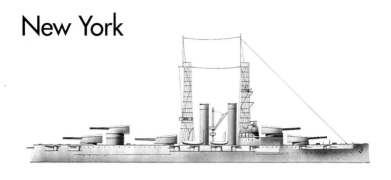

*N*ew York was laid down in September 1911 and completed in April 1914. Her engines developed 29,687hp and coal supply was 2964 tonnes (2917 tons), plus 406 tonnes (400 tons) of fuel oil. In 1916, she was the first American battleship to fit anti-aircraft guns. From 1914–19 she served with the US Atlantic Fleet, and for the last year of World War I she was assigned to the Royal Navy's Grand Fleet. After reconstruction work at Norfolk, during which her cage masts were replaced by tripods, she was again assigned to the Atlantic Fleet from 1936 to 1941, and in 1939 she was experimentally fitted with the first shipborne radar. Service in World War II took her to North Africa, Iwo Jima and Okinawa, where she was slightly damaged by a kamikaze. Having survived World War II, *New York* went on to survive the Bikini atomic bomb tests in 1946. She was sunk as a target off Pearl Harbor in 1948.

Country of origin:	USA
Crew:	1042
Weight:	28,854 tonnes (28,400 tons)
Dimensions:	174.6m x 29m x 9m (573ft x 95ft 2in x 29ft 6in)
Range:	12,708km (7060nm) at 12 knots
Armour:	304mm – 254mm (12in – 10in) belt and barbettes, 356mm (14in) on turrets
Armament:	10 356mm (14in), 21 127mm (5in) guns
Powerplant:	Twin screw, triple expansion engines
Performance:	21.4 knots

Nile

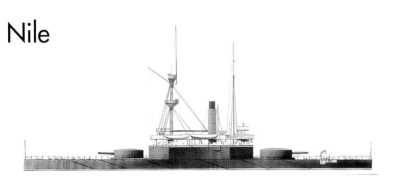

Nile and her sister *Trafalgar* were the heaviest battleships in the Royal Navy when construction. Launched in 1888, the *Nile*'s weaponry reflected the principle of combining the heaviest armament with maximum protection. The 343mm (13.5in) guns were mounted in twin, hydraulically operated, turrets on the centreline, some 4.2m (14ft) above the waterline. These were positioned fore and aft of the octagonal citadel. This held the 120mm (4.7in) guns, which were protected by bulkheads 127mm (5in) thick. Later the 120mm (4.7in) guns were replaced by more modern 152mm (6in) weapons. When she was completed in 1891, many naval officers felt that she would be one of the last capital ships to be built, because of the perceived threat of the torpedo boats then entering service. *Nile* spent most of her service in the Mediterranean before ending up as a training ship. She was scrapped in 1912.

Country of origin:	Great Britain
Crew:	577
Weight:	12,791 tonnes (12,590 tons)
Dimensions:	105m x 22m x 8.6m (345ft x 73ft x 28ft 6in)
Range:	12,044km (6500nm) at 10 knots
Armour:	500mm – 356mm (20in – 14in) belt, 450mm – 400mm (18in – 16in) on citadel, 450mm (18in) on turrets
Armament:	Four 343mm (13.5in), six 120mm (4.7in) guns
Powerplant:	Twin screw, triple expansion engines
Performance:	17 knots

North Carolina

North Carolina and her sister *Washington* were the first US battleships built after the lifting of the 1922 Washington Naval Treaty. However, the original design followed the later London Treaty which allowed for 355mm (14in) guns, but as the Japanese refused to restrict their main armament, the USA decided to fit *North Carolina* with triple 400mm (16in) gun turrets after her launch in 1940. By 1945 her weaponry had been replaced by mainly anti-aircraft weapons, namely 96 x 40mm (1.6in), and 36 x 20mm (0.8in) guns. She fought in the Pacific, from Guadalcanal to the final strikes on Japan. On 15 September 1942 she was torpedoed by the Japanese submarine *I-19* near Espiritu Santu, together with the destroyer USS *O'Brien*, which was sunk, and on 6 April 1945 she was hit by friendly fire off Okinawa. She was stricken in 1960, and is now preserved at Wilmington, North Carolina.

Country of origin:	USA
Crew:	1880
Weight:	47,518 tonnes (46,770 tons)
Dimensions:	222m x 33m x 10m (728ft 9in x 108ft 3in x 32ft 10in)
Range:	32,334km (17,450nm) at 12 knots
Armour:	304mm – 165mm (12in – 6.6in) belt, 140mm (5.5in) on deck, 400mm (16in) on barbettes and turrets
Armament:	Nine 400mm (16in), 20 127mm (5in) guns
Powerplant:	Quadruple screw turbines
Performance:	28 knots

Numancia

Numancia was an iron-hulled, broadside ironclad and was laid down at La Seyne in 1861. She was flagship during the war between Spain, Peru and Chile in 1865, and took part in the bombardment of Valparaiso on 27 March 1866. On 30 April she sustained 51 hits from shore batteries during an attack on Callao, but escaped undamaged. In 1867–68 she became the first armoured vessel to circumnavigate the world. In 1873 she was seized by insurgents during the Carlist civil war, and was damaged by gunfire and collision. Returned to the government, she operated against the Riffs in Spanish Morocco. She was completely rebuilt during 1897–98 when her armament was changed to include eight 254mm (10in), and seven 203mm (8in) rifled muzzle-loaders and two torpedo launchers. By 1914 she was a gunnery training ship. She sank while under tow to the breakers in 1916.

Country of origin:	Spain
Crew:	500
Weight:	7304 tonnes (7189 tons)
Dimensions:	96m x 17.3m x 8.2m (315ft x 57ft x 27ft)
Range:	5559km (3000nm) at 10 knots
Armour:	140mm – 102mm (5.6in– 4in) belt, 444mm (17.7in) wooden backing
Armament:	40 68-pounder guns (as launched)
Powerplant:	Single screw, non-compound engines
Performance:	13 knots

Oregon

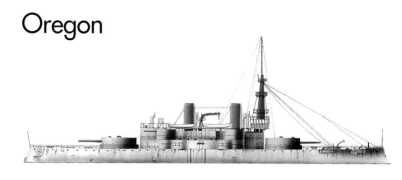

In 1889 the US Congress denied a request for 192 warships to be built over a 15-year period, and so the US Navy made do with three 'sea-going coastline battleships'. This designation was the only way the Navy could get the approval of Congress. The ships were the vessels of the Oregon class, and they carried heavy armament and protection on a small displacement which resulted in a low freeboard, limited endurance and low speed. In 1898 *Oregon* took part in the Battle of Santiago Bay during the war with Spain. After years as a floating monument, she was sold for scrap in 1942, but reprieved and in 1944 was used as an ammunition hulk in the Pacific. On 14 November 1948 she went adrift in a typhoon; she was not located until 8 December, when she was discovered 500 miles southeast of Guam and towed back. She was sold and broken up in Japan in 1956.

Country of origin:	USA
Crew:	636
Weight:	10,452 tonnes (10,288 tons)
Dimensions:	106.9m x 21m x 7.3m (351ft x 69ft 3in x 24ft)
Range:	8338km (4500nm) at 10 knots
Armour:	450mm – 102mm (18in – 4in), 425mm (17in) on barbettes, 380mm (15in) on turrets
Armament:	Four 330mm (13in), eight 203mm (8in), four 152mm (6in) guns
Powerplant:	Twin screw, vertical triple expansion engines
Performance:	15 knots

Palestro

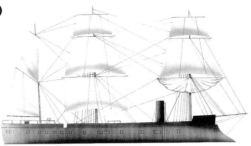

***P**alestro* was laid down at La Seyne in August 1864 and completed in January 1866. She and her sister ship *Varese* had iron hulls and a full barque rig. Her steam engines were capable of generating 930hp though it was intended that she should rely on her sails. On 20 July 1866, she and two other Italian ironclads, *Re d'Italia* and *San Martino*, met seven Austrian ironclads near Lissa. In the following battle *Palestro* suffered numerous hits. Fires were started, and she had to limp out of the fight. Two other Italian ships took her in tow, and boats were launched to take off the crew. Captain Capellini refused to abandon ship, and his crew volunteered to stay and fight the fire. It was to no avail and shortly afterwards she exploded and sank. Only 19 men from 250 survived. *Varese* served until 1891, although in her later years as a hospital ship.

Country of origin:	Italy
Crew:	252
Weight:	2642 tonnes (2600 tons)
Dimensions:	64.8m x 13m x 5.6m (212ft 7in x 42ft 8in x 18ft 4in)
Range:	3335km (1800nm) at 10 knots
Armour:	120mm (4.7in) belt, 120mm (4.7in) on battery
Armament:	Four 203mm (8in), one 164mm (6.5in) gun
Powerplant:	Single screw, reciprocating engines
Performance:	8 knots

Palestro

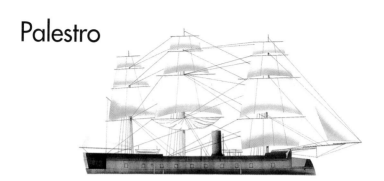

Palestro and her sister *Principe Amedeo* were the first ironclads to be built in Italian yards. They were also the last to have composite hulls with iron framing and wooden planking, and to carry sails. Due to the aftermath of the war with Austria in 1866, *Palestro* and her sister were six years on the stocks and took another four years to complete, *Palestro* entering service in July 1875. She had a full-length armour belt, a pronounced ram bow and 3413 sq m (36,740 sq ft) of canvas. She was used as a local defence vessel at La Maddalena after 1889, and was then assigned the role of boys' training ship at La Spezia. Her sister ship, *Principe Amedeo*, saw service in the Levant before also being relegated to the local defence role at Taranto. *Palestro* was removed from the effective list in 1900 and broken up in 1902–04.

Country of origin:	Italy
Crew:	548
Weight:	6374 tonnes (6274 tons)
Dimensions:	79.7m x 17.5m x 7.5m (261ft 6in x 57ft 5in x 24ft 7in)
Range:	3204km (1780nm) at 10 knots
Armour:	220mm (8.7in) belt, 140mm (5.5in) on battery
Armament:	12 160mm (6.3in) guns
Powerplant:	Single screw, single expansion engine
Performance:	12.85 knots

Pelayo

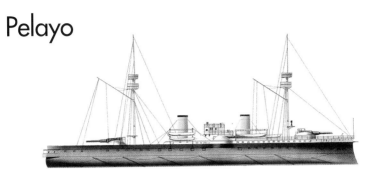

Launched in 1887, *Pelayo* was Spain's most powerful warship for over 20 years. She was built in France to designs by Lagane, one of the world's leading naval architects. She was based on the French *Marceau*, with slightly increased length and beam, and with reduced draught to allow her passage through the Suez Canal. *Pelayo* was rebuilt in 1897, and was given new boilers and armour over the midship battery. In 1898, at the time of the Spanish-American War, she set sail for the Philippines at the head of a squadron of warships, but was held up at Port Said and recalled when the conflict ended. The brief war with the USA cost Spain her entire Pacific Squadron, destroyed in the Battle of Manila Bay, and a second squadron, despatched to the Caribbean. It remained blockaded in Santiago harbour until it emerged and was sunk by waiting US warships. *Pelayo* was removed from the effective list in 1925.

Country of origin:	Spain
Crew:	520
Weight:	9900 tonnes (9745 tons)
Dimensions:	102m x 20m x 7.5m (334ft 8in x 66ft 3in x 24ft 9in)
Range:	3204km (1780nm) at 10 knots
Armour:	443mm – 293mm (17.75in – 11.75in) steel belt, 393mm – 293mm (15.75in – 11.75in) on barbettes
Armament:	Two 317mm (12.5in), two 279mm (11in), one 162mm (6.4in), 12 120mm (4.7in) guns
Powerplant:	Twin screw, vertical compound engines
Performance:	16.7 knots

Pennsylvania

***P**ennsylvania* was completed in 1916 and with her sister *Arizona* boasted a main armament of 12 356mm (14in) guns triple-mounted in four turrets. The triple mount later became a characteristic of American capital ships. *Pennsylvania* was reconstructed between the wars to include a large anti-aircraft armament, two aircraft catapults, two tripod masts and a strengthened submarine bulge and bulkheads. She came through World War II, though *Arizona* did not, being destroyed at Pearl Harbor in 1941. *Pennsylvania* herself was damaged by bombs while in dry dock at Pearl Harbor, and after reconstruction she fought at Attu, the Gilbert Islands, Kwajalein, Eniwetok, Saipan, Guam, Palau, Leyte Gulf, Surigao Strait and Lingayen. On 12 August 1945 she was severely damaged by an aerial torpedo. After the war she took part in two nuclear bomb tests, ending her days as a target ship.

Country of origin:	USA
Crew:	915
Weight:	33,088 tonnes (32,567 tons)
Dimensions:	182.9m x 185.4 x 29.6m x 8.8m (608ft x 97ft 1in x 28ft 10in)
Range:	14,400km (8000nm) at 12 knots
Armour:	343mm – 203mm (13.5in – 8in) belt, 450mm (18in) on turret
Armament:	12 356mm (14in), 22 127mm (5in) guns
Powerplant:	Four shaft, geared turbines
Performance:	21 knots

Petr Veliki

P*etr Veliki* was a large, breastwork turret ship with an iron hull and 2.4m (8ft) freeboard. Her armour belt was complete, but submerged at full load. Her side armour had 550mm (22in) of wood between two plates of 175mm (7in). Completed in 1872, she received new engines in a refit in 1881, and was reconstructed in 1905–06. Renamed *Barrikada* after the 1917 revolution, she served as a gunnery training ship with the Baltic fleet. She was scrapped in 1922. The Russian Revolution destroyed the effectiveness of the fleet, especially that of the larger ships, which were completely immobilised. Without their officers, who had either been killed or were with the White Russian forces, the ships were controlled by enlisted men, who had little idea of how to operate or maintain them. Many of the ships under White control sailed for Tunisia at the end of the civil war.

Country of origin:	Russia
Crew:	432
Weight:	10,572 tonnes (10,406 tons)
Dimensions:	103.5m x 18.9m x 8.2m (339ft 8in x 62ft 3in x 27ft)
Range:	3706km (2000nm) at 10 knots
Armour:	356mm (14in) wrought iron on belt, citadel and turrets
Armament:	Four 305mm (12in), six 86mm (3.4in) guns
Powerplant:	Twin screw, horizontal return connecting rod engines
Performance:	10 knots

Pobieda

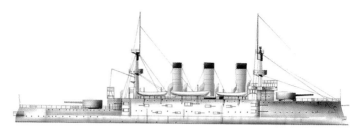

Completed in 1902, *Pobieda*'s engines developed 15,000hp, and coal supply was 2032 tonnes (2000 tons). *Pobieda*, *Peresviet* and *Osliabia*, all of the same class, were the first Russian warships to feature quick-firing guns. They had a high forecastle with their secondary armament mounted on two decks. *Pobieda* joined the Pacific squadron in 1903, in time for the war with Japan; in February 1904 she was slightly damaged by gunfire in action at Port Arthur, and further damaged by a mine in April, but survived thanks to the protection given by her coal bunker and internal armour. On 10 August she took 11 hits in the Battle of the Yellow Sea, and was again repeatedly hit by shore batteries in October–November. In December 1904 she was sunk by salvos of 279mm (11in) shells, but raised by the Japanese in 1905 and renamed *Suwo*. She was scrapped in 1922.

Country of origin:	Russia
Crew:	757
Weight:	12,872 tonnes (12,670 tons)
Dimensions:	133m x 21.7m x 8.3m (436ft 4in x 71ft 5in x 27ft 3in)
Range:	11,118km (6000nm) at 10 knots
Armour:	229mm – 127mm (9in – 5in) belt, 254mm – 127mm (10in – 5in) on turrets, 127mm (5in) on casemates
Armament:	Four 254mm (10in), 11 152mm (6in), 20 75mm (3in), guns
Powerplant:	Triple screw, vertical triple expansion engines
Performance:	18.5 knots

Prince Albert

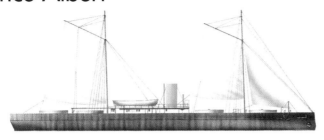

*P*rince Albert was Britain's first iron turret ship, and was built by Cowper Coles as a direct challenge to Admiralty policy. The turrets were all carried on the centreline, two forward of the midship superstructure and two aft. *Prince Albert* was originally designed with six turrets, but they were later reduced to four. Each turret weighed 112 tonnes (111 tons) and was hand-worked. The vessel was laid down in 1862, but construction was not completed until four years later, in 1866. Although *Prince Albert* enjoyed a fairly long military career, the warship had a singularly uneventful service life. She was on the reserve for most of her career and finished up in the Particular Service Squadron at Portsmouth in 1878. She was reboilered in the same year. *Prince Albert* was sold in 1899 and subsequently scrapped in 1904.

Country of origin:	Great Britain
Crew:	201
Weight:	3942 tonnes (3880 tons)
Dimensions:	73.1m x 14.6m x 6.2m (240ft x 48ft x 20ft 6in)
Range:	1500km (810nm) at 10 knots
Armour:	112mm (4.5in) belt with 450mm wood backing, 266mm – 140mm (10.5in – 5.5in) on turrets with 356mm (14in) wood backing
Armament:	Four 229mm (9in) muzzle-loading guns
Powerplant:	Single screw, horizontal direct acting engines
Performance:	11.2 knots

Prince of Wales

P*rince of Wales* was launched in 1939 and completed in 1941. Her main armament was housed in two quadruple 356mm (14in) gun turrets fore and aft and a double 356mm (14in) turret superfiring forward. She took part in the hunt for the *Bismark* in May 1941 with her construction incomplete and workers still on her. Whilst engaging the German battleship she took hits on her bridge and below her waterline but survived. In August 1941 she took Winston Churchill to an historic meeting with President Franklin D. Roosevelt in Newfoundland. Later in 1941 she was sent to the Far East as a last-minute defence against the Japanese invasion of Malaya. With the battlecruiser *Repulse* and four destroyers she sortied on 9 December. The next day she and *Repulse* were attacked by Japanese aircraft and within two hours both had been sunk. *Prince of Wales* had been operational for only seven months.

Country of origin:	Great Britain
Crew:	1422
Weight:	41,402 tonnes (42,076 tons)
Dimensions:	227.1m x 31.4m x 9.9m (745ft x 103ft x 32ft 7in)
Range:	25,942km (14,000nm) at 10 knots
Armour:	380mm – 112mm (15in – 4.5in) belt, 330mm – 279mm (13in – 11in) on barbettes, 330mm – 152mm (13in – 6in) on turrets
Armament:	10 356mm (14in), 16 131mm (5.25in) guns
Powerplant:	Four shaft, geared turbines
Performance:	28 knots

Principe di Carignano

P*rincipe di Carignano* was designed as a screw frigate by Engineer Mattei, but
was converted to an ironclad while still on the stocks, though she retained a
barquentine rig. Completed in 1865, she was a broadside vessel with most of her
armament carried on the main deck behind the iron armour. Her engine developed
1960hp, and range at 10 knots was around 2280km (1200 miles). In 1865–66 she
was in service in the Aegean, and in July 1866 she took part in the Lissa campaign,
during which she received some battle damage. After being refitted in 1869 she
was present at the liberation of Rome. She was rearmed in 1870, her 203mm (8in)
guns reduced to four in number, and her 164mm (6.5in) guns increased to 16.
She was discarded in 1875 and broken up between 1877 and 1879. The vessel was
named after Prince Eugenio of Savoy-Carignan (1816–1888), an Italian admiral.

Country of origin:	Italy
Crew:	572
Weight:	4152 tonnes (4086 tons)
Dimensions:	75.8m x 15.2m x 7.2m (248ft 8in x 50ft x 23ft 8in)
Range:	2160km (1200nm) at 10 knots
Armour:	118mm (4.75in) wrought iron on sides
Armament:	10 203mm (8in), 12 164mm (6.5in) guns
Powerplant:	Single screw, single expansion engine
Performance:	10.2 knots

Queen Elizabeth

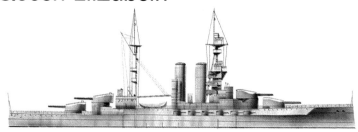

Completed in 1915, *Queen Elizabeth* was a major advance in battleship development, and was the first capital ship to be built with oil-burning boilers. She was fast, but her reliance upon oil fuel concerned critics, who foresaw disaster if oil supplies were ever interrupted. As a result, the following Revenge class carried both coal and oil fuel. She saw service in the Dardanelles in 1915, but missed the Battle of Jutland the following year due to a refit. Converted to a flagship, she was rebuilt between 1937–41. Assigned to the Mediterranean Fleet, she was in action off Crete in May 1941. In December that year she was severely damaged in a daring attack by Italian frogmen in Alexandria harbour. In 1943–44 she served with the Home Fleet, then sailed for the Indian Ocean, where she completed her war service. She was scrapped in 1948–49.

Country of origin:	Great Britain
Crew:	951
Weight:	33,548 tonnes (33,020 tons)
Dimensions:	196.8m x 27.6m x 10m (646ft x 90ft 6in x 30ft)
Range:	8100km (4500nm) at 10 knots
Armour:	330mm – 152mm (13in – 6in) belt, 254mm – 102mm (10in – 4in) on barbettes, 330mm (13in) on turrets
Armament:	Eight 380mm (15in), 16 152mm (6in) guns
Powerplant:	Quadruple screw turbines
Performance:	23 knots

Re d'Italia

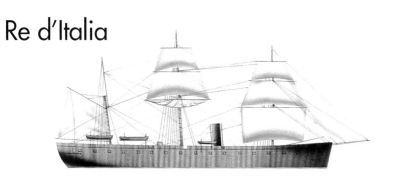

Upon completion *Re d'Italia* and her sister *Re di Portogallo* were Italy's heaviest warships. Being wooden-hulled, they had no internal subdivisions, and although the armour stretched end-to-end, the steering compartment was unprotected. *Re d'Italia* was rammed and sunk by the Austrian flagship *Ferdinand Max* at the Battle of Lissa in July 1866 after her steering had been disabled, with the loss of 383 lives. The vessel was named in honour of Victor Emmanuel II, the first king of a united Italy. Her sister vessel, *di Portogallo* (named in honour of Luis I, king of Portugal [1838–1889], the son-in-law of Victor Emmanuel II) was rammed by the Austrian central battery ship *Kaiser* at the Battle of Lissa, but survived to see further service as an artillery school ship at La Spezia. She was broken up in 1877–89. Lissa is now the Adriatic island of Vis.

Country of origin:	Italy
Crew:	565
Weight:	5791 tonnes (,700 tons)
Dimensions:	84.3m x 16.6m x 6.7m (276ft 7in x 54ft 6in x 22ft)
Range:	5781km (1800nm) at 12 knots
Armour:	118mm (4.75in) wrought iron sides
Armament:	Two 200mm (7.9in), two 72-pounder, 30 160mm (6.3in) guns
Powerplant:	Single screw, single compound engine
Performance:	12 knots

Re Galantuomo

The Italian Navy was founded in 1860 upon the unification of Italy, and the new government at once set about ordering the construction of ironclads in foreign shipyards, including two armoured frigates in the USA. *Re Galantuomo* was Italy's only wooden steam line-of-battle vessel. A two-decker, she was laid down at Cantiere di Castellammare di Stabia, and was completed in 1861. Her engines developed 1351hp, and she carried her guns on two decks. She was rearmed in the early 1870s, when she was given 18 160mm (6.3in) guns. In 1863, the ship transported the crews needed for *Re d'Italia* and *Re di Portogallo* from Italy to the Webbs yard in New York, where the ships were being built. *Re Galantuomo* then served as a coastal defence ship and was at Taranto during the war with Austria in 1866. She was scrapped in 1875.

Country of origin:	Italy
Crew:	976
Weight:	3860 tonnes (3800 tons)
Dimensions:	58.4m x 15.5m x 7m (191ft 7in x 50ft 10in x 23ft 3in)
Range:	4076km (2200nm) at 8 knots
Armour:	None
Armament:	64 cannon (as originally launched)
Powerplant:	Single screw, single direct acting engine
Performance:	9 knots

Re Umberto

Designed by Benedetto Brin, *Re Umberto* was one of three capital ships which, on completion, were the fastest of their type in the world. The two barbettes housing the 343mm (13.5in) guns were mounted on a central pivot, so allowing for all-round loading and a faster rate of fire. This system was adopted by the Royal Navy in 1898. *Re Umberto* was laid down in 1884 and was completed in 1893. She became a depot ship in 1912 and was stricken in 1914. Reinstated in 1915, she was converted into an armed assault ship in 1918, her principal task being to force the enemy-held harbour at Pola. For this purpose her turrets and barbettes were removed and 76mm (3in) guns were mounted, but the war ended before the operation could take place and she never saw action. She was scrapped in 1920. Her sister *Sardegna* was the first warship to have triple expansion engines and one of the first to carry wireless telegraph.

Country of origin:	Italy
Crew:	733
Weight:	15,701 tonnes (15,454 tons)
Dimensions:	127.6m x 23.4m x 9.3m (418ft 8in x 76ft 10in x 30ft 6in)
Range:	11,118km (6000nm) at 10 knots
Armour:	75mm (3in) on deck, 102mm (4in) on side and turrets, 343mm (13.5in) on barbettes
Armament:	Four 343mm (13.5in), eight 152mm (6in), 16 120mm (4.7in) guns
Powerplant:	Twin screw, vertical compound engines
Performance:	20 knots

Regina Margherita

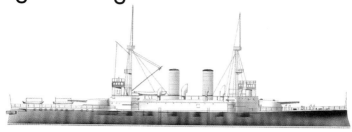

***R**egina Margherita* was designed by Benedetto Brin,with the emphasis placed on speed. As originally designed, the vessel was to have had four 304mm (12in) guns, together with 12 203mm (8in) weapons. However, after Brin's death the plans were revised to feature the mixed armament listed below. An unusual feature of her design was the double bridge fore and aft. *Regina Margherita* sank in 1916 after striking two German mines laid off Valona by the German submarine *UC14*. The loss of life (675) was heavy. They were casualties in a theatre of war often eclipsed by the carnage of the Western Front, but it was of vital importance to the eventual Allied victory. If the Central Powers had succeeded in securing Albania as one of their principalities and had fortified Valona, they could have closed the Adriatic. The Italians prevented them from doing so.

Country of origin:	Italy
Crew:	900
Weight:	13,426 tonnes (13,215 tons)
Dimensions:	138.6m x 23.8m x 8.8m (454ft 10in x 78ft 3in x 28ft 10in)
Range:	18,000km (10,000nm) at 12 knots
Armour:	152mm (6in) on side, 203mm (8in) on turrets, 152mm (6in) on battery
Armament:	Four 304mm (12in), 12 152mm (6in), 20 75mm (3in) guns
Powerplant:	Twin screw, triple expansion engines
Performance:	20.3 knots

Regina Maria Pia

Anxious to build a powerful fleet, Italy ordered four broadside ironclads from France, including *Regina Maria Pia*. She was laid down in 1862 and completed in 1864. Her engine developed 2924hp, and range at ten knots was 4940km (2600 miles). In 1866 she saw action at Porto San Giorgio. Her rig was altered from schooner to barque, and was eventually replaced with two military masts during a refit in 1888–90. She was rearmed to carry two 220mm (8.7in) and nine 203mm (8in) guns, and was later given eight 152mm (6in) and five 120mm (4.7in) guns. In 1886 she was damaged at the Battle of Lissa by shellfire and a collision with the broadside ship *San Martino*; in 1878, after a refit, she took part in a 'police action' to protect Italian interests at Salonika and in 1886 she participated in operations off Crete. In 1895 she was rebuilt as a coastal defence ship before being stricken in 1904.

Country of origin:	Italy
Crew:	900
Weight:	4599 tonnes (4527 tons)
Dimensions:	81.2m x 15.2m x 6.3m (266ft 5in x 50ft x 20ft 10in)
Range:	4940km (2600nm) at 10 knots
Armour:	118mm (4.75in) iron belt
Armament:	22 164mm (6.5in), four 72-pounder guns
Powerplant:	Single screw, single expansion reciprocating engine
Performance:	13 knots

Renown

Constructed in just a year, *Renown* and her sister *Repulse* were the last British battlecruisers. Heavily armed, but sacrificing protective armour for high speed, within a month of her launch in October 1916 *Renown* was back in dock to be fitted with another 492 tonnes (500 tons) of steel plate. Even then she was thought to be too lightly built – even for the recoil of her 380mm (15in) guns – and was to receive extra armour during refits in 1918 and 1923. Converted into a fast carrier escort in 1936, she took part in operations against commerce raiders in the South Atlantic in 1939 and was damaged in action off Norway in April 1940. She subsequently took part in the hunt for *Bismarck*, escorted convoys to Malta, in the Atlantic and the Arctic, and formed part of the covering force during the Allied landings in North Africa. She served with the Eastern Fleet in 1944–45. She was broken up at Faslane in 1948.

Country of origin:	Great Britain
Crew:	1200
Weight:	30,356 tonnes (30,850 tons)
Dimensions:	242.2m x 27.4m x 7.8m (794ft x 90ft x 25ft 6in)
Range:	6570km (3650nm) at 12 knots
Armour:	152mm – 37.5mm (6in – 1.5in) belt, 178mm – 102mm (7in – 4in) on barbettes, 279mm (11in) on turrets
Armament:	Six 380mm (15in), 17 102mm (4in) guns
Powerplant:	Four shaft, geared turbines
Performance:	30 knots

Retvisan

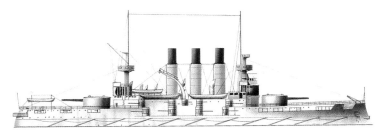

***R**etvisan* was the only capital ship to be built for the Russians by a US yard, and her design was standard US type, with a flush-deck and central superstructure. During the Russo-Japanese war in 1904 she was torpedoed off Port Arthur. She survived, but was later hit by howitzers during the Battle of the Yellow Sea and sunk. When Port Arthur fell in 1905 she was raised by the Japanese. Renamed *Hizen*, she was used as a target and finally sunk in 1924. Numerically, the Russian Far Eastern and Japanese fleets were not dissimilar, but Japan commanded the approaches to Port Arthur and Vladivostok. The former was attacked without declaration of war by Japanese destroyers on the night of 8/9 February 1904, two battleships (one the *Retvisan*) and a cruiser being damaged. Weeks later a Japanese invasion force laid siege to the base, precipitating the war that resulted in the destruction of the Russian fleet at Tsushima.

Country of origin:	Russia
Crew:	738
Weight:	13,106 tonnes (12,900 tons)
Dimensions:	117.8m x 22m x 7.9m (386ft 8in x 72ft 2in x 26ft)
Range:	7412km (4000nm) at 10 knots
Armour:	229mm – 127mm (9in – 5in) belt, 229mm – 203mm (9in – 8in) on turrets
Armament:	Four 304mm (12in), 12 152mm (6in), 20 11-pounder guns
Powerplant:	Twin screw, vertical triple expansion engines
Performance:	18.8 knots

Riachuelo

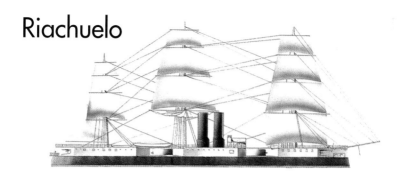

Launched in 1883, *Riachuelo* was a twin-turreted, fully-rigged ship and was built to replace *Independencia*, which had been sold to Britain. *Riachuelo* was an excellent example of armour and offensive power on a 6100-tonne (6000-ton) displacement and was the first warship to feature a steel, iron-backed composite armour. For many years she was a major unit in the Brazilian Navy. She had a steel hull with two twin turrets mounted in echelon amidships and two funnels. She was designed with a barque rig, but was completed with two masts. These were later replaced by two heavy military masts during reconstruction work in 1895, but they were removed in 1905. Named after a battle fought during the war with Paraguay on 11 June 1865, she foundered under tow while heading for a breaker's yard in Europe. She was scrapped in 1910.

Country of origin:	Brazil
Crew:	367
Weight:	6100 tonnes (6100 tons)
Dimensions:	92.9m x 15.8m x 6m (305ft x 52ft x 19ft 8in)
Range:	11,118km (6000nm) at 10 knots
Armour:	280mm – 178mm (11in – 7in) belt, 254mm (10in) on turrets and conning tower
Armament:	Four 234mm (9.2in), six 140mm (5.5in) guns
Powerplant:	Twin screw, vertical compound engines
Performance:	16.7 knots

Richelieu

*R*ichelieu was first in a class of four battleships planned between 1935 and 1938, but she was the only one completed in time to see action during World War II. Launched in March 1940, *Richelieu* escaped the fall of France and joined the Allies in 1942, forming part of a powerful battle group that included battleships *Valiant*, *Howe* and *Queen Elizabeth*, battlecruiser *Renown* and carriers *Victorious*, *Illustrious* and *Indomitable*. She escorted many attack sorties by the carriers on Java, Sumatra and the various enemy-held island groups in the Indian Ocean. She underwent a substantial refit in the USA in 1943, when radar and an extra 100 anti-aircraft guns were added. Joining the British Eastern Fleet in 1944, she served until the end of the war. She later operated off Indo-China during France's war there. *Richelieu* was paid off and hulked in 1959, and was broken up in 1964.

Country of origin:	France
Crew:	1670
Weight:	47,084 tonnes (47,850 tons)
Dimensions:	247.85m x 33m x 9.63m (813ft 2in x 108ft 3in x 31ft 7in)
Range:	10,800km (6000nm) at 12 knots
Armour:	343mm – 243mm (13.5in – 9.75in) belt, 437mm – 169mm (17.5in – 6.75in) on main turrets
Armament:	Eight 380mm (15in), nine 152mm (6in) guns
Powerplant:	Four shaft, geared turbines
Performance:	30 knots

Roanoke

Roanoke was the only multi-turreted ironclad to see service in the American Civil War, and the first to be commissioned with more than two turrets. Originally she was a wooden-hulled, 40-gun steam frigate laid down in 1853. On March 9 1862 there was a celebrated action at Hampton Roads between the Union ironclad *Monitor* and the Confederate ironclad *Virginia*. The action was inconclusive, but it proved once and for all that the day of the turret ship had finally arrived. In May 1862 she was cut down to just above the waterline and the low freeboard was plated with iron armour. Three turrets were installed in January 1865 and she was rearmed, though the hull proved too weak for the weight of the turrets. When the war ended in 1865 she was taken out of service, and sold in 1883.

Country of origin:	USA
Crew:	350
Weight:	4465 tonnes (4395 tons)
Dimensions:	80.7m x 16m x 7.4m (265ft x 52ft 6in x 24ft 3in)
Range:	Not known
Armour:	114mm (4.5in) on hull sides, 279mm (11in) on turrets
Armament:	Two 380mm (15in), two 280mm (11in), two 150-pounder guns
Powerplant:	Single screw, horizontal direct acting engines
Performance:	6 knots

Rolf Krake

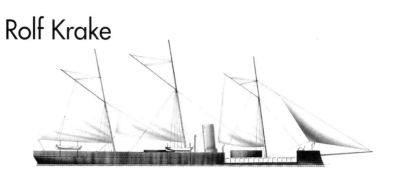

Denmark was the first Scandinavian country to possess an ironclad fleet of any size. In 1862, with increasing tension between Denmark and Prussia, the Danes boosted their defences. They ordered a coastal defence monitor-type vessel from Napier in Glasgow, which was laid down in December 1862. In 1864 she fought an action with Prussian shore batteries at Egernsund. *Rolf Krake* had a shallow draught, and low freeboard. Her main armament was mounted in pairs, in two of the new Coles turrets. She had a low silhouette, with her turrets mounted directly on the maindeck and only a small armoured bridge towards the rear of the ship. Hinged metal bulwarks gave the deck protection from high seas, and these were dropped down when in action. In 1867 the forward guns were replaced by a 203mm (8in) weapon. She became a training ship in 1893 and was sold in 1907.

Country of origin:	Denmark
Crew:	150
Weight:	1341 tonnes (1320 tons)
Dimensions:	56m x 11.6m x 3.2m (183ft 9in x 38ft 2in x 10ft 6in)
Range:	2130km (1150nm) at 8 knots
Armour:	112mm – 76mm (4.5in – 3in) hull, 112mm (4.5in) on turrets with 229mm (9in) wood backing
Armament:	Four 68-pounder guns
Powerplant:	Single screw, single expansion compound engine
Performance:	9.5 knots

Roma

***R**oma*, a wooden-hulled broadside ironclad with 2960 sq m (31,933 sq ft) of sail, was laid down in 1863 and completed in 1869. She was rearmed in 1874–75 with 11 254mm (10in) guns. In 1870 she was present at the liberation of Rome, and in 1873 she took part in the blockade of Cartagena, Spain. This action was taken by leading European powers in the wake of the civil uprisings that followed the proclamation of Don Carlos as Charles VII of Spain in the previous year. Its aim was to prevent the exit of warships seized by revolutionary forces. In 1886 *Roma* served as the flagship of the defending force guarding La Spezia. She was removed from the effective list in 1895, and used as a floating ammunition depot ship until she was scuttled to prevent an explosion after being set ablaze by lightning in July 1896. She was refloated in August, and was then broken up.

Country of origin:	Italy
Crew:	551
Weight:	6250 tonnes (6250 tons)
Dimensions:	79.6m x 17.5m x 7.6m (261ft 2in x 57ft 5in x 25ft)
Range:	3492km (1940nm) at 10 knots
Armour:	150mm belt (5.9in)
Armament:	Five 254mm (10in), 12 203mm (8in) guns
Powerplant:	Single screw, single expansion engine
Performance:	13 knots

Royal Sovereign

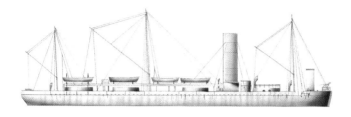

The battle of Hampton Roads between the turret ship *Monitor* and the broadside ship *Virginia* had a profound effect on British naval thinking. It was clear that the turret ship was far superior, so experimental ships, such as *Royal Sovereign*, were built. With the introduction of the ironclad, Britain was left with a large fleet of obsolete wooden battleships. In 1862, work began to convert one such vessel, the 121-gun three decker, *Royal Sovereign*, into Britain's first ironclad turret ship. The top two decks were cut off and five 266mm (10.5in) guns were mounted in four turrets, the fore turret housing two guns and the single turrets being placed on the centreline. The turrets weighed 153–165 tonnes (151–163 tons) and were manually operated. A light steadying rig was fitted. With the increased weight of her new armour, her speed fell from 12.2 to 11 knots. She was sold for scrap in 1885.

Country of origin:	Great Britain
Crew:	300
Weight:	5161 tonnes (5080 tons)
Dimensions:	73.3m x 18.9m x 7.6m (240ft 6in x 62ft x 25ft)
Range:	2779km (1500nm) at 10 knots
Armour:	140mm – 112mm (5.5in – 4.5in) belt, 140mm – 254mm (10in – 5.5in) on turrets
Armament:	Five 266mm (10.5in) guns
Powerplant:	Single screw, return connecting rod engine
Performance:	11 knots

Royal Sovereign

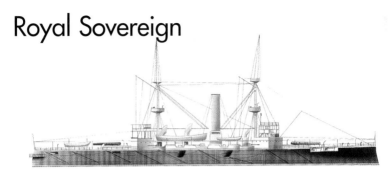

Designed by Sir William White, *Royal Sovereign* was laid down at Portsmouth Dockyard in September 1889 and was completed in 1892. She was one of 70 vessels ordered under the Naval Defence Act of 1889, and set the standard for most of the pre-dreadnought capital ships that followed. The idea of the new design was increased fighting efficiency, plus the maintenance of speed in a seaway. These requirements were only possible in a barbette ship carrying its guns high above the waterline, with a high freeboard for better seakeeping. *Royal Sovereign* was scrapped in 1919. Other ships in the Royal Sovereign class were *Empress of India*, *Ramillies*, *Repulse*, *Resolution*, *Revenge* and *Royal Oak*. Of these, only *Revenge* served in World War I, being returned to service as a bombarding ship in 1914. In August 1915 she was renamed *Redoubtable*. She was broken up in 1919.

Country of origin:	Great Britain
Crew:	712
Weight:	15,830 tonnes (15,580 tons)
Dimensions:	125m x 22.8m x 8.3m (410ft 6in x 75ft x 27ft 6in)
Range:	15,750km (4720nm) at 15 knots
Armour:	450mm – 356mm (18in – 14in) belt, 425mm – 279mm (17in – 11in) on barbettes, 152mm (6in)
Armament:	Four 343mm (13.5in), 10 152mm (6in) guns
Powerplant:	Twin screw, triple expansion engines
Performance:	16.5 knots

Ryujo

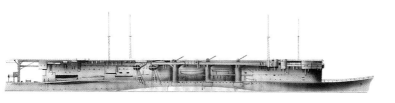

Launched in 1931, *Ryujo* was Japan's first major purpose-built aircraft carrier. She was designed with a cruiser hull, which restricted her width, and so a second hangar was built above the first. This resulted in increased top weight and instability, and almost immediately after her completion in May 1933 she was back in the dockyards for modification. Between 1934 and 1936 her hull was strengthened and her bulges widened. In December 1941 she was one of the ships covering the Japanese landings in the Philippines, followed by the Dutch East Indies in February 1942. The following April, she formed part of the Japanese carrier task force that made a major sortie into the Indian Ocean to strike at Ceylon. She subsequently moved back to the Pacific for operations against Midway Island, and was sunk by aircraft from USS *Saratoga* in August 1942 during the battle of the Eastern Solomons.

Country of origin:	Japan
Crew:	924 (after 1936)
Weight:	10,150 tonnes (9990 tons)
Dimensions:	175.3m x 23m x 5.5m (575ft 5in x 75ft 6in x 18ft 3in)
Range:	18,530km (10,000nm) at 14 knots
Armour:	Light plate around magazines and machinery
Armament:	12 127mm (5in) guns
Powerplant:	Twin screw, turbines
Performance:	29 knots

Sachsen

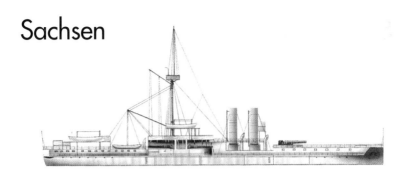

Completed in 1878, *Sachsen* was one of a class of four units which broke away from previous designs for German central battery and broadside ironclads. Two of the 260mm (10.25in) guns were carried in a pear-shaped redoubt on the forecastle, the rest being positioned in a rectangular barbette abaft the funnels. Armour covered the central citadel, and the armoured deck protected her ends. *Sachsen* did not have sails, but she carried a single military mast aft. In 1886 she was given three torpedo tubes, and in the late 1890s she was given new armour and engines. She was discarded in 1910. The other units in this class were *Baden*, *Bayern* and *Wurttemberg*. *Baden* was fleet flagship; she was used as a target hulk in 1920 and broken up at Kiel in 1938. *Bayern* suffered a similar fate, while *Wurttemberg* served as a torpedo school ship before being broken up at Wilhelmshaven in 1920.

Country of origin:	Germany
Crew:	317
Weight:	5767 tonnes (5677 tons)
Dimensions:	98.2m x 18.3m x 6.5m (322ft 2in x 60ft 4in x 21ft 5in)
Range:	9265km (5000nm) at 12 knots
Armour:	254mm – 203mm (10in – 8in) on citadel, 63.5mm – 51mm (2.5in – 2in) on deck
Armament:	Six 260mm (10.25in), six 86mm (3.4in) guns
Powerplant:	Twin screw, horizontal single expansion engines
Performance:	13.5 knots

Salamander

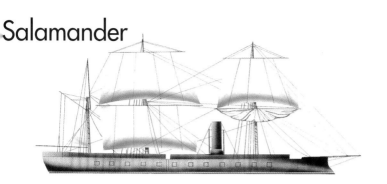

Salamander was Austria's first ironclad. She was laid down in 1861 and completed in 1862, one of the fastest building times for a new type of vessel. She was a wooden-hulled broadside, with a full-length waterline belt which rose at the foremast to protect the battery. She was refitted and rearmed between 1869–70 and given an increased sail area. Stricken in 1883, she then served as a mine store until she was scrapped in 1896. The other vessel in this class was *Drache* (Dragon), which was completed in November 1862. Like her sister ship, she took part in the Battle of Lissa in 1866, where she received some damage. She was refitted and rearmed in 1867–68, stricken in 1875 and broken up in 1883. Both vessels were designed as a response to Sardinia'a Formidabile class of iron hull armoured corvettes, which were originally designed as floating batteries.

Country of origin:	Austria
Crew:	346
Weight:	3075 tonnes (3027 tons)
Dimensions:	62.8m x 13.9m x 6.3m (206ft x 45ft 7in x 20ft 8in)
Range:	2779km (1500nm) at 10 knots
Armour:	115mm (4.4in) belt
Armament:	14 150mm (5.9in), 14 68-pounder guns
Powerplant:	Single screw, horizontal low pressure engines
Performance:	11.3 knots

Scharnhorst

Launched in 1936, *Scharnhorst* and her sister *Gneisenau* were designed as fast commerce raiders. Though outgunned by the 400mm (16in) weapons of British battleships, plans existed to improve the main armament to 380mm (15in). War intervened and proposed turrets for bigger guns went to the *Bismark*. *Scharnhorst* took part in the invasion of Norway in April 1940 where she was damaged. Despite this, she sank the carrier *Glorious* the following month. Considered a deadly threat, she was attacked for the next two years by surface ships, aircraft and mini-submarines, but remained operational. In February 1942 she escaped from the French port of Brest, to make a famous dash through the English Channel. She was mined and damaged en route. *Scharnhorst* was finally sunk in December 1943 by *Duke of York* and three cruisers on her way to attack an Arctic convoy.

Country of origin:	Germany
Crew:	1840
Weight:	38,277 tonnes (38,900 tons)
Dimensions:	229.8m x 30m x 9.91m (753ft 11in x 98ft 5in x 32ft 6in)
Range:	16,306km (8800nm) at 19 knots
Armour:	343mm – 168mm (13.75in – 6.75in) belt, 356mm – 152mm (14in – 6in) on main turrets, 75mm (3in) on deck
Armament:	Nine 279mm (11in), 12 150mm (5.8in) guns
Powerplant:	Three shaft, geared turbines
Performance:	32 knots

Sevastopol

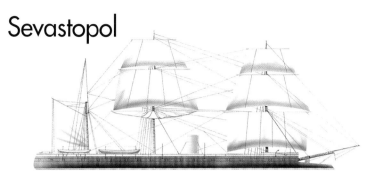

Sevastopol was Russia's first ocean-going ironclad. She was laid down in 1860 as a wooden-hulled, unarmoured frigate mounting 28 60-pounder guns. Conversion began in 1862, and she was completed as a battleship in 1865. Her armoured battery was 60m (195ft) long, and was positioned amidships. Two of the 203mm (8in) guns were placed outside the battery. Armoured bulkheads ran the length of the battery. *Sevastopol* was removed from the effective list during the 1880s. She was one of two wooden vessels converted to ironclads. They were followed by Russia's first armoured warship, *Pervenietz*, and more advanced ironclads such as the armoured frigates *Pozharski*, *Minin* and *General Admiral*. Some rather novel ships were designed by Russian naval constructors during this period, including a class of circular ironclads by A.A. Popov.

Country of origin:	Russia
Crew:	607
Weight:	6228 tonnes (6130 tons)
Dimensions:	89.9m x 15.8m x 7.9m (295ft x 52ft x 26ft)
Range:	4632km (2500nm) at 10 knots
Armour:	112mm (4.5in) wrought iron on sides and battery
Armament:	16 203mm (8in), one 152mm (6in), eight 86mm (3.4in) guns
Powerplant:	Single screw, horizontal return engines
Performance:	12 knots

Shinano

At the time of her completion, *Shinano* was the world's largest aircraft carrier, but she was to have the shortest career of any major warship of her type when, on 29 November 1944, she was sunk by the US submarine *Archerfish*. *Shinano* was a Yamato class battleship, but after carrier losses at the Battle of Midway she was converted into an auxiliary carrier with massive internal capacity for transporting supplies of fuel and spares, plus aircraft, to the Japanese task forces. Her single storey hangar was 168m (550ft) long, and her own air group of 40–50 planes were housed forward, with the replacement aircraft for the task forces stowed aft. She was torpedoed and sunk while on her way to Kure for final fitting out. There is little doubt that the decisive Battle of Midway turned the tide of the Pacific war. The lack of strong carrier forces afterwards put an end to Japanese hopes of further conquest.

Country of origin:	Japan
Crew:	2400
Weight:	74,208 tonnes 973,040 tons)
Dimensions:	266m x 40m x 10.3m (872ft 9in x 131ft 3in x 33ft 9in)
Range:	13,340km (7200nm) at 16 knots
Armour:	202mm (8.1in) belt, 77.5mm (3.1in) on flight deck, 187mm (7.5in) on hangar deck
Armament:	16 127mm (5in), 145 25mm (1in) guns, 336 rocket launchers, 70 aircraft
Powerplant:	Quadruple screw turbines
Performance:	28 knots

South Dakota

Commissioned into service in 1942, *South Dakota* was the first in a class of four battleships designed specifically to survive hits from 400mm (16in) shells while being able to perform at up to 27 knots. Launched in June 1941, *South Dakota* was fitted as a purposely designed force flagship. She saw service off Guadalcanal in 1942 where she was instrumental in defending the *Enterprise* task group, and later took part in the night action which saw the destruction of the Japanese battleship *Kirishima*. In 1944 she was in action during the Battle of the Philippine Sea, and was present at Tokyo Bay at the formal Japanese surrender in August 1945, when she flew the flag of the commander of the US Pacific Fleet, Admiral Halsey. She was damaged in action three times: at the Battle of Santa Cruz, at Guadalcanal, and off Saipan. *South Dakota* was withdrawn from service in 1946 and sold in 1962.

Country of origin:	USA
Crew:	1793
Weight:	43,806 tonnes (44,519 tons)
Dimensions:	207.3m x 34m x 10.7m (680ft x 108ft 2in x 35ft 1in)
Range:	27,000km (15,000nm) at 12 knots
Armour:	304mm (12in) belt, 282mm – 432mm (11.3in – 17.3in) on barbettes, 450mm (18in) on turrets
Armament:	Nine 400mm (16in), 20 127mm (5in) guns
Powerplant:	Four shaft turbines
Performance:	27.5 knots

Sparviero

In 1936 it was suggested that the large liner *Augustus* could provide the possible basis for an aircraft carrier. Although the idea was initially rejected, it was revised in 1942, when it was decided to convert *Augustus* into an auxiliary carrier. She was renamed *Falco*, then *Sparviero*. Just as her upper works had been removed, she was seized by the Germans in 1944 for use as a blockship. She was scuttled in 1944. Although Italy, with four battleships, was the major power in the Mediterranean when she declared war in 1940, the battle fleet was always used in a defensive manner, especially after the strike on Taranto by British naval aircraft when three capital ships were put out of action. If Italy had had one or two aircraft carriers at the outset, armed with suitable aircraft, the war in the Mediterranean might have taken a different turn, as she could have then adopted an offensive posture.

Country of origin:	Italy
Crew:	–
Weight:	30,480 tonnes (30,000 tons)
Dimensions:	202.4m x 25.2m x 9.2m (664ft 2in x 82ft 10in x 30ft 2in)
Range:	–
Armour:	–
Armament:	Six 152mm (6in), four 102mm (4in) guns (proposed)
Powerplant:	Quadruple screw, diesel engines
Performance:	18 knots (as liner)

Stonewall

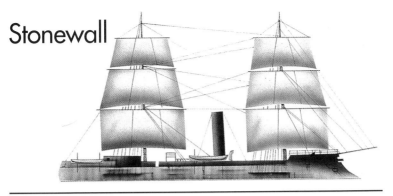

Built in Bordeaux and commissioned in 1863, *Stonewall* was the last ironclad to serve in the Confederate Navy. The 229mm (9in) gun was housed in the bows above the ram, and could fire directly ahead or through a port on either side. Because of French neutrality, the vessel was delivered via Denmark, where she went under the names of *Staerkodder* and *Olinde*. Crossing the Atlantic, she arrived in Havana in May 1865 to find the Civil War over. *Stonewall* was handed over to Union forces. She was sold to Japan and renamed *Adzuma*. In 1888 she was removed from the effective list and used as an accommodation ship. In Confederate service, she was named in honour of General Thomas Jonathan 'Stonewall' Jackson (1824–1863), who was killed at the Battle of Chancellorsville. *Adzuma* saw brief action in Japanese service, against rebel forces at Hakodate.

Country of origin:	Confederate States of America
Crew:	130
Weight:	1585 tonnes (,560 tons)
Dimensions:	60m x 32m x 16m (194ft x 31ft 6in x 15ft 8in)
Range:	3706km (2000nm) at 8 knots
Armour:	112mm – 89mm (4.5in – 3.5in) belt, 140mm (5.5in) over bow gun, 850mm (24in) wooden backing behind side armour
Armament:	One 228mm (9in), two 70-pounder guns
Powerplant:	Twin screw, horizontal direct-acting engines
Performance:	10 knots

Sultan

Sultan was laid down in 1868 and launched in 1870. All her 254mm (10in) rifled muzzle-loaders were in a 25.3m- (83ft-) long armoured battery, with the forward gun firing through an embrasured port to give ahead fire. She was ship-rigged, spreading 4589 square metres (49,395 sq ft) of canvas when carrying studding sails, but was a slow ship. Sultan was a very powerful vessel and one of the most heavily armed central battery ships ever built. In 1882 she took part in the bombardment of Alexandria, but hit a rock off Malta the same year. After salvage, she was reconstructed in 1893–96. In 1906 she saw inactive service as an artificers' training ship at Portsmouth, and was renamed *Fisgard IV*. She was used as a mechanical training ship for many years, reverting to her original name in 1932. Her final days were spent as a mine-sweeping depot ship and she was scrapped in 1945.

Country of origin:	Great Britain
Crew:	633
Weight:	9693 tonnes (9540 tons)
Dimensions:	99m x 18m x 8m (324ft 10in x 59ft x 26ft 3in)
Range:	3965km (2140nm) at 10knots
Armour:	304mm – 152mm (12in – 6in) belt with 304mm – 254mm (12in – 10in) wood backing, 229mm (9in) on main battery, 203mm (8in) on upper battery
Armament:	Eight 254mm (10in), four 228mm (9in) guns
Powerplant:	Single screw, horizontal trunk engine
Performance:	14.13 knots

Taiho

Taiho (Giant Phoenix) was Japan's largest purpose-built aircraft carrier and the first to feature an armoured deck. She was laid down in July 1941 and went into service in March 1944. The two-tier hangars were 150m (500ft) long and unarmoured at the sides. The lower hangar was 124mm (4.9in) thick over the boiler and machinery spaces, which also had 150mm- (5.9in-) thick side armour; the flight deck had 75mm- (3in-) thick armour to withstand a 455kg (1,000lb) bomb. Total armour protection came to 8940 tonnes (8800 tons). *Taiho* was blown up within a few weeks of entering service by the US submarine *Albacore* on 19 June 1944 during the Battle of the Philippine Sea. Two more vessels of this class were planned (Nos 801 and 802) together with five more of a modified Taiho type (Nos 5021 to 5025) but none was ever laid down. *Taiho* was similar in design to the earlier *Shokaku*.

Country of origin:	Japan
Crew:	1751
Weight:	37,866 tonnes (37,270 tons)
Dimensions:	260.6m x 30m x 9.6m (855ft x 98ft 6in x 31ft 6in)
Range:	14,824km (8000nm) at 18 knots
Armour:	150mm – 55mm (5.5in – 2.2in) belt, 77.5mm (3.1in) on flight deck
Armament:	12 100mm (3.9in), 71 25mm (1in) guns
Powerplant:	Quadruple screw turbines
Performance:	33.3 knots

Tegetthoff

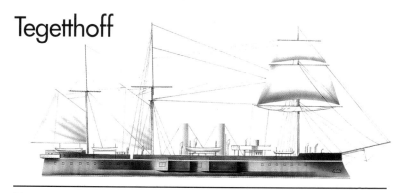

Launched in 1878 and commissioned in 1881, *Tegetthoff* was Austria's last central battery ironclad and was the largest capital ship to be added to the navy for over 20 years. She was named after Admiral Wilhelm von Tegetthoff, victor of the Battle of Lissa. In 1897 she became a floating battery at Pola, and in 1912 was renamed *Mars*. She was ceded to Italy in 1918 as a war reparation and scrapped in 1920. After a period in the doldrums, the Austrian Navy underwent a time of rebirth at the end of the 19th century, starting with the construction of the Monarch class of second class battleship in 1893. Six years later the Habsburg class was laid down; there was an increase in the pace of new building, but progress continued to be dogged by a shortage of funds. There was also a lack of expertise on the part of some shipbuilding yards, which resulted in the production of inferior vessels.

Country of origin:	Austria
Crew:	575
Weight:	7550 tonnes (7431 tons)
Dimensions:	92.5m x 21.8m x 7.6m (303ft 4in x 71ft 6in x 24ft 10in)
Range:	6114km (3300nm) at 10 knots
Armour:	356mm (14in) belt and casemates
Armament:	Six 280mm (11in), six 90mm (3.5in) guns
Powerplant:	Single screw, horizontal low-pressure engine
Performance:	14 knots

Temeraire

Commissioned in 1877, *Temeraire* was Britain's first barbette ship, with one 280mm (11in) gun mounted at each end of the upper deck in a pear-shaped barbette. The 254mm (10in) guns were in a central battery. The largest of her type, she was originally brig-rigged carrying 2322 square metres (25,000 sq ft) of canvas, though her rig was later reduced. She took part in the bombardment of Alexandria in 1882. In 1902 she became a depot ship and workshop. She was renamed *Indus II* in 1904 and later *Akbar*, and was sold in 1921. *Temeraire* saw her peak at a time when Europe was undergoing significant change. A new and mighty German state had forged a triple alliance with Austria and Italy. In 1892 a dual alliance was concluded between Russia and France; the power blocs that would be the catalyst of World War I were taking shape. Britain remained aloof; her fleet still ruled the oceans.

Country of origin:	Great Britain
Crew:	580
Weight:	8677 tonnes (8540 tons)
Dimensions:	86.9m x 18.9m x 8.2m (285ft x 62ft x 27ft)
Range:	5003km (2700nm) at 10 knots
Armour:	279mm – 5.5mm (11in – 5.5in) belt with 305mm (12in) wooden backing, 203mm (8in) on battery
Armament:	Four 280mm (11in), four 254mm (10in) guns
Powerplant:	Twin screw, vertical inverted compound engines
Performance:	14.7 knots

Tennessee

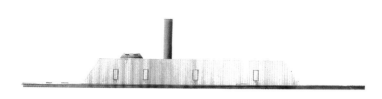

When the Confederate States of America came into existence on 21 February 1861 it had no navy, apart from a few vessels captured at Norfolk, Virginia; construction of warships and weapons presented major problems. When ships were built, they were casemate ironclads similar to the successful *Merrimac*, and all were isolated in the southern ports. *Tennessee* was the largest ironclad built in the Confederacy and was the main force in the defence of Mobile Bay in Alabama. Laid down in 1862, she was towed down to Mobile after launching by the ironclad *Baltic* for completion. The falling waters of the river made it almost impossible to get Tennessee over the bars and giant wooden pontoons were constructed and lashed to the vessel to lift her over. *Tennessee* was captured by Union forces on 5 August 1864 after a three-hour battle. She was later commissioned into the US Navy.

Country of origin:	Confederate States of America
Crew:	113
Weight:	1293 tonnes (1273 tons)
Dimensions:	64m x 14.6m x 4.3m (209ft x 48ft x 14ft)
Range:	Not known
Armour:	152mm – 127mm (6in – 5in) on sides, 50mm (2in) on deck
Armament:	Two 181mm (7.1in), four 152mm (6in) guns
Powerplant:	Single screw, non-condensing engines
Performance:	7 knots

Texas

Texas was the last major warship to be launched in the Confederacy. She was one of the most powerful ironclads, and the only twin-screw, to be built in the South. She was laid down at Rocketts, a suburb just outside Richmond, and was moved into the city after launching to be fitted out. Four of her guns were mounted on pivots, giving direct ahead and astern fire, as well as broadside firing through ports. The two remaining guns were positioned on each broadside. The guns were Brooke rifles – powerful, advanced weapons. When Richmond fell to the Union Army on 3 April 1865, the Confederates failed to blow up Texas, and she was seized by the Union and moved to the Norfolk Navy Yard. Throughout the Civil War, the Confederate Navy was never able to bring its forces together, and no attempt could be made to gain command of the seas. In the end, all its vessels were sunk, captured or scuttled.

Country of origin:	Confederate States of America
Crew:	50
Weight:	Unknown
Dimensions:	66m x 15.3m x 3.9m (217ft x 50ft 4in x 13ft)
Range:	Not known
Armour:	102mm (4in) on battery
Armament:	Six 163mm (6.4in) guns
Powerplant:	Twin screw, horizontal direct-acting engines
Performance:	8 knots

Texas

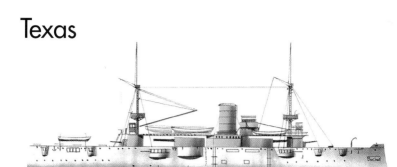

Texas was authorised in 1886, laid down in June 1889 and completed in 1895. She was designed in Britain and proved to be a good seaboat, but after initial trials the hull needed strengthening. By 1904, the funnel had been raised and more armour added to the turret hoists. She took part in the Battle of Santiago Bay in 1898 during the Spanish-American War. During this battle, which was fought on 3 July, the Spanish cruisers stood little chance against the American warships, which included the battleship *Iowa*, armed with four 12in and eight 8in guns. However, the battle underlined the need for improved naval gunnery; the victorious Americans expended 9,500 shells and registered only 123 hits, a hit rate of 1.2 per cent. In 1911 *Texas* was renamed *San Marcos*, and was destroyed as a target in 1912.

Country of origin:	USA
Crew:	508
Weight:	6772 tonnes (6665 tons)
Dimensions:	91m x 19.5m x 6.8m (299ft x 64ft x 22ft 6in)
Range:	5373km (2900nm) at 10 knots
Armour:	305mm – 152mm (12in – 6in) belt, 305mm (12in) on turrets and redoubt
Armament:	Two 305mm (12in), two 152mm (6in) guns
Powerplant:	Twin screw, vertical triple expansion engines
Performance:	17 knots

Tiger

Completed in 1914, it had been intended to fit *Tiger* with small tube boilers and geared turbines, and had this suggestion been adopted her top speed may have been 32 knots. However, as it was, *Tiger* was still the fastest, as well as the largest, capital ship of her day. She was also the last coal-burning capital ship in the Royal Navy, and was the only British battlecruiser to carry 152mm (6in) guns. She took part in the battles of Dogger Bank in 1915 and Jutland in 1916, receiving 15 direct hits during the latter. Battlecruisers, such as *Tiger*, were vulnerable when unable to exploit their speed and firepower, but survival depended on where they were hit, not the number of times. *Tiger* took 15 hits and survived, but the three that were sunk were struck by just six 11in and 12in shells. After World War I *Tiger* served in the Atlantic Fleet until becoming a training ship in 1924. She was paid off in 1933.

Country of origin:	Great Britain
Crew:	1121
Weight:	35,723 tonnes (35,160 tons)
Dimensions:	214.6m x 27.6m x 8.6m (704ft x 90ft 6in x 28ft 5in)
Range:	8370km (4650nm) at 12 knots
Armour:	229mm – 75mm (9in – 3in) belt, 229mm (9in) on turrets and barbettes
Armament:	Eight 343mm (13.5in), 12 152mm (6in) guns
Powerplant:	Quadruple screw turbines
Performance:	30 knots

Tsessarevitch

Tsessarevitch was part of the Russian naval expansion programme of 1898. She was laid down at La Seyne in June 1899, and was completed in 1903. Her design followed the French practice of the period, having a pronounced tumble-home and high forecastle. Assigned to the Pacific Fleet, where she flew the flag of Rear-Admiral Vitgeft, commanding the First Pacific Squadron, she was damaged in the surprise Japanese attack on Port Arthur on 9 February 1904. On 7 August that year she was hit by siege batteries at Port Arthur, and three days later she was damaged by 15 hits in the Battle of the Yellow Sea, Rear-Admiral Vitgeft being killed in the action. She was afterwards interned at Kiauchau, China. While serving in the Baltic in World War I, during which time she engaged the German dreadnought *Kronprinz*, she was renamed *Grazhdanin*. She was scrapped in 1922.

Country of origin:	Russia
Crew:	782
Weight:	13,122 tonnes (12,915 tons)
Dimensions:	118.5m x 23.2m x 7.9m (388ft 9in x 76ft x 26ft)
Range:	10,192km (5500nm) at 10 knots
Armour:	254mm – 178mm (10in – 7in) belt, 254mm (10in) on main turrets, 152mm (6in) on secondary turrets
Armament:	Four 304mm (12in), 12 152mm (6in), 20 3-pounder guns
Powerplant:	Twin screw, vertical triple expansion engines
Performance:	18.5 knots

Tsukuba

Tsukuba was ordered in 1904 as a replacement for one of two powerful battleships lost during the war with Russia. She was laid down at Kure Naval Dockyard in 1905, and originally classified as an armoured cruiser. By the time she was completed in 1907, much more powerful battlecruisers were being built for the Japanese Navy, and in 1921 her sister *Ikoma* was rerated as a first-class cruiser. In January 1917 her magazine caught fire and she blew up in Yokosuka Bay killing 305 crew. She was later raised and broken up. In 1914, as part of the Imperial Japanese Navy's 1st South Seas Squadron, *Tsukuba* took part in the search for the German Admiral von Spee's battle squadron, which had been sighted east of the Marshall Islands. Admiral von Spee eluded his pursuers and went on to win the Battle of Coronel in November 1914, but was defeated and killed off the Falklands on 8 December.

Country of origin:	Japan
Crew:	879
Weight:	15,646 tonnes (15,400 tons)
Dimensions:	137m x 23m x 8m (449ft 10in x 75ft 6in x 26ft 3in)
Range:	7412km (4000nm) at 14 knots
Armour:	178mm – 102mm (7in – 4in) belt, 178mm (7in) on turrets and barbettes, 75mm (3in) on deck
Armament:	Four 304mm (12in), 12 152mm (6in) guns
Powerplant:	Twin screw, vertical triple expansion engines
Performance:	20.5 knots

Unicorn

Launched in 1941, *Unicorn* was built as part of the 1938 Naval Expansion Programme, and was intended to be a depot/maintenance support ship. She was modified during construction so that she could operate her own aircraft, as well as maintain aircraft from other carriers. Her engines developed 40,000hp, and range at 13 knots was 20,900km (11,000 miles). After completion in 1943 she served in the Mediterranean, then on Atlantic patrols, before moving to the Pacific. She later became a depot ship in Hong Kong, and was scrapped in 1959–60. In Royal Navy circles, *Unicorn* is well remembered for her role in the Korean War, ferrying aircraft, spare parts and personnel to the theatre. The British Commonwealth air commitment in Korea comprised a squadron of Gloster Meteor fighters (RAAF) and thirteen naval air squadrons on five light fleet carriers.

Country of origin:	Great Britain
Crew:	1200
Weight:	20,624 tonnes (20,300 tons)
Dimensions:	186m x 27.4m x 7.3m (610ft x 90ft x 24ft)
Range:	20,900km (11,000nm) at 13 knots
Armour:	112.5mm (4.5in) flight deck, 2in (100mm) belt
Armament:	Eight 102mm (4in) guns
Powerplant:	Twin screw turbines
Performance:	24 knots

Vanguard

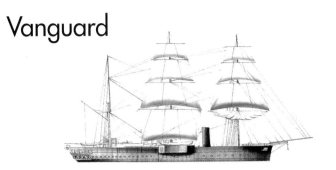

Vanguard was a successful central battery ship built for overseas service, in which great reliance was placed upon good sailing qualities, and where the cruising ironclads of other navies were likely to be encountered. The ships of this class (the others were *Audacious*, *Invincible* and *Iron Duke*) were designed as a response to the French Alma class, which were the first ironclads to feature guns mounted in barbettes. *Vanguard* and her sisters were designed from the outset to provide a steady gun platform under steam in a seaway with good sailing performance and axial fire from the main armament. Completed in 1870 and originally ship-rigged, from 1871 she was barque-rigged and carried 2202 sq m (23,700 sq ft) of canvas. In 1875 she sank after being accidentally rammed by *Iron Duke* in thick fog off the Irish coast.

Country of origin:	Great Britain
Crew:	450
Weight:	6106 tonnes (6010 tons)
Dimensions:	85.3m x 16.4m x 6.8m (280ft x 54ft x 22ft 7in)
Range:	2334km (1260nm) at 10 knots
Armour:	203mm – 152mm (8in – 6in) belt, 254mm – 203mm (10in – 8in) teak backing, 152mm (6in) on battery
Armament:	10 229mm (9in), four 152mm (6in) guns
Powerplant:	Twin screw, horizontal return connecting rod engines
Performance:	14.5 knots

Vanguard

Vanguard was the last battleship built for the Royal Navy. She was ordered in 1941 under the Emergency War Plan of 1940, but did not enter service until 1946. *Vanguard* was basically a lengthened *King George V*, and could accommodate four twin turrets on the centreline. In 1947 she took members of the British Royal Family on tour to South Africa, and after a refit she served in the Mediterranean in 1949–51, primarily as a training ship. In the 1950s she became part of the NATO reserve. The decision to complete the building of *Vanguard* was prompted both by the desire to have at least one modern capital ship embracing war experience (which in the event she did not have) and the availability of the twin 15in guns removed from *Courageous* and *Glorious* when the latter ships were converted to aircraft carriers. She was sold for scrap in 1960.

Country of origin:	Great Britain
Crew:	1893
Weight:	52,243 tonnes (51,420 tons)
Dimensions:	248m x 32.9m x 10.9m (813ft 8in x 108ft x 36ft)
Range:	16,677km (9000nm) at 20 knots
Armour:	356mm – 112mm (14in – 4.5in) belt, 330mm – 152mm (13in – 6in) on main turrets, 330mm – 280mm (13in – 11in) on barbettes
Armament:	Eight 380mm (15in), 16 140mm (5.5in) guns
Powerplant:	Quadruple screw turbines
Performance:	30 knots

Vasco da Gama

Vasco da Gama was Portugal's only capital ship, and was originally intended primarily for the defence of Lisbon. She was built by the Thames Ironworks, London, and was a compact and powerful vessel. Launched in 1876, her octagonal battery rose up above the main deck, housing the two 260mm (10.2in) guns. It had a 0.9-metre (3ft) overhang on each side, so providing axial fire. In the 1890s the rig was reduced to two masts. Between 1901 and 1903 she underwent a major refit, which included new armament and structural modifications. Severely damaged and beached during revolutionary fighting near Lisbon in 1917, she was not stricken and broken up until 1936. The fact that she survived for much longer than her contemporaries was due entirely to the fact that a plan of 1895 to increase the size of Portugal's navy, including the building of two coastal battleships, came to nothing.

Country of origin:	Portugal
Crew:	232
Weight:	2518 tonnes (2479 tons)
Dimensions:	65.8m x 12m x 5.4m (216ft x 40ft x 18ft)
Range:	3335km (1800nm) at 10 knots
Armour:	228mm (9in) belt and (10in) battery, 254mm wood backing
Armament:	Two 260mm (10.2in), one 152mm (6in), two 40-pounder guns
Powerplant:	Twin screw, compound engines
Performance:	10.3 knots

Vauban

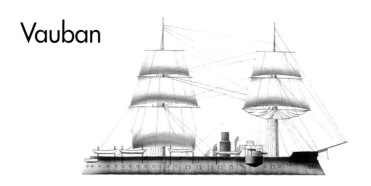

The French battleship *Vauban* was the epitome of the French ironclad cruising ship. She was based on the preceding Bayard class, but instead of having a wooden hull, she had a steel hull, sheathed with wood and coppered. As completed in 1885, *Vauban* was brig-rigged and carried 2155 square metres (23,200 sq ft) of canvas, but this was later removed and she was given two military masts instead. She was discarded in 1905. *Vauban* was built at a time when the French Navy was going through a period of crisis; in 1884 Admiral Aube, a significant naval reformer, had suspended battleship construction, turning French naval policy on its head. A few years earlier, France had captured the technological maritime lead with the launching of *Gloire*, the world's first ironclad, which development started a naval race with Britain.

Country of origin:	France
Crew:	440
Weight:	6210 tonnes (6112 tons)
Dimensions:	81m x 17.5m x 7.7m (265ft 9in x 57ft 3in x 25ft 3in)
Range:	4632km (2500nm) at 12 knots
Armour:	254mm – 150mm (10in – 5.9in) belt, 198mm (7.8in) on barbette
Armament:	Four 238mm (9.4in), one 190mm (7.5in), six 150mm (5.9in) guns
Powerplant:	Twin screw, vertical compound engines
Performance:	14.5 knots

Vitoria

Upon her completion in 1867, *Vitoria* helped to push Spain into fifth place among the world's naval powers behind Britain, France, Italy and Austria. She was an iron-hulled, broadside frigate with a ram bow. All her guns were mounted on the main deck. *Vitoria* had a chequered career; in 1873 she was seized by insurgents at Cartagena, and afterwards she surrendered to the British battleship *Swiftsure* and the German *Friedrich Carl* after her crew went ashore at Escombera. She was returned to the Spanish government, and in October 1973 she saw action against insurgent warships off Cartagena. In January 1874 she was involved in a collision with the British steamer *Ellen Constant*, which sank. She was rebuilt in France in 1897–98 and was given quick-firing guns. She was used as a training ship after 1900 and stricken in 1912.

Country of origin:	Spain
Crew:	500
Weight:	7250 tonnes (7135 tons)
Dimensions:	96.3m x 17.3m x 8m (316ft 2in x 57ft x 26ft 3in)
Range:	4447km (2400nm) at 10 knots
Armour:	140mm (5.5in) iron belt, 125mm (5in) on battery
Armament:	30 68-pounder guns
Powerplant:	Single screw, single compound engine
Performance:	12.5 knots

Vittorio Emanuele

Vittorio Emanuele was one of a quartet of battleships of the Regina Elena class. They were built to a revolutionary design which combined a powerful armament with good protection and high speed on a relatively light displacement. The 304mm (12in) guns were mounted in single turrets, one forward and one aft, and the 203mm (8in) guns were in twin turrets at main deck level. *Vittorio Emanuele* was laid down in 1901 and completed in 1908. In 1911 she took part in naval operations off Tobruk and in the bombardment of Benghazi; the following year found her in the Aegean, providing support for Italian forces occupying the island of Rhodes. In 1915–17 she served in the southern Adriatic, returning to the Aegean in 1918. Her last active service was at Constantinople in 1919, during a period of civil unrest in Turkey. She was removed from service in 1923.

Country of origin:	Italy
Crew:	764
Weight:	12,800 tonnes (12,600 tons) (approx)
Dimensions:	144.6m x 22.4m x 8m (474ft 4in x 73ft 6in x 26ft 3in)
Range:	18,000km (10,000nm) at 12 knots
Armour:	245mm (9.8in) on sides, 37.5mm (1.5in) on deck, 203mm (8in) on turrets
Armament:	Two 304mm (12in), 12 203mm (8in), 16 76mm (3in) guns
Powerplant:	Twin screw, vertical triple expansion engines
Performance:	21.3 knots

Vittorio Veneto

*V**ittorio Veneto* was badly damaged several times during World War II. She was hit by a torpedo during the Battle of Matapan in March 1941. During this attack, which was carried out by Swordfish aircraft from the carrier HMS *Formidable*, *Veneto* narrowly escaped destruction; out of three torpedoes dropped at close range to port and two to starboard, one struck her just above her port outer propeller, quickly flooding her with thousands of tons of water. She managed to get away, but the Italians lost three cruisers, two destroyers and 2400 men. Having been repaired she was torpedoed again, this time by the submarine *Urge*. As a finale she was bombed in 1943 on her way to Malta to surrender. After Italy joined the Allies, she was laid up in the Suez Canal. She was broken up between 1948 and 1950.

Country of origin:	Italy
Crew:	1950
Weight:	46,484 tonnes (45,752 tons)
Dimensions:	237.8m x 32.9m x 9.6m (780ft 2in x 108ft x 31ft 6in)
Range:	8487km (4580nm) at 16 knots
Armour:	279mm – 75mm (11in – 3in) belt, 350mm – 279mm (13.6in – 11in) on barbettes, 350mm – 200mm (13.6in – 7.8in) on turrets
Armament:	Nine 381mm (15in), 12 152mm (6in), four 120mm (4.7in), 12 89mm (3.5in) guns
Powerplant:	Quadruple screw turbines
Performance:	31.4 knots

Vittorio Veneto

***V**ittorio Veneto* was a purpose-built helicopter cruiser that followed on from the smaller Andrea Doria class of the 1950s. The addition of a second deck aft gave her greater hangar capacity. A large central lift is set immediately aft of the super-structure, and two sets of fin stabilisers make her a steady helicopter platform. Laid down in 1965 and completed in 1969, she underwent a major refit between 1981 and 1984 which upgraded her missiles and radar. Her normal air group comprises six anti-submarine Sea King or nine AB212 helicopters. She is fitted with an Aster SAM/ASW launcher system with three rotary drums loaded with 40 surface-to-air missiles and 20 ASROC anti-submarine missiles; her operations centre can elect the missile type to be fired according to the nature of the threat detected. He role as the Italian Navy's flagship was handed over to carrier *Giuseppe Garibaldi* in 1995.

Country of origin:	Italy
Crew:	550
Weight:	8991 tonnes (8850 tons)
Dimensions:	179.5m x 19.4m x 6m (589ft x 63ft 8in x 19ft 8in)
Range:	9000km (5000nm) at 10 knots
Armour:	100mm (4in) belt
Armament:	12 40mm (1.6in), eight 76mm (3in) guns, four Teseo SAM launchers, one ASROC launcher
Powerplant:	Twin screw turbines
Performance:	32 knots

Von der Tann

Completed in 1911, *Von der Tann* was Germany's first battlecruiser, and the first major German warship to have turbines. On 16 December 1914, following an earlier attack on Yarmouth, *Von der Tann* and other warships shelled Hartlepool, Whitby and Scarborough on the northeast coast of England, killing 127 civilians and wounding 567. The fact that 38 women and 39 children were among the dead caused a great anti-German outcry in Britain. *Von der Tann*'s protection was good, and though she was hit by four shells at the Battle of Jutland in 1916, which caused severe fire damage and put all her main guns out of action, she reached home without difficulty. She was surrendered at the end of World War I, and scuttled at Scapa Flow in June 1919. She was raised in December 1930, and was broken up at Rosyth between 1931 and 1934.

Country of origin:	Germany
Crew:	1174 (at Jutland)
Weight:	22,150 tonnes (21,802 tons)
Dimensions:	172m x 26.6m x 8m (563ft 4in x 87ft 3in x 26ft 7in)
Range:	7920km (4400nm) at 10 knots
Armour:	248mm – 100mm (9.6in – 3.9in) belt, 228mm (8.8in) on barbettes and turrets
Armament:	Eight 280mm (11in), 10 150mm (5.9in) guns
Powerplant:	Quadruple screw turbines
Performance:	27.7 knots

Voragine

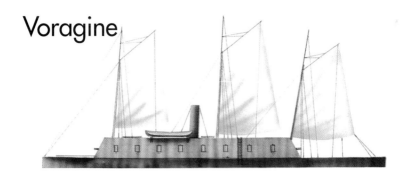

Launched in 1866, *Voragine* was built at La Foca, Genoa, for coastal defence purposes (Italy has an extremely long coastline, which had to be defended). The guns were positioned in a large raised battery amidships. Engines developed 588hp, and a light rig was carried for steadying sails. She was discarded in March 1875. A sister vessel, *Guerriera*, was launched in May 1866. Gun-makers were ahead of naval designers when it came to battle, for they had developed weapons that could penetrate armour. Ship designers responded with even thicker armour, but iron plate is heavy and there were many square metres on the sides of warships. Therefore they developed the central battery ship in which a few big guns were mounted in a short, well-protected battery amidships above a narrow armour belt which protected the full length of the waterline.

Country of origin:	Italy
Crew:	Unknown
Weight:	2389 tonnes (2352 tons)
Dimensions:	56m x 14.4m x 4.2m (183ft 9in x 47ft 4in x 14ft)
Range:	Unknown
Armour:	140mm (5.5in) on battery and waterline
Armament:	12 guns
Powerplant:	Single screw, single expansion engine
Performance:	6.9 knots

Warrior

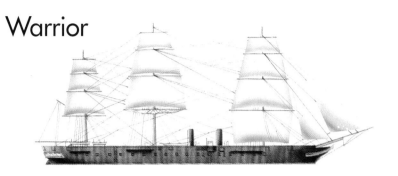

Warrior was the world's first iron-hulled capital ship. Designed by Isaac Watts, she was laid down in May 1859 and on completion was the most powerful warship in the world, faster and more heavily armed than even the French *Gloire*. High speed was achieved by the 'V' formation of the forward part of the hull. Originally designated as a frigate because she only had one deck, *Warrior* and her sister *Black Prince* were reclassified as armoured cruisers in 1880. *Warrior* became a depot ship in 1902 and was hulked in 1923 after which she was used a pipeline pier. Her hulk was rediscovered and restored during the 1980s, and she is now stationed at Portsmouth, England. As a depot ship she was briefly renamed *Vernon III* before reverting to her original name. Her sister, *Black Prince*, became a boys' training ship at Queenstown and was renamed *Emerald* then *Impregnable III*.

Country of origin:	Great Britain
Crew:	707
Weight:	9357 tonnes (9137 tons)
Dimensions:	115.8m x 17.8m x 8m (420ft x 58ft 4in x 26ft)
Range:	3780km (2100nm) at 12 knots
Armour:	114mm (4.5in) on belt and battery, 457mm (18in) wood backing
Armament:	10 110-pounder, four 70-pounder, 26 68-pounder guns
Powerplant:	Single screw, single expansion trunk engine
Performance:	17 knots with combined steam and sail

Warspite

Completed in 1916, *Warspite* belonged to the Queen Elizabeth class, developed from the Iron Duke class, but her displacement was increased by 2540 tonnes (2500 tons), and 6m (20ft) were added to the length. The 380mm (15in) guns fired an 871kg (1916lb) shell to a range of 32,000m (35,000yd) with extreme accuracy. She was badly damaged at Jutland taking 15 hits from 279mm (11in) 304mm (12in) shells.*Warspite* was extensively modernised between 1934 and 1937. During operations in World War II she was severely damaged by German bombs off Crete, and later by German radio-controlled bombs off Salerno, Italy, when covering the Allied landings. She was partially repaired, and used as part of the bombardment force covering the D-Day landings in Normandy. She was further damaged by a mine off Harwich on 13 June 1944. She was paid off in 1945 and scrapped in 1948.

Country of origin:	Great Britain
Crew:	951
Weight:	33,548 tonnes (33,020 tons)
Dimensions:	197m x 28m x 9m (646ft x 90ft 6in x 29ft 10in)
Range:	8100km (4500nm) at 10 knots
Armour:	330mm – 168mm (13in – 6.6in) belt, 330mm – 127mm (13in – 5in) on turrets, 254mm – 102mm (10in – 4in) on barbettes
Armament:	Eight 380mm (15in), 16 152mm (6in) guns
Powerplant:	Quadruple screw turbines
Performance:	23 knots

Washington

Washington and her sister *North Carolina* were the first US battleships built after the lifting of the 1922 Washington Naval Treaty. Original designs complied with the 356mm (14in) gun limitations of the later London Treaty, but when Japan refused to ratify the agreement the design was recast to carry three triple 400mm (16in) gun turrets. The additional weight of the larger weapons caused a two-knot reduction in top speed. *Washington* began her World War II service escorting Arctic convoys to Russia, then transferring to the Pacific Theatre, where she fought at Guadalcanal, Leyte, Okinawa and Iwo Jima and took part in many raids on Japanese-held territory. She suffered damage in a collision with the battleship *Indiana* in February 1944. *Washington*, along with *South Dakota*, sank the Japanese battlecruiser *Kirishima* at Guadalcanal in November 1942. She was scrapped in 1960–61.

Country of origin:	USA
Crew:	1880
Weight:	47,518 tonnes (46,770 tons)
Dimensions:	222m x 33m x 10m (728ft 9in x 108ft 4in x 33ft)
Range:	31,410km (17,450nm) at 12 knots
Armour:	168mm – 304mm belt (6.6in – 12in), 178mm – 406mm (7in – 16in) on main turrets
Armament:	Nine 400mm (16in), 20 127mm (5in) guns
Powerplant:	Quadruple screw turbines
Performance:	28 knots

Wivern

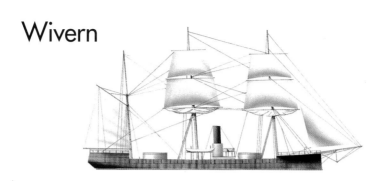

The Confederate Navy agent John Bullock commissioned *Wivern* from Laird Brothers in 1861. She was laid down as *Mississippi*, but was seized by the neutral British government in 1864 and became HMS *Wivern*. Completed in 1865, she was the first vessel to have Cowper Coles' new tripod masts. She was found to be unstable in heavy seas and was used for coastal defence instead. In 1898 she took up duties in Hong Kong harbour. She was sold in 1922. Wivern's sister, *Scorpion*, was also laid down for the Confederate States of America under the name *North Carolina*, and was built under the cover name *El Tousson*. She was also seized by the British government, completed in 1865 and sent to Bermuda, where she saw service as a coastal defence ship. She was sunk as a target vessel in 1901 and her hulk sold two years later. She foundered in 1903, on her way to a Boston breaker's yard.

Country of origin:	Great Britain
Crew:	153
Weight:	2794 tonnes (2750 tons)
Dimensions:	68.4m x 12.9m x 4.9m (224ft 6in x 42ft 6in x 16ft 3in)
Range:	2409km (1300nm) at 10 knots
Armour:	112mm – 50mm (4.5in – 2in) belt with 254mm – 203mm (10in – 8in) wood backing, 254mm – 127mm (10in – 5in) on turrets
Armament:	Four 228mm (9in) guns
Powerplant:	Single screw, horizontal direct acting engine
Performance:	10.5 knots

Yamato

Yamato, together with her sister *Musashi*, were the world's largest and most powerful battleships ever built when they were launched. No fewer than 23 designs were prepared for *Yamato* between 1934 and 1937 when she was laid down. When she was launched, her displacement was only surpassed by that of the British liner *Queen Mary*. Her main turrets each weighed 2818 tonnes (2774 tons), and each 460mm (18.1in) gun could fire two 1473kg (3240lb) shells per minute over a distance of 41,148m (45,000yds). As flagship of the Combined Fleet she saw action in the battles of Midway, the Philippine Sea and Leyte Gulf. On 25 December 1943 she was torpedoed by the US submarine *Skate* south of Truk, and in October 1944 she was damaged by two bomb hits at Leyte Gulf. On 7 April 1945 she was sunk by US carrier aircraft 130 miles southwest of Kagoshima with the loss of 2498 lives.

Country of origin:	Japan
Crew:	2500
Weight:	71,110 tonnes (71,659 tons)
Dimensions:	263m x 36.9m x 10.3m (862ft 10in x 121ft x 34ft)
Range:	13,340km (7200nm) at 16 knots
Armour:	408mm (16.1in) belt, 231mm – 200mm (9.1in – 7.9in) deck, 546mm (21.5in) on barbettes, 650mm – 193mm (25.6in – 7.6in) on main turrets
Armament:	Nine 460mm (18.1in), 12 155mm (6.1in), 12 127mm (5in) guns
Powerplant:	Quadruple screw turbines
Performance:	27 knots

Zaragosa

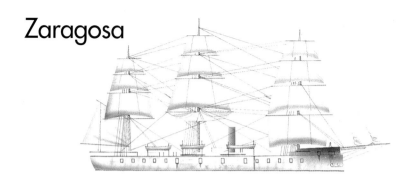

Zaragosa was a wooden-hulled broadside battleship. She was originally armed with 68-pounder guns, but in 1885 she was given four 228mm (9in) guns on the main deck, one 180mm (7.1in) gun under the forecastle and two more 180mm (7.1in) weapons on sponsons. She formed part of the Spanish force sent to Cuba in 1873. She was recalled to Spain upon the outbreak of the civil war, and became a torpedo training ship in 1895. She was stricken in 1899. Mainly because of corruption in the Spanish colonial government, there was continual unrest in Cuba at this time, and various attempts at independence – often influenced by external enouragement, not least from the USA – were met with ruthless military repression, supported by the Spanish Navy. The result was a bitter and bloodthirsty civil war in the closing years of the 19th century.

Country of origin:	Spain
Crew:	500
Weight:	5618 tonnes (5530 tons)
Dimensions:	85.3m x 16.6m x 8m (280ft x 54ft 7in x 26ft 6in)
Range:	3335km (1800nm) at 6 knots
Armour:	127mm – 102mm (5in – 4in) belt, 133mm (5.25in) on battery, 660mm (26in) wood backing
Armament:	21 68-pounder guns
Powerplant:	Single screw, horizontal single expansion engines
Performance:	8 knots

Zealous

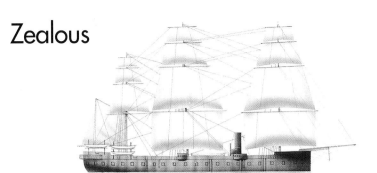

In 1861 seven wooden two-deckers were selected for conversion into ironclads in answer to France's ambitious building programme. Only four were completed, of which *Zealous* was one. Her engines could give her a speed of only 11.7 knots and in later service in the Pacific she operated entirely under sail. However, with 2713 square metres (29,200 sq ft) of canvas she could cover greater distances with sail than her contemporaries. She became a guardship in 1873 and was sold in 1886. The Pacific, where *Zealous* spent six years of her active service, was only one of fifteen independent commands. It was a remote outpost, and a Royal Commission was appointed to discuss the provision of coaling stations. These were eventually established in such places as Labuan (Borneo) and the Cape York peninsula in Australia, but the Pacific remained an area of low priority for the Royal Navy.

Country of origin:	Great Britain
Crew:	510
Weight:	6197 tonnes (6100 tons)
Dimensions:	76.8m x 17.8m x 7.7m (252ft x 58ft 6in x 25ft 5in)
Range:	2779km (1500nm) at 10 knots
Armour:	114mm – 63.5mm (4.5in – 2.5mm) belt, 114mm (4.5in) on battery
Armament:	20 178mm (7in) guns
Powerplant:	Single screw, return connecting rod engine
Performance:	12.5 knots

Zuikaku

Zuikaku and her sister *Shokaku* were the most successful carriers operated by
the Japanese Navy. They were considerably larger than previous purpose-built
carriers, and were better armed, better protected and carried more aircraft. The
wooden flight deck was 240m (787ft) long and 29m (95ft) wide, and was serviced by
three lifts. She formed part of the carrier task force whose aircraft attacked the US
Pacific Fleet base at Pearl Harbor in December 1941, and subsequently participated
in every notable fleet action of the Pacific war – Java, Ceylon, the Coral Sea, the
Eastern Solomons, Santa Cruz, the Philippine Sea and Leyte Gulf. Her name means
Lucky Crane and her sister ship was *Shokaku* (Happy Crane), sunk in June 1944
by the US submarine *Cavalla*. *Zuikaku* was sunk in action by American forces on
25 October 1944, during the Battle of Cape Engano in Leyte Gulf.

Country of origin:	Japan
Crew:	1660
Weight:	32,618 tonnes (32,105 tons)
Dimensions:	257m x 29m x 8.8m (843ft 2in x 95ft x 29ft)
Range:	17,974km (9700nm) at 18 knots
Armour:	45mm (1.8in) belt, 162.5 (6.5in) over magazines, 97.5mm (3.9in) on flight deck
Armament:	16 127mm (5in) guns
Powerplant:	Quadruple screw turbines
Performance:	34.2 knots

Index

Note: Page numbers in **bold** refer to main entries.